SALT OF THE EARTH

SALT OF THE EARTH

A SOCIO-POLITICAL HISTORY OF MEXICO CITY EVANGELICAL PROTESTANTS (1964-1991)

LINDY SCOTT

Editorial Kyrios

CUPSA

Published by Editorial Kyrios and Centro de Comunicación Cultural CUPSA, A.C.

Editorial Kyrios is the book-publishing division of Centro Comunitario Koinonia A.C., a wholistic Christian ministry in Mexico. Requests for information should be addressed to:

Editorial Kyrios
Apdo. 121-001
Santo Domingo, Coyoacán
México, D.F. 04369 MEXICO

Cover illustration: *Joel Medina Palacios*

ISBN 968-7011-28-9

First Printing, 1991

Library of Congress Cataloging-in-Publication Data

Scott, Lindy B., 1951-

Salt of the Earth: A Socio-Political History of Mexico City Evangelical Protestants (1964-1991)

Includes bibliographical references.

ISBN 968-7011-28-9

1. Evangelicalism--Mexico--History--20th century. 2. Mexico--Church history--20th century. 3. Protestant churches--Mexico--20th century. 4. Church and Social Problems.

I. Title.

BX4833. S25 1991

280'.409/S427

Printed in Mexico

To the Christians in Mexico

You are the salt of the earth...

Jesus Christ

ACKNOWLEDGMENTS

This dissertation has involved the help of numerous people who kindly gave of their time, knowledge, and wisdom to see it through to completion. I would like to thank all who have helped in the process of this dissertation.

First of all, I wish to thank my family for their constant encouragement and sacrifices on my behalf. My wife and best friend, Dinorah, accompanied me, day in and day out, through the entire process. My children, John, Jennifer, and Stephanie, through their gestures of encouragement showed me that they believed in me. My parents, John and Mary Jane Scott, not only provided a loving family in my early life, but also encouraged me in the writing of the dissertation. My sister and brother-in-law, Jane and Michael Cleary, offered words of encouragement and helpful suggestions regarding style.

My dissertation committee, Rosemary Ruether, Frank Safford, Richard Tholin, and Phyllis Bird, provided insightful comments and suggestions. Their sacrifices of time are greatly appreciated.

Church leaders from Mexico were very gracious in both the time they gave to me for the interviews as well as the use of their Sunday School class time for the election questionnaires.

The library staff at the following institutions were very helpful in the search for printed materials: Garrett-Evangelical Theological Seminary, Northwestern University, El Colegio de México, El Instituto Evangelístico de México, El Seminario Teológico Presbiteriano de México, La Comunidad Teológica, El Seminario Metodista de México, El Seminario Bautista de México, Ohio State University, Otterbein College, The University of Texas, Trinity Evangelical Divinity School, and Northern Baptist Theological Seminary.

Christian friends from the Des Plaines Evangelical Free Church and the Comunidad de Jesús in Mexico City offered encouragement and prayers. Dave and Karen Anderson deserve special mention for the support and friendship offered. Other friends, too numerous to mention, in Latin America and throughout the world kindly shared many insights and words of encouragement.

I remain, however, totally responsible for the deficiencies of this dissertation.

TABLE OF CONTENTS

LIST OF TABLES

CHAPTER 1

INTRODUCTION

In the Sermon on the Mount (Matthew 5:13-16), Jesus called his disciples "salt of the earth." The principal role of Christians as salt is to work together with God in the transformation of their society, promoting God's justice in a fallen world.[1] They are to demonstrate that they are children of God by their lifestyle of costly discipleship. Their visible actions are to be lived out in society. These good deeds will powerfully persuade others that there is a loving and just God.[2]

Christians, down through the ages and all over the world, have had this same challenge to be salt in their society. Evangelical Protestants in Mexico City are no exception. Mexican Protestants[3] are a growing minority within their country. They currently comprise 10% of their nation's population. These Evangelicals are, to a large degree, shaped by the culture that surrounds them. They, in turn, influence their society in different ways.

In the nineteenth century, Mexican Protestants were closely identified with the liberal governments of Juárez, Lerdo, and Porfirio Díaz. In the last years of the Porfiriato, many Evangelicals opposed the dictatorship and began to work for a change.[4] Evangelical Christians played a significant role in the Revolution

---

[1]Delegates to the Lausanne conference on the Church's Response to Human Needs stated that "we should not be either naively optimistic nor falsely critical. We are called to be a new community that seeks to work with God in the transformation of our societies; men and women of God in society, salt of the earth, light of the world (Matthew 5:3-16)." La Iglesia en Respuesta a las Necesidades Humanas: Wheaton '83 (Mexico City: Visión Mundial de México, nd), 10.

[2]The phrase "salt of the earth" is commonly used by Latin American Evangelicals to describe their influence and participation in society. For example, Pablo Alberto Deiros, ed. Los Evangélicos y el Poder Político en América Latina (Grand Rapids and Buenos Aires: Nueva Creación, 1986), 9-10, affirmed that "due to his or her serious commitment to and contact with the world in terms of 'salt' and 'light,' the believer cannot avoid involvement in the political area. As a child of God, he/she is called to interject into the social sphere those values that spring from his/her faith. There is not one single space of human existence in which the Christian cannot find a place of testimony for the redeeming power of God in Jesus Christ. The light and the salt of the Gospel need to reach all the areas of personal and social experience, through believers committed to the Kingdom of God in the world."

[3]Although the words Protestant and Evangelical have somewhat different meanings in the Anglo American context, in Latin America they are synonyms as all Protestants are known as "Evangélicos." Therefore, in this study, the terms will be used interchangeably.

[4]See Jean Pierre Bastian, Los Disidentes: Sociedades Protestantes y Revolución en México (Mexico City: Fondo de Cultura Económica and El Colegio de México, 1989) and Deborah Jo Baldwin, Protestants and the Mexican Revolution: Missionaries, Ministers, and Social Change (Urbana: University of Illinois Press, 1990).

(1910-1917) and in the post-revolutionary regimes. As the Revolution became "institutionalized," the ruling political party (Partido Revolucionario Institucional or PRI) became much more conservative in its national policies. The clearest shift took place in 1940 when the populist president Lázaro Cárdenas left office and was replaced by Avila Camacho who brought about a reconciliation with the Roman Catholic Church. Recent presidents (Díaz Ordaz, Echeverría, López Portillo, De la Madrid, and Salinas) have maintained that conservative political stance in Mexico's internal affairs, defending the privileges of the ruling classes, while at the same time verbally advocating the "revolutionary" cause of the poor.[5]

Certain questions arise regarding the social and political involvement of Protestants in Mexico. These can be grouped in three different areas: (1) historical; (2) socio-economical; and (3) theological.

(1a) As the PRI shifted from a liberal to a conservative political stance, did Protestants also shift to a more conservative political posture, or did they maintain their liberal persuasion? (1b) Accordingly, has the Protestant alliance with the PRI been weakened in the last quarter of a century, and if so, why? (1c) How have the anti-clerical laws of the 1917 Constitution, although originally directed against the Catholic Church, affected Evangelical participation in society?

It is commonly assumed that evangelistic missionary work produces an upward mobility among its adherents. An emphasis upon education and hard work, combined with a renunciation of alcoholic beverages, tobacco, and other "vices," tends to promote second and third generation Evangelicals into the middle class. Social organizations, such as schools and clubs, usually accompany this phenomenon in Latin America. Mexico, given its particular constitutional legislation, has limited some of these social expressions of the Evangelical Church. (2a) Has the upward social mobility of Mexican Protestants been a factor in shaping Evangelical socio-political action? (2b) On a related note, has the reduction in social organizations caused Mexican Evangelicalism to be more "isolationist"?

It is commonly thought that a conservative theology produces either an "apolitical" or a conservative political posture. An "apolitical" stance is rarely such, for it usually means supporting the social, economic, and political forces that are in power. But is it true that a conservative theology comes down on the side of defending the status quo? Mexican Evangelical participation in the Revolution of 1910 seems to challenge that assumption. (3a) Have Mexican Evangelicals, with their conservative theology, been defenders of the status quo? (3b) If not, have they taken "prophetic" stands on any major issues in the recent past?

---

[5]This is true even of those presidents who were left of center in their international political posture, eg. Echeverría. Cf. Arthur Liebman, Kenneth N. Walker, and Myron Glazer, Latin American University Students: A Six-Nation Study (Cambridge: Harvard University Press, 1972), 174-75, where the authors affirm and demonstrate that "despite the PRI's own claim to be 'leftist,' there have been a variety of indications to the contrary."

Mexican Evangelicals affirm that God's revelation in Scripture is their maximum authority for faith and practice. (3c) Has their theological understanding of Scripture, therefore, guided their political and social involvement, or, conversely, has their socio-economic setting greatly conditioned their reading of the Bible? Finally, (3c) what theologies have they developed to articulate their understanding of Christian participation in the social and political spheres?

This dissertation will attempt to answer these questions and to show the interrelationships between the various historical, social, legal, political and theological components. The time frame studied is 1964 to 1991.[6] To limit the scope of this paper three denominations were chosen which reflect part of the great diversity of Mexican Protestantism--the Iglesia Presbiteriana Nacional, the Convención Nacional Bautista de México, and the Iglesia de Dios en la República Mexicana. The first two are historical denominations, having existed for more than a hundred years in Mexico. The third is a fairly typical Pentecostal denomination dating from the early 1920's. All three are well established in Mexico and are of comparable size. In addition, each of these denominations has several local churches in the Mexico City metropolitan area.

Justification for this Dissertation

The Protestant presence in Latin America has grown steadily over the last few decades and Evangelicals now exercise a certain amount of power and influence in some countries.[7] Although not as large a percentage of the total population as Protestants in countries such as Brazil, Chile, or Guatemala, Mexican Evangelicals have now become a significant minority in their country.[8] In spite of their growing numbers, however, their participation in Mexican society has been given very little space in Mexican historiography. The separation of church and state in Mexico has been interpreted in such a way that courses on the

---

[6]A good overview of this period in Mexican history can be found in Michael C. Meyer and William L. Sherman, The Course of Mexican History 3d ed. (New York: Oxford University Press, 1987), 663-91.

[7]Protestant support of Fujimori in the recent Peruvian elections and the choice of Evangelicals as President and Vice-President in the 1991 Guatemalan elections are but two examples of significant Protestant political clout in the last few years. Recent studies have highlighted growing Evangelical influence in Latin America. See David Martin, Tongues of Fire: The Explosion of Protestantism in Latin America (Oxford: Blackwell, 1990) and David Stoll, Is Latin America Turning Protestant? The Politics of Evangelical Growth (Berkeley: University of California Press, 1990).

[8]It is officially reported that 6 to 8% of Mexican citizens consider themselves to be Protestants. The Catholic Bishops in Mexico estimate that 10% are Evangelicals. Catholic studies show that there has been a 400 percent increase in conversions to Protestantism since 1968; "Evangelicals in Mexico," The Christian Century (January 17 1990):41-42. Many rumors have circulated that the Catholic hierarchy has held up the release of religious data from the 1990 census due to the high percentage of Evangelicals in the southern states.

Sociology of Religion are virtually unknown in Mexican universities.[9] Literature on the topic of Evangelical participation in Mexican society can be classified into four categories.

The first genre of literature consists of books and magazine articles written to recruit missionary personnel and resources for Protestant ministry in Mexico. Written primarily by North American missionaries, these works appeared early on the scene in Mexico. Especially among the historical denominations that depended to a large degree on funding from outside the country, there was a steady stream of literature promoting the work. Presbyterian books include Twenty Years among the Mexicans (1881), Sunrise in Aztec Land (1922), Modern Missions in Mexico (1925), Mission to Mexico (1960), and Margaret Shelby Erdman's Contentedly Yours, Alice J. McClelland (1969) written just three years before the Presbyterian missionaries left Mexico. Baptist books include James Chastain's Thirty Years in Mexico (1930), The Challenge of Mexico to Missions (1952), Stronger than Mushrooms: The Various Facets of Baptist Student Work in Mexico (1976), and A Century of Baptist Work in Mexico (1979). Much additional information of a similar nature can be found in the Southern Baptist missionary magazine The Commission and the Presbyterian Mission Yearbook for Prayer and Study. Given the lack of formal relations between the Iglesia de Dios en la República Mexicana and churches in the United States, there are no comparable works written for this denomination.

A second genre of literature is made up of articles and books that are self-descriptive of Evangelical thought and practice. Included here are the official denominational magazines. For the three groups under study, these are El Faro, La Luz Bautista, and El Camino a la Vida. Some interdenominational magazines such as the Boletín Teológico of the Fraternidad Teológica Latinoamericana and Continente Nuevo of the Billy Graham Association include articles written by Mexican Evangelicals. This genre also includes reports of denominational meetings, bulletins, manuals, strategies, yearly reports and a few historical studies such as José Coffin's El General Gutiérrez, Eduardo Carrero's La Iglesia Presbiteriana en México: Sus Conquistas, Sus Problemas, Su Actitud and Alejandro Treviño's Historia de los Trabajos Bautistas en México.

A limited number of books have been authored by Mexican Evangelicals on topics that treat social issues. Some of the more notable studies include several Presbyterian articles in Un Pueblo con Mentalidad Teológica, Edesio Sanchez Cetina's Fe Bíblica: Antiguo Testamento y América Latina (Ensayos Exegéticos), and several volumes by the Baptist pastor Rolando Gutiérrez. The most prolific Mexican Evangelical author was the Methodist lay preacher Gonzalo Báez

---

[9]Only recently have sociological courses on religion in Mexico been offered at Mexican universities. For example, in 1990 the Universidad Iberoamericana offered a special team taught course on Christian Religion in Mexico. The Protestant section was taught by Jean Pierre Bastian.

Camargo who wrote for the daily newspaper Excelsior for more than fifty years.[10]

The third type of literature is of a more academic nature. This genre includes theses and dissertations and articles in scholarly journals written both within and outside of Mexico. As paradigms of Protestant socio-political participation, the most informative works are Jean Pierre Bastian's Los Disidentes: Sociedades Protestantes y Revolución en México, 1872-1911,[11] Deborah Baldwin's Protestants and the Mexican Revolution: Missionaries, Ministers, and Social Change, Edwin Rosser's Beyond Revolution: The Social Concern of Moisés Sáenz, Mexican Educator, and Marianne McKechnie's The Mexican Revolution and the National Presbyterian Church of Mexico, 1910-1940. Compared to the extensive scholarship devoted to these earlier periods, it appears that the 1940's and 1950's are given almost a cursory glance by academic historians. For example, Mary Cassaretto's El Movimiento Protestante en México (1956) and Marvin Penton's Mexico's Reformation: A History of Mexican Protestantism (1965) only briefly examine the previously mentioned time frames in terms of socio-political activity.

Evangelical socio-political activity over the last thirty years has received scant attention by academicians. Although certain recent sociological and anthropological studies such as Carlos Garma's Protestantismo en una Comunidad Totonaca (1987) and Pedro Carrasco's Protestantismo y Campo Religioso en un Pueblo del Estado de Oaxaca (1983) do analyze the social and political influence of Mexican Evangelicals, these deal almost exclusively with rural areas. The most useful theses written in Mexican seminaries are Eliezer Arteaga's Proyección de Nuestra Iglesia en la U.N.A.M. (1964), Rebeca Montemayor de Ulloa's Ministerio Social Cristiano: Conceptualización y Praxis (1981), Raul Tec's La Necesidad de Cumplir en su Totalidad la Misión de la Iglesia (1975), Samuel Villagran's Encarnación de la Iglesia en la Sociedad: Coyuntura Actual (1985), and Sergio Estrada's La Mujer en el Pensamiento de Jesucristo Aplicado a las Iglesias Bautistas en México (1982).

Within this section can be included studies dealing with church growth in Mexico. These are generally academic studies, but contain a definite pro-evangelical stance. Donald McGavran, one of the leading scholars of the church growth movement, wrote a classical study on Mexico entitled Church Growth in Mexico (1963). More recent works include Charles Bennett's Tinder in Tabasco: A Study of Church Growth in Tropical Mexico (1968), Manuel Gaxiola's La Serpiente y la Paloma: Análisis del Crecimiento de la Iglesia Apostólica de la Fe in Cristo Jesús de México (1970), James Mitchell's The Emergence of a Mexican

---

[10] He used the pseudonym Pedro Gringoire for his newspaper articles and for some of his numerous books.

[11] Bastian is by far the most prolific recent author on Mexican Protestantism (see bibliography), but most of his work is concentrated in the Porfiriato and Revolutionary periods.

Church (1970), Julian Bridges' Expansión Evangélica en México (1973), Rex Ralph Jones' Church Planting among Middle Class Families in Mexico City (1984), and Boyce Wilson's Church Growth by Church Division: A Mexican Model for Urban Church Growth (1985).

The fourth genre of literature consists of works written about Mexican Evangelicals by non-evangelical authors. Many were composed by Catholic authors and frequently reflect heated debate or sound a warning about Protestant advances in Mexico, such as Joaquín Cardoso's La Historia del Protestantismo en México (1946) and Pedro Rivera's Protestantismo Mexicano: Su Desarrollo y Estado Actual (1961) and Instituciones Protestantes en México (1962). Others have written about Mexican Protestants within the context of Church-State relations, human rights, persecution, or through the involvement of Wycliffe missionary linguists with ethnic groups in Mexico. Some have been sympathetic to the Evangelical cause such as Roberto Blancarte and Carlos Monsiváis, while others have criticized the Protestants quite vehemently.

Methodology

As can be easily observed, very little research has been published concerning the recent social and political involvement of Mexican Evangelicals. Consequently, it was necessary to employ several research methods for this dissertation.

First, a thorough survey of the pertinent literature was made in order to provide the necessary historical background. Recent Evangelical literature, although usually not written with a focus on social and political participation,[12] did provide much helpful information.

The second methodology used was that of observation. The author was invited to teach at theological institutions of all three denominations and was therefore able to observe each group from the "inside."[13] In addition, the author attended several events sponsored by a wide diversity of religious groups (see Appendix A). These provided many opportunities for key conversations and observations.

The third instrument employed was a semi-structured interview.[14] More than one hundred interviews were conducted with Evangelical leaders. These

---

[12]Usually its focus was on topics such as evangelism, discipleship, or church growth.

[13]The author taught Biblical Greek and Exegesis at the Seminario Teológico Presbiteriano de México, the Instituto Bíblico de Reflexión Pastoral (Baptist), and the Seminario de la Iglesia de Dios en la República Mexicana at different times from 1988 to 1991. The danger of subjective "bias" was recognized, but the need for an "insider's perspective" seemed to justify taking that risk. See Julian L. Simon, Basic Research Methods in Social Science: The Art of Empirical Investigation (New York: Random House, 1969): 75-173.

[14]Ibid., 228-55.

enabled the author to obtain valuable information about Protestant involvement in three specific events: the student Movement of 1968, the earthquake relief of 1985 and 1986, and the 1988 national elections. These interviews also revealed some of the Evangelical thinking that shaped their particular action.

Given the confidential nature of voting in Mexico, a survey was used to obtain information about the 1988 political involvement of Mexican Evangelicals (a copy of the survey and a summary of its findings can be found in Appendix B). More than 500 surveys representing over twenty local churches of the three denominations were analyzed.

The next chapter of this dissertation provides an overview of Protestant history in Mexico until 1964. Specific incidents demonstrating social and political participation by Protestants are highlighted. Chapters 3, 4, and 5 deal with the Presbyterians, the Baptists, and the Church of God respectively. The historical background of each denomination is presented first, followed by a description of its participation in each of the three selected events. At the end of each chapter an analysis is given of their involvement (or lack of it). Chapter 6 provides a summary of the dissertation which includes a critique of the theological articulation that has been employed to justify the socio-political stance of the three churches.

Selected Events

Three significant events were chosen as loci around which Protestant socio-political participation could be examined. They were the student movement of 1968 leading up to the massacre of several hundred people in Tlatelolco, Mexico City on October 2, the earthquakes of 1985, and the general elections of 1988.

These events have certain similarities which make them appropriate for this study. In addition to involving large segments of the population,[15] each event had special significance for Mexico City. The student movement not only started in Mexico City but the "noche triste" of October 2 took place in Tlatelolco near the heart of the capital. The earthquakes also caused their greatest destruction in the older sections of the capital. The 1988 elections were hotly contested in Mexico City with candidates from opposition parties winning important seats in both houses of Congress.[16]

All three events have also had long lasting consequences for life in Mexico. The student movement of 1968 has been called a watershed event of recent Mexican history leading to the political awakening of an entire generation. It also

---

[15]Instead of concentrating on a few prominent Evangelicals who might be socially or politically noteworthy for reasons having little to do with their religious faith, this study, by focusing on these three events, enabled the analysis of a larger number of Evangelicals. Research on this broader cross section of Protestantism should result in more reliable conclusions.

[16]It is generally claimed that less election fraud took place in Mexico City due to the large number of poll watchers from the opposition parties.

challenged the then current international opinion that the PRI government in Mexico had the broad backing of its population. Author Carlos Monsiváis has demonstrated how the earthquakes of 1985, and the rescue and reconstruction activities afterwards, were the most important factors in the mobilization of Mexico's "civil society" in the decade of the 1980s.[17] By President Salinas' own admission the elections of 1988 marked the end of the one party domination of Mexican politics.[18]

Finally, each of these three events have had a strong "moral" component that called into question the action of the government. Liebman notes that the major force behind the 1968 student movement was the "moral outrage of thousands of students."[19] Fish and Kretzmann describe how the 1985 earthquakes "revealed the government's widespread corruption and paralysis."[20] The accusations of fraud in the 1988 elections touch at the heart of ethical outrage. If the Protestant community contributed at all to the social conscience of Mexico, its participation in these events should have been noticeable.

The Student Movement of 1968[21]

On July 22, 1968, a fairly typical skirmish took place in Mexico City between students of the private high school Isaac Ochoterena and students from the Vocational High Schools numbers two and five. Members of the gangs "los

---

[17]Carlos Monsiváis, Entrada Libre: Crónicas de la Sociedad que se Organiza (Mexico City: Ediciones Era, 1987), 11-122.

[18]See "Terminó la Era del PRI," Visión (August 8 1988): 6-7. Election results in the three years following the national election of 1988 have produced victories for some of the opposition candidates (mostly from the PAN party), yet the rapid demise of the PRI does not appear on the visible horizon.

[19]Liebman, Latin American University Students, 190.

[20]John H. Fish and John Kretzmann, "Reviving Mexico City: Neighborhood by Neighborhood," The Christian Century (29 November 1989): 1118.

[21]Some of the classical literature regarding the Mexican student movement of 1968 include Elena Poniatowska, La Noche de Tlatelolco: Testimonios de Historia Oral, (Mexico City: Ediciones Era, 1971); Luis González de Alba, Los Días y los Años (Mexico City: Ediciones Era, 1971); Jose Revueltas, México 68: Juventud y Revolución (Mexico City: Ediciones Era, 1978); Herman Bellinghausen, comp. Pensar el 68 (Mexico City: Cal y Arena, 1988), and Sergio Zermeño, México: Una Democracia Utópica, El Movimiento Estudiantil del 68, (Mexico City: Siglo Veintiuno Editores, 1978). A non-governmental running account of the events can be found in the independent magazine ¿Por Qué? A description in English of the student movement events can be found in John Womack, Jr., "Unfreedom in Mexico: Government Crackdown on the Universities," The New Republic (12 October 1968): 27-31; Paul E. Sigmund, ed. "Documents on the Student Revolt of 1968," chapter in Models of Political Change in Latin America (New York: Frederick A. Praeger, 1970), 33-44; Liebman, Latin American University Students, 166-200; and Kenneth F. Johnson, "The Saliency of Alienation: Mire + Muro + Sph = Tlatelolco," chapter in Mexican Democracy: A Critical View (Boston: Allyn & Bacon, 1971), 148-164.

arañas" and "los ciudadelos" were also involved. As damage was done to the Ochoterena school, it was announced that the battle would continue the next day. Police (granadero) intervention on July 23 provoked a confrontation with about 3000 students using rocks, tear gas, and sticks. The Federación Nacional de Estudiantes Técnicos (FNET)[22] subsequently protested the excess of force used by the police. On Friday, July 26 a protest march organized by the FNET drew more than 5000 students. Several battles ensued between police and students. On Sunday the Comité Coordinador de Huelga (CCH) of the Instituto Politécnico Nacional (IPN) met with representatives of the UNAM, the Normal, and the Chapingo Agricultural School to discuss plans for a general strike of all schools.[23] On July 30, police used bazooka fire to destroy the 300 year old door of the Preparatoria #1. More than 400 students were injured, several were killed, and 1000 were jailed. Police occupied several schools.

On August 1, Javier Barros Sierra, rector of the UNAM, gave much credibility to the emerging student movement by leading a protest march involving 80,000 people. The general director of the IPN, Guillermo Massieu, also defended the students against the attacks of the police. President Gustavo Díaz Ordaz offered his "hand" as an olive branch of peace to the students.[24] Accusations arose that the student movement was infiltrated with official agitators from the "corrientes del maoísmo y el trotskismo." On August 8 the Consejo Nacional de Huelga (CNH) was organized with members from the IPN, UNAM, Chapingo, the Normal, the Colegio de México, the Universidad Iberoamericana, the Universidad Lasalle, and universities from other parts of the country. Over 150,000 students and professors had joined the strike. On August 13, 200,000 protestors marched from the Casco of Santo Tomás to the Zócalo. On August 22, Luis Echeverría, Secretario de Gobernación, informed that the government was willing to discuss

---

[22]This was a government controlled student organization. Although the FNET protested the excess of police violence on this occasion, it later sided with the government. It was therefore repudiated by the majority of the student movement.

[23]The strike would last until the following six demands were met: (1) the dissolution of the FNET, the Porra Universitaria, and the MURO (student political groups controlled by the government authorities); (2) expulsion of students who were members of said groups; (3) indemnization by the government for students injured or killed by the police; (4) freedom for all students detained in jails; (5) the dissolution of the "granaderos" police unit; and (6) abolishment of article 145 of the Penal Code.

[24]In Guanajuato he declared, "Una mano está tendida, la de un hombre que a través de la pequeña historia de su vida, ha demostrado que sabe ser leal. Los mexicanos dirán si esa mano se queda tendida en el aire. . . ."

the problems with the "true teachers and students."[25] The CNH asked the government to name the date, time, and place for the discussions, with the only condition that they be public.

On August 27 the largest protest march took place with 400,000 people gathering in the Zocalo. At 1 am on the next morning the police and army used force to remove the student guards from the Zocalo. From this date on, the police and army always used force in their confrontations with the demonstrators. Various government spokesmen defended the use of this force.[26] Respected professor and engineer Heberto Castillo was beaten by policemen and demanded the re-establishment of the "implementation of the Constitution." Accused of using the student movement to disrupt the Olympics, the CNH denied the validity of such charges.

In his State of the Union address on September 1, President Díaz Ordaz warned that he was willing to use the "totality of the armed forces" if necessary to restore tranquility to the capital. On September 10, the Senate gave complete support to the President. On September 13, 250,000 protestors participated in a "march of silence." One leader affirmed that "we are demonstrating that there are millions of honorable Mexicans willing to make sacrifices. We desire to have public discussions (with the government), so that the people be not deceived any longer."

On Wednesday September 18, the army took over the Ciudad Universitaria of the UNAM with tanks, jeeps, and 10,000 soldiers. The PRI supported the invasion and expressed "solidaridad y confianza al Gobierno," but UNAM Rector Barros Sierra urged the university students to maintain "the moral defense of the UNAM." Some divisions within the PRI surfaced as Diputado leader Guillermo Morfín "respetuosamente" asked the army to leave the university premises and that he "was in agreement with the conduct of the rector." Octavio Hernández, another PRI diputado, blamed the rector for the disturbances.

On September 21, violent confrontations erupted between students of the Vocational School #7 and the police. On September 23, Rector Barros Sierra resigned protesting that "it is obvious that university autonomy has been violated." The army also occupied the Casco de Santo Tomás campus of the IPN. Two days later, the university "junta" rejected the resignation of Barros Sierra. On September 30, the army abandoned the CU campus of the UNAM.

---

[25] Bellinghausen, Pensar el 68, 261, cites Echeverría as saying that the government "is willing to examine, together with the interested sectors, through its appropriate public officials, in their respective spheres, the points of view of the authentic teachers and students." Echeverría proposed "a frank and peaceful dialogue that would result in the solution to this deplorable problem."

[26] Fidel Velázquez, leader of the PRI controlled labor conglomeration CTM affirmed that "whatever means the authorities use to repress the current situation is fully justified and will be backed by the people and I believe that the time has come to use them."

On Wednesday, October 2, a crowd of students, adults, and children gathered in the Plaza of the Three Cultures in Tlatelolco. Some 5000 soldiers armed with machine guns, pistols, and high powered rifles attacked the crowd. Hundreds of participants were killed.[27] Two thousand protestors were detained, including the majority of the leaders of the CNH. On the following day, the Senate issued a statement affirming that the "conduct of the Federal Executive has been in accordance with the Political Constitution of the country and with its laws in effect." For several days family members looked for missing relatives in the Campo Militar #1 and in various hospitals. On October 5, the CNH cancelled all public demonstrations.

The Olympics[28] began without incident on October 12. Little by little, the Student Movement became weakened. On October 29, the army vacated the Casco of Santo Tomás campus of the IPN. During the month of November certain confrontations between police and students continued. Leopoldo Zea and Luis Villoro proposed continuing the protest movement while returning to classes. Gradually that idea gained the approval of the majority. On December 4 the CNH resolved to end the strike and two days later, the CNH was formally dissolved. The "Comités de Lucha" of the various schools were given the responsibility to continue the movement. Their "Gran Marcha de Protesta" on December 13 resulted in the arrest of 500 persons and was the last major event of the movement.

Although the Protestant community publicly commented very little about the student movement in the summer and fall of 1968,[29] certain debates were raised later.[30] For example, two years after the event, Methodist Pastor Raúl Macín accused his own denomination of having been indifferent to the events of 1968,

---

[27]"Mexico: Night of Sadness," Newsweek (October 14, 1968): 45-48 records the "official" statistics of 29 killed, 80 injured, and 363 jailed. Cf. Alfredo Márquez Campos, México, 1968 (Mexico City: Editorial Estela, 1969), 254, and "Spell of the Olympics," Newsweek (October 21 1968): 64. Interviews by the author have shown that many Mexicans did not have much faith in those official figures.

[28]The importance of the Olympics for both the government and for the students cannot be over emphasized. It was the first time that the Olympics were held in Latin America and the first time in a "developing country." The Mexican government's reputation was on the line, and therefore had invested eighty million dollars in the construction of sports and tourist facilities. The students used the international publicity of the upcoming Olympics as leverage for their cause.

[29]An exception was Pedro De Koster. This Methodist was widely known in the Evangelical community and was a respected business consultant in the Díaz Ordaz administration. He publicly gave thanks to God for the decisive police action of October 2. More than twenty years later, he maintained his support of that "gutsy" decision by Díaz Ordaz; Pedro De Koster, interview by author, 13 April 1991, Mexico City.

[30]The Baptists, Presbyterians, and Church of God denominations are omitted here due to the extensive coverage given them in chapters 3, 4, and 5.

even though many Methodist youth participated in the student movement.[31] In some cases, that indifference yielded to open hostility against students who participated.

> In the student movement there was a strong participation by youth of different denominations, Protestant youth who acted with a clear Christian conscience. Nevertheless, they did not have the support of the Church; that is, there were again isolated, individual actions, without the consent, nor the support, nor the interest of the Church. In some cases, as in the Gante Church, the youth were even persecuted by their own church, criticized, attacked, and finally some were expelled.[32]

The elder Methodist statesman, Gonzalo Báez Camargo, challenged Macín's comments. He defended the non-involvement by the Methodist Church during the student movement precisely because the issues were not clear-cut.[33] He also denied that youth had been persecuted by or expelled from the Gante Church due to their participation in the student movement.[34] Macín later became a political activist, running for the office of Representative (diputado) on the leftist PSUM party in 1982. He also left the Methodist Church.[35]

The Olympic Games scheduled to begin on October 12, 1968 were very important for Mexican Protestants. The more main-line denominations had planned several ecumenical worship services and activities.[36] The more evangelistic groups had organized several outreach activities. These activities tended to distract Protestant attention given to the student movement.

The Catholic Church hierarchy, with few exceptions (eg. Sergio Méndez Arceo), provided little official comment during the more active months of the

---

[31]Raúl Macín, "El Compromiso de un Pastor Evangélico Mexicano: Entrevista con el Pbro. Raúl Macín," Estudios Ecuménicos 9 (December 1970): 57-60.

[32]Ibid., 60. The Gante church was one of the principal Methodist churches in the city situated in a prominent location a few blocks from the Zócalo. For a history of the church see Gonzalo Báez Camargo, Biografía de un Templo (Mexico City: Ediciones Luminar, 1953).

[33]One of the most important questions for Mexican evangelicals was the amount of outside influence in the student movement. The period was definitely influenced by the student movement in France and the early protests against the Viet Nam war on university campuses in the United States. But the degree of outside involvement in the Mexican student movement has still not been clarified.

[34]Gonzalo Báez Camargo, "Rectificaciones que Son de Justicia," Estudios Ecuménicos 11 (1971): 82-84. At that time, Báez Camargo was a member of the leadership of the Gante Church.

[35]Others affirm that he was expelled from the denomination.

[36]Lutherans, Episcopalians, and Methodists, together with non-evangelical groups such as Catholics, Jews, and oriental religions.

student movement. Base communities and certain Catholic organizations such as the Centro de Estudios de Comunicacion Social participated actively alongside the students.[37] Their participation was a factor in their marginalization by the hierarchy. Successive student generations have generally seen the Catholic Church as being unconcerned about student issues.[38]

The student movement of 1968 contributed powerfully to the political awareness and activities of Mexican youth throughout the 1970s. It also marked a change in the relationship between the Mexican government and the general populace. Evangelicals in Mexico both participated in and were affected by these events. This dissertation attempts to identify and make explicit that involvement.

The Earthquakes of 1985[39]

On September 19, 1985 at 7:19 in the morning a tremendous earthquake measuring 8.1 on the scale of Richter jolted Mexico City and the states of Jalisco, Michoacán, Guerrero, and Colima as well as other parts of the Mexican Republic. It was the most violent earthquake that has struck the Western Hemisphere in this century.[40]

The following day at 7:40 in the evening another temblor (7.9 on the Richter scale) again struck the Mexican Republic. Together, these two earthquakes wreaked havoc upon Mexico City causing thousands of deaths,[41] uprooting tens of thousands of Mexican lives, and destroying homes and buildings worth millions of dollars.

Relief work and emergency aid were hampered by difficult and unforeseen circumstances. Three of the largest government hospitals (Hospital General, Centro Médico, Hospital Juárez) were seriously damaged resulting in the transfer of thousands of patients and the loss of more than 5000 hospital beds in the most

---

[37] José Alvarez Icaza, "Las Comunidades Cristianas de Base, Marginadas por la Iglesia al Dar su Apoyo al Movimiento Estudiantil," Uno Más Uno (Mexico City), 3 October 1988.

[38] A survey of Mexican college students in 19?? revealed widespread rejection of the Catholic Church precisely due to this apathy and lack of concern. See... CIDOC,

[39] The "official" report of the earthquakes can be found in Presidencia de la República: Unidad de la Crónica Presidencial. Terremotos de Septiembre: Sobretiro de las Razones y las Obras: Crónica del Sexenio 1982-1988, Tercer Año (Mexico City: Fondo de Cultura Económica, 1986). An extensive summary of the periodical literature covering this period is contained in María Teresa Camarillo, coord., Memoria Periodística del Terremoto (19 de Septiembre - 10 de Octubre 1985), (Mexico City: UNAM, 1987).

[40] "Disaster in Mexico," Newsweek (30 September 1985): 16-21; "Mexico: Killer Quake," Time (30 September 1985): 34-43; Allen A. Boraiko, "Earthquake in Mexico," National Geographic (May 1986): 654-75; and Terremoto de la Ciudad de México, Visión Mundial de México, 1986, videocassette.

[41] Official government estimates place the death toll at 7,000. Others calculate the figure at nearer 20,000.

affected areas.

In the midst of this disaster tens of thousands of Mexicans participated in rescue work, counseling, food and medicine distribution, and other forms of humanitarian aid. The international community also sent large quantities of food and medicine. There were many "complaints among Mexicans and some foreign relief workers that the government of President Miguel de la Madrid Hurtado had handled the crisis less than adequately."[42] Over the next several months, scores of humanitarian and religious organizations (both Catholic and Protestant) participated in the long and arduous task of rebuilding homes and lives. Much of this initiative sprang from the victims themselves and their neighbors. Again there were numerous accusations that the government of De la Madrid had mismanaged the situation, by siphoning off funds and delaying the construction of homes.[43]

Mexican Protestants were not mere bystanders during the rescue efforts and reconstruction process. On an individual basis, they became involved just like many of their non-evangelical neighbors. Yet they also participated in specifically Christian projects. This study will make explicit that participation and explore some of the longer lasting consequences of that involvement.

The National Elections of 1988

The national elections of 1988 were the most disputed in recent Mexican history. The Partido Revolucionario Institucional (PRI) had dominated the political scene in Mexico since the Revolution. It had never lost a presidential, gubernatorial, or senate election. But the contest developed into a three way race when one of the PRI's up and coming stars, Cuauhtémoc Cárdenas, deserted the party and challenged the PRI's candidate Salinas de Gortari. Being the son of one of the most popular Mexican presidents, Lázaro Cárdenas (1934-40), Cuauhtémoc was able to form a coalition of centrist and leftist parties including the Partido Auténtico de la Revolución Mexicana (PARM), the Partido Popular Socialista (PPS), the Partido de Frente Cardenista de la Restructuración Nacional (PFCRN), and the Partido Mexicano Socialista (PMS). The Partido de Acción Nacional (PAN), traditionally the main opposition, appealed to many among the middle class, the Catholics,[44] and those favoring a more capitalistic system. Their

---

[42]"Miracles Amid the Ruins," Time (7 October 1985): 36-38. The leader of the West German sixty-eight member rescue delegation claimed that "more people could have been saved from the rubble if there had been better coordination with troops and police"; also see "Against All Odds," Newsweek (7 October 1985): 38-40; cf. Monsiváis, Entrada Libre, 17-122.

[43]Ibid.

[44]. Since its beginning the Partido Acción Nacional (PAN) has had the support of many Catholics. Although official ties with the Catholic Church are difficult to demonstrate, many Protestants believe this party to be controlled by the Catholic bishops.

candidate was Manuel Clouthier. The official results gave the presidential victory to the PRI's Salinas with 50.4%. Cárdenas came in second with 31.1% and Clouthier was third with 17.1%. There were numerous accusations of voter fraud,[45] followed by large protest demonstrations.[46] In the Federal District (Mexico City), where the polls could be watched more closely, the PRI actually lost the election by a wide margin. According to the official results of the Comisión Federal Electoral, Cárdenas received 48% of the capital's vote, the PRI 27%, and the PAN came in a close third with 22%.[47]

Protestant leaders spoke very little publicly about the elections, either before or after. Catholic voices revealed a wide range of opinions and revealed the non-monolithic nature of Mexican Catholicism. Many poorer neighborhoods with strong Catholic base communities voted for Cardenas in large numbers. One leader of the San Pedro Mártir neighborhood ironically expressed the anti-PRI sentiment of his community, "With or without Cárdenas, we are all Cardenistas."[48]

It is commonly thought that the Catholic hierarchy is associated with the PAN party. Therefore, a large number of the more devout Catholics voted for Clouthier for religious reasons. And, of course, many Catholics voted for the PRI, the PAN, or Cárdenas, for reasons that had little to do with their religious convictions.

No study to date, however, has analyzed the voting preferences of Mexican Protestants. The survey used in this dissertation (see Appendix B) reveals not only how Evangelicals in Mexico City voted in the 1988 presidential election, but also describes related political behavior, such as party affiliation and participation in the pre-election campaign and/or post-election protests.

---

[45]Andrew Bilski, "A Tarnished Victory," Macleans (25 July 1988): 18; Stryker McGuire, "A Compromised Election: Despite Cries of Fraud, Mexico's Ruling Party Claims a Close Victory," Newsweek (18 July 1988): 36; Oscar Hinojosa, "Damaged Goods: Did Salinas Really Win?" World Press Review (September 1988): 17-18; Stephen Baker, "For Salinas, The Real Campaign is just Beginning," Business Week (5 December 1988): 48; and Robert J. Samuelson, "The Mexican Connection," Newsweek (12 December 1988): 53.

[46]Felipe Vargas, "México: Avance Democrático," Visión (25 July 1988).

[47]Iván Zavala, "Encuestas: La Brújula Loca." La Jornada (Mexico City), 5 March 1991.

[48]Fish and Kretzmann, "Reviving Mexico City," 1117.

CHAPTER 2

PROTESTANTS IN MEXICO UP TO 1964

Conquest and Colonization (1521-1810)

The Spanish Conquest of Mexico during the early sixteenth century was as much a religious conquest as it was a military one. For better or worse, the Spanish Monarchs had a wholistic[1] understanding of their presence in the New World, with the political, religious, military, social, and economic dimensions intertwined and blended together. The Spaniards, under the reign of King Ferdinand and Queen Isabella, finally defeated the Moors in 1492 killing them, converting them, or forcing them out of Spain. Thus, it was natural and logical for the Spaniards to extend the Christianization of Spain to all of the newly discovered lands. Soon after Columbus' first voyage, Ferdinand and Isabella appealed to the Pope to grant them title to the new lands. They insisted that their most ardent aim was to increase the dominion of the Roman Catholic faith.[2] Pope Alexander VI responded most favorably to their petition, granting them both the dominion of the Indies as well as the exclusive responsibility of Christianizing the natives.[3] Ferdinand and Isabella, as well as their successor Charles V, carried out this mandate with holy zeal and fervor.

From the first contact between the Spanish Conquistadors under Cortés and the Indian natives, the Spaniards tried to destroy the Indian religions and replace them with the Catholic faith. Bernal Díaz del Castillo, who accompanied Cortés on that first expedition throughout Mexico, relates that on the day following the first battle between the Spaniards and Mexican Indians, Cortés tried to Christianize the Tabascan Indians.

---

[1]Some recent commentators have made a distinction between the two spellings "wholistic" and "holistic." The first refers to the wholeness of interdependent components. The second is similar but has acquired certain unique characteristics due to its use within the New Age Movement. Given the polemical nature of that movement for conservative Protestants, the more general term "wholistic" is used throughout this dissertation to avoid confusion.

[2]This was especially true for Isabella, for in her letter of instructions to Columbus (Barcelona, May 29, 1493), she affirmed as her principal concern the conversion of the natives. See J. Lloyd Mecham, Church and State in Latin America: A History of Politico-Ecclesiastical Relations, rev. ed., (Chapel Hill: The University of North Carolina Press, 1966), 13.

[3]Ibid., 12-13. Ribadeneyra describes this Real Patronato de Indias as "la piedra más rica, la más preciosa Margarita de su real diadema." It was based on three main documents: (1) the bull of Alexander VI, May 4, 1493, which conceded to the Catholic Kings the dominion of the Indies and exclusive privilege of converting the natives; (2) the bull of Alexander VI, November 16, 1501, which gave the Spanish crown the tithes and first fruits of the churches of the Indies; and (3) the bull of Julius II, July 28, 1508, which granted to the monarchs of Spain the right of universal patronage over the Catholic Church in the new lands.

> One other thing Cortés asked of the chiefs and that was to give up their idols and sacrifices, and this they said they would do, and, through Aguilar, Cortés told them as well as he was able about matters concerning our holy God, and he showed them an image of Our Lady with her Precious Son in her arms and explained to them that we paid the greatest reverence to it as it was the image of the Mother of our Lord God who was in heaven.[4]

Díaz goes on to remark that the Indians were attracted to the image of Mary, and indeed begged to be able to keep it.[5]

Within the next three years the Aztec Empire had been completely conquered. Millions of natives came under the Spanish crown and evangelization began on a massive scale in New Spain.[6] In 1524, twelve Friars Minor of the Order of St. Francis arrived in New Spain, in response to a request made by Cortés to Emperor Charles V. These dozen men, considered the spiritual fathers of the Mexican Catholic Church, evangelized the Indians throughout the Valley of Mexico.[7] Other Franciscans joined in the work a few months later, founding a monastery in Cuernavaca.[8] The Dominicans arrived in 1526 and members of the Augustinian order in 1533.[9] Bishop Zumárraga estimated that 1,500,000 Indians had been baptized by 1531.[10] Just five years later, the famous Franciscan historian Motolinia claimed that five million Indians had been baptized.[11] The last quarter of the sixteenth century saw a marked change in the state of the Church.

---

[4]Bernal Díaz del Castillo, The Discovery and Conquest of Mexico, trans. A. P. Maudslay (New York: Grove Press, 1956), 63.

[5]Ibid.

[6]Gomara estimated that between six and ten million Indians were baptized during Cortes' conquest and that "in short they converted as many as they conquered"; quoted in Orvil W. Reid The Challenge of Mexico to Missions (Guadalajara: Baptist Student Home Print Shop, 1952), 36.

[7]Mariano Cuevas S. J., Historia de la Iglesia en México, 3d ed. (El Paso: Editorial "Revista Católica", 1928), Vol. I. quoted by Marvin James Penton, "Mexico's Reformation: A History of Mexican Protestantism from its Inception to the Present" (Ph.D. dissertation, Iowa State University, 1965), 8.

[8]Charles S. Braden, Religious Aspects of the Conquest of Mexico (Durham, North Carolina: Duke University Press, 1930), 136.

[9]Ibid.

[10]Ibid., 222-23.

[11]Ibid., 224. There are reasons to doubt Motolinia's figures but there is general agreement that by 1550, at least, the overwhelming majority of Indians in New Spain had been "converted" by the Catholic missionaries.

The great burst of missionary activity had run its course and those already "Christianized" displayed many pagan, idolatrous characteristics.[12]

While the Roman Catholic Church was expanding in the New World, it was being torn asunder in the Old. The year 1517 not only saw Europeans reach the shores of Yucatan but also the beginning of the Protestant Reformation. Luther, the "father" of Protestantism, initially attempted to improve the Church from within, as an Augustinian monk. But by the time Cortés conquered the island city of Tenochtitlán (Mexico) in 1521, Luther's break with Catholicism had become definitive. Europe was divided into those who remained loyal to the old Church and those who aligned themselves with Luther and the Protestants. Spain remained extremely loyal to the Roman Catholic Church. Emperor Charles V (Charles I of Spain) and his son Philip II led the movement known as the Counter-Reformation. They promulgated royal decrees prohibiting non-Catholics from entering any of the Spanish colonies overseas.[13] Before the Protestant Reformation began, these decrees were directed against Jews, Moslems, and "New Christians."[14] With the expansion of the Reformation in northern Europe, the Spanish monarchs banned all "Lutheran heretics" as well from their colonies in the New World.

Protestants, nevertheless, soon entered New Spain despite the decrees. The Spanish government was not completely able to enforce the ban. Most of the early Protestants were traders or settlers. During the reign of Charles V, some of his Dutch, German and Italian subjects came to his American colonies. His son Philip II, at times, claimed to be king of England and Portugal, and even France in the name of his daughter. It is not surprising that some of the subjects from those countries came to the Spanish colonies, and some of them were

---

[12]It is generally accepted that 1572 marks the end of the fervent missionary or primitive period of the Mexican Church. In that year the Jesuits arrived with their emphasis on the education and spiritual strengthening of the Creole society. In the same year a secular archbishop, Dr. Pedro Moya de Contreras, was appointed to the metropolitan see. Robert Ricard, The Spiritual Conquest of Mexico: An Essay on the Apostolate and the Evangelizing Methods of the Mendicant Orders in New Spain: 1523-1572, trans. Lesley Byrd Simpson (Berkeley: University of California Press, 1966), 2-4. The degree of Christopagan syncretism can be seen from the following comment of Motolinia: "Just when the friars were thinking that since they had taken away the idolatry of the temples of the demon, and the people had come to the doctrine and to baptism, all was accomplished, they found the most difficult thing of all, one which required a longer time to destroy, namely the natives gathered together at night and made feasts to the demon according to various rites. Later the friars were told how the Indians were hiding their idols and putting them at the foot of the crosses or in the steps below the stones so that while they appeared to adore the cross, they were really adoring the demon." Braden, Conquest, 251.

[13]Henry Charles Lea, The Inquisition in the Spanish Dependencies (New York: The Macmillan Company, 1908), 191-97.

[14]"New Christians" were those who had recently converted to Catholicism from either Judaism or Islam. Their Christianity was suspect because many of their conversions were motivated by economic reasons or even mere survival. Many continued to practice their old religions secretly.

Protestants.[15]

The first known Protestant in what is today Mexico was Andrés Moral, a Moravian lapidary.[16] He was arrested in Mexico City in 1536 for the crime of heresy. He admitted having fallen into the following ten "heresies": (1) verbal confession should be made to God and not to another man; (2) the Church could not curse or excommunicate because such actions were contrary to God and love; (3) the clergy would be better off married and the bishops had no right to collect revenues; (4) it was wrong for one man to confess to another because he had seen confessions divulged; (5) papal bulls were worth nothing and carried no value because the Pope sold them; (6) it was foolish for those dying as Franciscans or Dominicans to obtain indulgences; (7) he had always doubted the authority of the Church; (8) the Holy Spirit could come upon Luther, as upon other saints so that he could expound upon the Scriptures as had they; (9) Luther had power to expound the Scriptures; and (10) it was unnecessary for the Church to have images and it was unnecessary for Christians to adore them.[17] Moral was sentenced to wear the Sanbenito, to perpetual banishment from New Spain and to present himself before the Inquisition in Seville.[18]

Many "Lutheran heretics" traveled the same path as Moral. During the last half of the sixteenth century the more missionary minded Catholic orders were forced westward and northward to evangelize the Indians, as a greater number of "secular" clergy took over the Indian parishes in the central area and continued the Christianizing process. These were specially concerned to maintain the purity of the Holy Catholic faith and were eager to eradicate any form of heresy in their midst. Officials of the Inquisition brought many charges against the "Lutheran heretics." An Englishman, Robert Tomson, was imprisoned and had his possessions confiscated for his open criticism of the use of images in worship. He was sent to Spain to serve his three year term of imprisonment.[19] A fellow prisoner, Augustin Boacio, a Genoese, was accused of Lutheran doctrines and sentenced to perpetual imprisonment. Boacio jumped ship near the island Tercera of the Azores and swam naked to shore. He made good his escape and ended

---

[15]Penton, "Reformation," 12.

[16]This first "Mexican" Protestant was also known as Morel, Morab, Juan Alemán, or simply "the Moravian." See Gonzalo Báez Camargo, Protestantes Enjuiciados por la Inquisición en Iberoamerica: Documentos Inéditos o muy Raros para la Historia del Protestantismo en Iberoamerica (Mexico: Casa Unida de Publicaciones, 1959), 46-47.

[17]J. T. Medina, La Primitiva Inquisición Americana (Santiago, Chile: Imprenta Elzeviriana, 1914), 137.

[18]Báez Camargo, Protestantes Enjuiciados, 46-48.

[19]Penton, "Reformation," 14-17.

up in London.[20]

In 1571 a tribunal of the Inquisition was established in Mexico with two inquisitors. Only a few Spaniards were ever suspected of Protestant heresy. Indians were usually excused for their errors due to their "immaturity" in the Catholic faith.[21] Most of the charges were brought against foreigners, frequently English or French sailors and merchants.[22] In response, British privateers like Hawkins and Drake began attacking Spanish possessions at every possible opportunity. During the sixteenth century most of the "heresy" revolved around issues already raised by Luther and other Reformers in Europe. The Protestants in New Spain generally did not get involved in the debates of Bartolomé de Las Casas and others regarding the protection and evangelization of the native Indians.

The seventeenth century saw the Catholic Mendicant Orders continue their missionary work in the west and north. The secular priests consolidated the work throughout the rest of Mexico. The number of Protestants "discovered" in New Spain began to decline, although there were usually a few foreign residents or a few captured foreign sailors who could be presented at the occasional autos (trials) as "Lutheran or Calvinist heretics." For example, in 1601 some thirty-three Protestants appeared.[23] Most were reconciled to the Catholic Church but four were burned at the stake as "obdurate and impenitent heretics."

During the middle of the century a "Protestant Crusade" was directed against Spain's Empire in the Americas. Oliver Cromwell, Lord Protector of England, Scotland and Ireland from 1653 to 1658, commissioned a powerful fleet of thirty-eight ships and 2,500 troops known as the "great Sea Armament." They were to attack Hispaniola and establish a British colony there which would serve as a base to attack Spain's other American possessions. Their attack failed completely, and they were only able to take the island of Jamaica in May, 1655. After the restoration of Charles II to the throne of Great Britain in 1660, no Protestant state actively engaged in attacks upon the Spanish American Empire

---

[20]Ibid., 17.

[21]Mecham, Church and State, 35.

[22]Strained relations between Spain and other European powers played a major role in the establishment of the Inquisition in New Spain in 1571. An English fleet under the command of John Hawkins brought African slaves to sell in the Spanish Indies in 1568. His fleet was defeated and many of his men were captured. They were considered "English dogs, Lutherans, and enemies of God." Two years later a group of French Huguenots attacked a settlement on the Yucatan peninsula and left some prisoners in the wake of their defeat. These two large groups of non-Catholics in New Spain motivated Philip II to send inquisitors to Mexico City. Throughout the colonial period the Inquisition was used more and more for political purposes. Penton, "Reformation," 19-26.

[23]Báez Camargo, Protestantes Enjuiciados, 65.

for religious reasons.[24] Religious politics gradually gave way to secular politics in European affairs as the Protestant states of Great Britain and Holland were frequently allies of the king of Spain. A growing spirit of toleration in Europe also contributed to a softening of the Inquisition's treatment of "heretics" in New Spain.

The eighteenth century continued to witness this general lessening of religious animosity both in the New World and in the Old. Although several Protestants appeared before the Holy Office of the Inquisition, none were handed over to the secular authorities for execution.[25] For three centuries Protestantism had not been able to gain a foothold in New Spain. But winds of change were blowing. In many ways the Catholic Church was entering into a period of decadence.[26] The Enlightenment began to influence literate classes of Mexican society. This new philosophy became an ally of Protestantism, for in Europe many of its adherents advocated religious freedom as well as other civil liberties. The expulsion of the Jesuits in 1767 was another factor that weakened the Catholic Church in New Spain.[27] Colonists acquired many of their reducciones, and their work with the Indians was left in shambles.[28]

Independence (1810-1910)

The first half of the nineteenth century saw major changes take place in Mexico that paved the way for the future development of Protestantism, although little of this activity involved Protestants themselves. The Roman Catholic Church

---

[24]Although no Protestant nation would subsequently launch a religious crusade upon Spanish America, certain individual Protestants did continue to dream of the evangelization of Hispanic America. The famous Bostonian Puritan, Cotton Mather, was so inclined. Cotton Mather, Diary of Cotton Mather (Boston: Massachusetts Historical Society, 1912), 7:420.

[25]Some of the accusations seem quite contradictory. One Galician Spaniard named Francisco Laxe was accused of being "the most evil man who has been seen during these times since he reached the point of being an Anabaptist and an Atheist." A Frenchman, Juan Langouran, was charged with Protestantism, although, at the same time, he was considered a "Deist and a Judaizer"; see Báez Camargo, Protestantes Enjuiciados, 95. Many American Protestants appeared before the Inquisition tribunal as part of their "conversion" process; see Richard E. Greenleaf, "North American Protestants and the Mexican Inquisition, 1765-1820," Journal of Church and State 8, no. 2 (Spring 1966): 186-199.

[26]Enrique Dussel describes various aspects of this "Bourbon Decadence" in his A History of the Church in Latin America, trans. Alan Neely, (Grand Rapids: Eerdmans Publishing Company, 1981), 60-61.

[27]Although the Catholic historian Mariano Cuevas has argued for a Protestant conspiracy lurking behind the expulsion of the Jesuits, there is little evidence to support his claim. For a refutation of his theory see Dennis R. Palmer, "The American Protestant Conspiracy Theory of Mexican History: A Case Study in the Literature of Mexican Militant Catholicism" (Ph.D. dissertation, Graduate Theological Union, 1978).

[28]Dussel, History, 60.

was sharply divided on the issue of Mexican independence. The higher clergy, primarily composed of peninsular Spaniards (gachupines), opposed any type of revolution. The lower clergy, mainly creole in origin, mostly favored independence. In fact, it was the leadership of Mexican priests like Hidalgo and Morelos that ignited the revolutionary process. On September 16, 1810, Father Miguel Hidalgo issued the "grito de Dolores" calling the Mexicans to independence in the name of the Virgin of Guadalupe and of Jesus Christ. A class war had begun. Morelos established a Constitution modeled on the Spanish Constitution of 1812 and on earlier French Revolutionary documents.[29] He urged that all taxes that supported the church, except the tithe, be abolished. The actions of these two priests could not be tolerated by the Catholic hierarchy. Both were condemned to death by the Mexican Inquisition[30] for, among other things, having adopted the heretical ideas of Luther. Such charges had little foundation in fact and were primarily used as anti-revolutionary propaganda.[31] Nevertheless, it is important to note that the Inquisition, by proclaiming that Hidalgo and Morelos had read and appropriated Luther's doctrines, desired to discredit the two leaders by associating them with the "great evils" of Protestantism.

With the execution of Morelos in 1815, the revolutionary movement almost died out, with only small bands of rebels continuing to fight. Then, suddenly, in 1821, the opposing sides were able to unite under the leadership of Agustín Iturbide and the terms of the Plan of Iguala. The rise of liberal anti-clericalism in Spain in 1820 motivated the Mexican hierarchy to escape from the control of the Spanish Bourbons. Thus Iturbide was able to win over the majority of the royalists because his program did not contain anti-clerical elements and he was able to convince most of the revolutionaries because their goal of independence from Spain would be achieved.

During the three year reign of Emperor Agustín I (Iturbide), the Catholic Church enjoyed the support of the government. Even after Iturbide's demise, the republican Constitution of 1824 continued to guarantee obedience to the Catholic Church, protection of all of the Church's privileges, and prohibition of Protestant denominations. Foreign Protestants living in Mexico were not allowed to practice their religion. It was even difficult for foreign Protestants who died in Mexico to be

---

[29]For a description of the Constitution of Apatzingan see Herbert I. Priestley, The Mexican Nation (New York: The Macmillan Company, 1926), 234-35.

[30]Morelos and Hidalgo were the last persons to be condemned to death by the Mexican Inquisition before its final suppression in 1820.

[31]Hidalgo was also accused of "Judaizing" and Morelos was charged with "the ugly, impure and abominable of the heresies of Hobbes, Helvetius, Voltaire, Luther and other pestilential deistic, materialistic and atheistic authors that he has surely read. . . ." J. T. Medina, Historia del Tribunal del Santo Oficio de la Inquisición en México, 2d ed. (Mexico City: Ediciones Fuente Cultural, 1952), 354, 380.

buried on Mexican soil.[32]

One of the major organizations favoring political liberalism, and to a lesser degree religious freedom, was the York Rite Masonic Lodge. It became established in Mexico City in 1825 with the aid of the American ambassador Joel Poinsett. These liberal "yorkinos" maintained their struggles against the rival Scottish Rite Masonic Lodge, which grouped together political, economic, and religious conservatives.[33] Although the year 1830 marked the end of the "Masonic Wars," the York Rite Masons and the lodge that was begun later, the Rito Nacional, provided an ideological framework that was conducive to Protestantism.

The spring of 1827 saw the arrival of James Thomson to the shores of Mexico. He had served as an agent of the British and Foreign School Society since 1818, with the purpose of establishing Lancasterian primary schools throughout Latin America.[34] These schools used the Bible as one of their main textbooks. Prior to his arrival in Mexico, he had established such schools in Argentina, Chile, Peru, Uruguay, Ecuador and Colombia. Thomson also represented the British and Foreign Bible Society, a Protestant non-sectarian organization, and had brought with him a supply of Bibles and New Testaments. Although the government prohibited Protestant proselytism, it did permit the circulation of the Scriptures. Thomson's supplies were soon exhausted and he had to order more. Thousands of Bibles, New Testaments, and portions of Scriptures were sold during the next three years. Catholic opposition began to appear[35] and with the establishment of the Bustamante regime in 1830 Thomson

---

[32] A rather amusing debate ensued in the Senate regarding the burial of British subjects. When some Senators objected to the burial of heretics on Mexican soil, Senator Canedo responded that "...although he perfectly agreed with his worthy colleagues in principle, he foresaw some practical difficulties in the accomplishment of their wishes, which would compel him, though most reluctantly, to vote against them. The melancholy influx of foreigners could not be denied, nor was it to be expected that amongst so many, some should not be summoned, during their residence in the Republic, to receive, in another world, the penalty of their unbelief in this. What, then was to be done with the bodies? He saw but four modes of disposing of them; namely to bury, burn, eat or export them. To the first, his Reverend colleagues seemed to object; the second, might prove inconvenient for the scarcity of fuel; in the third, he, for one, must decline any participation; and as for the fourth, dead heretics not being included amongst the exportable commodities mentioned in the tariff, he feared that such an innovation might seriously embarrass the custom-house officers on the coast. He should, therefore, upon the whole, incline for burial, as amongst four serious evils it appeared to him to be the least." Quoted in Penton, "Reformation," 49-50.

[33] Wilfrid H. Callcott, Church and State in Mexico: 1822-1857 (Durham, N.C.: Duke University Press, 1926), 37.

[34] For a thorough treatment of Thomson's life see Juan C. Varetto, Diego Thomson, Apóstol de la Instrucción Pública e Iniciador de la Obra Evangélica en la América Latina (Buenos Aires: Imprenta Evangélica, 1918), 5-116.

[35] The Metropolitan See published an edict prohibiting the sale, purchase, or possession of any Bible

was forced to return to England.[36] But the groundwork for Protestantism had been laid.

One man reached by Thomson's work was Dr. José María Luis Mora. Mora not only became an official member of the Bible Society but also publicly praised and defended the Society's objectives in his magazine, El Observador de la República Mexicana.[37] In fact, upon Thomson's departure in 1830, Mora became the Bible Society's official representative in Mexico. He labored incessantly for the spread of the Scriptures among his fellow Mexicans in Spanish, Náhuatl, Tarasco, Otomí and Huasteco. Mora also advanced the Protestant cause by urging religious tolerance through his writings and as a political advisor to Gómez Farías.[38]

During this period important changes occurred in the field of higher education which paved the way for the later development of Protestantism. The establishment of the republic in 1824 deepened the conviction that the colonial educational structure could not adequately meet the needs of an independent Mexico.[39] Demands increased for greater educational opportunities and new courses in the fields of economics, constitutional and statutory law, and the natural and physical sciences. A shift in theoretical orientation gradually took place from traditional Scholasticism to a greater reliance on empirical methods. Mora championed this liberal cause and argued "that clerical domination of the colegios produced graduates who seemed more fit for the cloistered life of the monastery than for leadership positions in the economy or government of the new republic."[40] In the majority of cases the government was able to establish civil institutes of education independent of clerical control without inspiring united opposition from the ecclesiastical leaders.[41]

---

published by the British and Foreign Bible Society. Frank W. Patterson, A Century of Baptist Work in Mexico (El Paso: Baptist Spanish Publishing House, 1979), 24.

[36]For a detailed account of Thomson's work in Mexico see Horacio Westrup P., Paladines del Evangelio en México (Mexico City: Casa Unida de Publicaciones, 1953).

[37]Pedro Gringoire, El Doctor Mora: Impulsor Nacional de la Causa Bíblica en México (Mexico: Sociedad Bíblica de México, A.C., 1978), 15

[38]Although Genaro García claimed that Mora himself became a Protestant, Pedro Gringoire found insufficient evidence to support that claim; Gringoire, Doctor Mora, 48.

[39]James H. Lee, "Church and State in Mexican Higher Education, 1821-1861," Journal of Church and State 20, no. 1 (Winter 1978): 59.

[40]Ibid.

[41]Ibid., 60-72. Lee describes in detail how hostile conflict over higher education between the government and the Catholic Church was avoided until the War of the Reform (1858-60).

By 1833, the conservative government of Anastasio Bustamante was overthrown. Although Santa Anna was officially President, most of the executive authority was exercised by the liberal Vice President, Valentín Gómez Farías. The liberal congress, urged on by Gómez Farías, produced far-reaching legislation that curbed the power of the Catholic Church. Priests were prohibited from participation in politics, the government stopped enforcing the collection of tithes, education was secularized, and monks and nuns were permitted by law to forswear their vows.[42] An immediate clerical outcry took place. The masses were persuaded by the Church to oppose the Liberals. Santa Anna returned as the savior of "religión y fueros," forcing the exile of the Vice President. The conservatives, with the support of the Church, won the victory as the legislation of 1833-1834 was repealed. Santa Anna did indeed appear to be a savior for the Catholic Church. But his actions over the next twenty years lost credibility not only for him but also for the Church. In 1836, Texas seceded. In 1845 Mexico was conquered by American troops and lost half of her territory through the Treaty of Guadalupe Hidalgo. Then in 1853 Mexico suffered humiliation as Santa Anna sold the Mesilla Strip (the Gadsden Purchase) to the United States for ten million dollars. The old "caudillo" had gone too far, and in 1855 he was overthrown for the last time.[43]

The new government headed by Ignacio Comonfort had many able, liberal leaders such as Benito Juárez (Minister of Justice), Miguel Lerdo de Tejada (Secretary of the Treasury), and Melchor Ocampo (Secretary of State). Gómez Farías was still living and provided inspiration as the "Liberal Patriarch." The Catholic Church hoped that President Comonfort would be able to moderate his more liberal cabinet, but that was not the case. On November 23, 1855, the Ley Juárez went into effect. It restricted the judicial fueros of both the clergy and the military, thus forcing both groups to be subject to the civil jurisdiction of the public courts. In June, 1857, the Ley Lerdo became the law of the land. Its articles stipulated that the Church sell its real properties, except for Church buildings, and dispose of its investments. Although the Church was to be duly compensated, this law had the effect of reducing ecclesiastical power over the economy. The Constituent Congress of 1856-57 included these two laws, as well as other anti-clerical measures, in the new Constitution. Article 5 declared religious vows to be unconstitutional.[44] Articles 56 and 57 prohibited priests from being elected to the

---

[42]Mecham, State, 348-52.

[43]For a good treatment of the political ups and downs of this "Benemérito de la Patria, General de División, Gran Maestre de la Nacional y Distinguida Orden de Guadalupe, Gran Cruz de la Real y Distinguida Orden Española de Carlos III, y Presidente de la República Mexicana," see Mecham, Church and State, 348-59.

national Congress or to the presidency. An article advocating religious toleration was proposed, but after a week of fiery debate, it was shelved by a vote of 65 to 44.[45] Yet, the final effect of the Constitution of 1857 was indirectly to grant religious liberty. The Roman Catholic Church was not recognized as the state church nor given special protection. Other churches could operate in the country under the authority of the freedom of speech, the press, and assembly granted under the new Constitution.

The Catholic Church reacted strongly even before the Constitution was officially adopted. Pope Pius IX attacked Mexican liberalism in no uncertain terms:

> The Chamber of Deputies among the many insults it has heaped upon our Most Holy Religion and its ministers, as well as upon the Vicar of Christ on Earth, has proposed a new constitution containing many articles, not a few of which conflict with Divine Religion itself, its salutary doctrines, its most holy precepts, and with its rights. . . . For the purpose of more easily corrupting manners and propagating the detestable pest of indifferentism and tearing souls away from our Most Holy Religion, it allows the free exercise of all cults and admits the right of pronouncing in public of every kind of thought and opinion. . . . And so that the Faithful who reside there may know, and the Catholic world may understand, that we energetically reprove everything the Mexican government has done against the Catholic Religion, against its Church, its sacred ministers and pastors, and against its laws, rights, and properties, as well as against the authority of this Holy See, We raise our Pontifical voice in apostolic liberty . . . <u>to condemn, to reprove, and declare null and void the said decrees and everything else that the civil authority has done in scorn of ecclesiastical authority and of this Holy See</u>. . . .[46]

The liberal reformers would not back down. Comonfort tried to effect a compromise but to no avail. General Zuloaga led the conservative forces and seized Mexico City in January 1858. Comonfort fled the country and Benito Juárez became president of the liberal government which made its temporary headquarters in Guadalajara. Three years of fierce fighting followed in the War of the Reform. This marked a turning point in Mexican liberalism's attitude towards Catholicism. Up until now most of the Liberals were practicing Catholics who only wanted to reform the Church and limit its power. But now they became anti-

---

[44]Article 5 declares that "the law cannot recognize any contract which has as its object the loss or irrevocable sacrifice of the liberty of man, whether for cause of work, education or <u>religious vow</u>...." (emphasis mine).

[45]Callcott, <u>Church and State</u>, 209.

[46]Simpson, <u>Many Mexicos</u>, 244-45.

Catholic. In July, 1859, with a desire to break the power of the clergy once and for all, Juárez issued the first of his famous wartime Reform laws. These laws stipulated that all church properties, including church buildings, were to be nationalized. No reimbursement was to be given to the priests. All male orders were suppressed. Only certain churches could remain open and only upon petition of the state governors. Marriage was declared to be a civil contract and divorce became legal. Cemeteries were taken from the clergy and placed under secular control.

The Catholic Church responded by anathematizing the liberal leaders and protesting against the imminent dangers of Protestantism.[47] Juárez countered by banishing the Bishop of Chiapas and by opening the door to the Protestants.[48] Just before the end of the War of the Reform on December 4, 1860, the liberals issued a decree establishing freedom of religion for all Mexicans. Juárez returned to Mexico City on January 11, 1861, and soon expelled the Archbishop of Mexico and other important clergy. Later, he expropriated all of the properties of the Church.

Hopes for a thorough Reform in Mexico were short-lived. 6000 Spaniards landed at Vera Cruz on December 14, 1861, followed by 3000 French soldiers and 700 Englishmen. After two years of fighting, the Austrian Archduke Maximilian was installed as the Mexican Emperor. The Catholic Church rallied to his side, hoping that Maximilian would restore their privileged status. Surprisingly, the Emperor refused to restore the Church's properties and only slowly abolished religious freedom.[49] With the end of the American Civil War, the liberals received the help of American pressure against Napoleon, compelling him to withdraw his armies. The Empire fell and on June 19, 1867, Maximilian died before a firing squad.

Once again Benito Juárez returned to Mexico City to continue his Reform. As a related goal, he promoted the development of Protestantism. His support of

---

[47]The liberals were frequently accused of being allied with the Protestants. One Manifestación al Clero warned of "that other reformed Church, which demagoguery pretends to establish in Mexico, it is the synagogue of Satan, it is the Protestant Church, the meeting-place of the adherents of Luther and Calvin, an invention of Jansenism and regalism; in short, it is anything it likes, but not the Church recognized by Jesus Christ. . . ." quoted in Wilfrid Hardy Callcott, Liberalism in Mexico 1857-1929 (Stanford University: Stanford University Press, 1931), 25-26.

[48]The liberals used the old adage "the enemy of my enemy must be my friend". If the Catholics hated Protestantism so much, the Protestants would probably make good allies for the liberals.

[49]In February 1865, Maximilian responded to a letter from Pope Pius IX, requesting the restoration of the privileges of the Catholic Church. He stated that he "was protecting the Catholic, Apostolic, and Roman religion as the State religión," but that he was at the same time authorizing "ample and open tolerance for all religions." Quoted in Jean Pierre Bastian, "Las Sociedades Protestantes en México, 1872-1911: Un Liberalismo Radical de Oposición al Porfirismo y de Participación en la Revolución Maderista" (Ph.D. dissertation, El Colegio de México, 1987), 54.

Protestantism had evolved over the years. Early on he had preferred and encouraged a Mexican Catholic Church, independent of Rome.[50] A small number of the lower clergy had supported the Constitution of 1857. These "padres constitucionalistas" began to organize in 1859. They received official support from Juárez upon his return to Mexico City in 1861.[51] Although Maximilian did not quench this "schismatic church" neither did he support it. With the removal of government funds, the independent Catholics established contact with the Episcopal Church headquarters in New York. The Episcopalians showed interest, and even sent a delegate to examine the situation in Mexico, but did not take immediate action in funding nor in the ordination of a bishop.

The return of Juárez in 1867 gave new impetus to the schismatic church. They were given two new church buildings and took on the name "Iglesia Mexicana de Jesús." Fourteen priests joined their ranks. In December 1868, the promised help of the Episcopalians finally arrived in the person of their first missionary, Henry Riley. By 1870 there were 23 schismatic congregations in the Valley of Mexico. Benito Juárez had now become quite favorable to the Protestants. He practically gave the church of San Francisco to Henry Riley.[52] He claimed that "the future happiness and prosperity of my nation depend on the development of Protestantism."[53] He went so far as to state, "I could wish that Protestantism would become Mexican by conquering the Indians; they need a religion which will compel them to read and not to spend their savings on candles

---

[50]A Mexican Church, subordinate to and supportive of the liberal government was more attractive to Juárez than religious groups of foreign origin. A thorough discussion of the internal schism within the Catholic Church in Mexico can be found in Bastian, "Sociedades Protestantes en México," 47-75.

[51]This support consisted of public recognition of the "padres constitucionalistas", the donation of two church buildings in Mexico City, the Templo de la Merced and the Templo de la Santísisma Trinidad, and the naming of Rafael Díaz Martínez as the "agente del gobierno para comenzar la reforma religiosa de la Iglesia Católica en México" with compensation.

[52]Matías Romero, who was the Secretary of the Treasury at the time, describes both his and Juárez' opinions regarding this transaction, "I strongly favored the implantation of a protestant community to restrain the abuses of the clergy. . . . I had to send for Protestants and bring them here, because only a few foreigners professed any religion other than the Catholic. . . . I then favored a Protestant community presided over by Mr. Riley, who wished to establish a National Mexican Church in competition with the Roman Catholic. . . . With the cordial cooperation of President Juárez who shared my sentiments and was perhaps more radical than I in these matters, I sold them the Church of San Francisco, one of the most beautiful in Mexico, located in the best neighborhood, and equal to which another could not have been built without great expense"; quoted in Lee R. Gandee, "The Introduction and Nineteenth Century Development of Protestantism in Mexico" (M.A. thesis, Mexico City College, 1949), 35.

[53]Gonzalo Báez Camargo and Kenneth G. Grubb, Religion in the Republic of Mexico (London: World Dominion Press, 1935), 89.

for the saints."[54] The schismatic church never really prospered due to various factors,[55] but many of the participants and congregations did become part of the Protestant movement in the 1870's.

After the Constitutionalists, the Baptists were the first Protestants to organize a church in Mexico. In 1862, James Hickey, an Irishman by birth, and his wife were forced to leave Texas due to their abolitionist convictions. They settled in Monterrey and immediately began to establish a church. In August of 1863 he was appointed agent of the American Bible Society. On January 30, 1864, three converts were baptized and the church was organized. One of these three, Thomas Westrup, was selected to be their pastor. The church was not affiliated with any denomination, but was doctrinally Baptist. Several converts were added in Monterrey over the next few years, in addition to a small congregation that was begun in Cadereyta, a town twenty-eight miles to the east of Monterrey. A schism developed in 1868. An American Cumberland Presbyterian missionary, Miss Melinda Rankin,[56] had moved to Monterrey in 1866 and began working with the Monterrey congregation. At her invitation, the Presbyterian minister John Parks moved from Brownsville to Monterrey to pastor the church. She alleged that Westrup could not properly pastor the congregation because he was an agent of the American Bible Society. The majority of the Protestants stayed with Westrup who had by 1870 accepted a position with the Baptist Home Mission Society. A small number of Protestants united with Rev. Parks to form a Presbyterian Church.

Sebastián Lerdo de Tejada became president upon the death of Benito Juárez in July 1872. The Catholics hoped that Lerdo would maintain a moderate position regarding their church, but that was not the case. Lerdo's presidency turned out to be very favorable to the Protestants as they began their work and very detrimental to the Catholics.

Many North American Protestant mission boards began work in Mexico in the early 1870's.[57] Mexico had long been considered a prime target for missionary work, but due to the American civil war and the unstable situation in Mexico, the

---

[54]Ibid.

[55]Bastian cites a lack of a unified, centralized leadership, geographic dispersion of the congregations, and the opposition of the Roman Catholic Church as the main factors. "Sociedades Protestantes en México," 72-75.

[56]Melinda Rankin has described her ministry in Mexico in her auto-biographical history, Twenty Years Among the Mexicans (Cincinnati: Central Book Concern, 1881).

[57]Some missionary work had already been started in Mexico by some Protestants, but this was primarily done by independent individuals. James Hickey, an Irish-American Baptist organized a church in Monterrey early in 1864. An American Cumberland Presbyterian missionary, Melinda Rankin, also organized a congregation in Monterrey at about the same time. These initial mission works will be studied in more detail in Chapters 3 and 4, respectively.

mission boards had postponed their plans. By 1872 the situation had become very favorable because the Mexican "government had broken the chains of Rome, abolished the convents, established religious freedom and confiscated all of the properties of the Church except those used for worship."[58]

The Society of Friends (Quakers) sent the missionary Samuel A. Purdie and his wife to Matamoros, Tamaulipas in 1871. Within one year they had organized a church and had reached 36 members. Three missionary couples of the Northern Presbyterian Church in the U.S.A. arrived in Mexico City in October 1872. Each couple was able to establish relations with some of the schismatic Catholics. The first couple moved to Villa de Cos, Zacatecas, and began to work with Juan Amador and Severo Cosio.[59] The second went to San Luis Potosí, due to the openness of the ex-governor, General Juan Bustamante. The third couple stayed in Mexico City for a time to study the Iglesia Mexicana de Jesús, before moving to Guanajuato. Two Congregationalist missionary couples arrived in Guadalajara in November 1872. They immediately began to make contacts with the liberal elements in the city. Five missionaries sent to Monterrey in 1873 began to work with the dozen congregations formed by Juan A. Sepúlveda and Melinda Rankin. The Northern Methodists preferred to send, first (in December 1872), Bishop Gilbert Haven, and then, Bishop William Butler (two months later) to effect the purchase of two large Catholic churches in Mexico. Thus the Methodist missionaries could build upon the tradition of the schismatic churches. The Southern Methodists also purchased a Catholic Church, that of the Capilla de San Andrés, through their Bishop Otto Keener. Keener left Alejo Hernández, a Mexican preacher who was converted in Texas, in charge of the church. The Southern Presbyterians began work early in 1874 in the city of Matamoros, Tamaulipas, with the missionary Anthony Graybill.

During the long dictatorship of General Porfirio Díaz (1876-80, 1884-1911), the government developed a more conciliatory position toward the Catholic Church, thus permitting the Church to regain much of its previous strength.[60] Although the

---

[58]35th Annual Report of the Missionary Society of the Presbyterian Church in the USA to the General Assembly celebrated in Detroit, Michigan, May 16-29, 1872.

[59]Presbyterian work in Villa de Cos had been started much earlier. Dr. Grayson Prevost had been spreading Protestant ideas for many years there. He had married the daughter of Don Severo Cosío in a Protestant wedding in Brownsville, Texas and had the encouragement of his father-in-law for his religious activities. Several Presbyterian workers, under the guidance of Melinda Rankin, had come from Monterrey in 1868 to help Prevost in his work. Thomas Westrup, representing the American Bible Society, had baptized 40 converts in a single mass baptism. These believers requested an ordained minister. Their petition resulted in the sending of the Northern Presbyterian missionaries. See Joel Martínez López, Orígenes del Presbiterianismo en México (Matamoros, Tamaulipas: n.p., 1972), 45-87.

[60]It is estimated that the value of ecclesiastical properties doubled from 1874 to 1910. In the area of education, the Catholic Church also regained its prime position. The number of Catholic schools

Laws of Reform were not removed from the statute books, neither were they totally enforced.[61]

At the same time that Díaz aided the Catholics, he was also quite willing to allow favors to the Protestants, thus limiting the strength of the Catholic Church. The Protestants thrived in this political environment. By 1903 the Presbyterians had organized 198 churches and congregations throughout the northern and central parts of the country.[62] Several new evangelical denominations and groups began work in Mexico during this period, bringing the total number of Protestant denominations to almost twenty.

As a corollary to their evangelistic work, the Protestants emphasized education. The Presbyterian pioneer, Melinda Rankin, was a teacher by trade, and established a primary school for Mexican girls in Brownsville, Texas, as early as 1852.[63] During her stay in Matamoros, Tamaulipas, in 1862-63, she opened a primary school there, and another in Monterrey, Nuevo León as of 1866. The level of this school was raised in 1879 to include a Normal school to prepare Mexican elementary teachers. In 1890 this school was moved to Saltillo under the direction of Jennie Wheeler. Over the next 26 years 175 women were graduated, of which the majority entered the teaching field, in private or public schools. Similar Normal schools were begun by many denominations, with the result that many Protestant congregations began to operate primary schools, as an evangelistic and social ministry.[64] The educational outreach reached into different strata of the Mexican population, ranging from the very poorest to the quite wealthy, depending on the locality and the denomination.

Most denominations also organized Bible Institutes or Seminaries for the training of pastors and evangelists. Quite often, this included elementary education as many men had not previously attended any school.

Evangelicals were divided along national lines regarding their evaluation of

---

jumped from 276 in 1885 to 593 in 1905. The prosperity of the Church can also be noted in the creation of five new archbishoprics (Durango, Linares, Oaxaca, Puebla, and Yucatán) and eight new bishoprics (Cuernavaca, Chihuahua, Saltillo, Tepic, Tehuantepec, Aguascalientes, Tabasco, and Campeche).

[61]Díaz moved very cautiously in relaxing the sting of the Reform Laws, and it was not until after 1890 that his "policy of conciliation" began to be discussed in the press. By then, his dictatorship had become firmly established and the old Liberal guard was too weak to challenge his policy. Mecham, Church and State, 376-79.

[62]Martínez, Presbiterianismo, 5.

[63]This later became known as the Instituto Femenino del Río Grande, where Rankin served as teacher and director until 1864.

[64]The Presbyterians began a primary school in Mexico City in 1872, which likewise was transformed into a Normal school in 1881.

the Porfiriato. Most North American missionaries described Porfirio Díaz in glowing terms.[65] Many Mexican evangelicals were dissatisfied with the dictatorship and began to oppose it openly.[66] The time was ripe for a revolution and the Mexican Protestants were ready to play an important role.

Revolution and Post-Revolution (1911-1940)

When Francisco I. Madero launched his campaign for President, most Mexican Protestants eagerly supported him.[67] They were ready for a change, and Madero offered alternatives that seemed congruent with Gospel.[68] Some Evangelicals, like the Methodist Andrés Osuna, were close friends with Madero.[69] There was nothing in Madero's program that went directly against the Catholic Church, but Catholics, fearing financial and political losses due to agrarian reform and lay education, established a National Catholic Party to counteract the Maderistas. When Madero was murdered, the Catholic Party backed the usurper Victoriano Huerta. Charges were made that the Catholic Church had supplied Huerta with money and arms.[70]

---

[65]The Methodist Bishop, William Butler, Mexico in Transition (New York: Hunt and Eaton, 1892) is totally uncritical in his praise of Porfirio Díaz. His son, John Wesley Butler, as late as 1907, Mexico: Coming into Light (Cincinnati: Jennings and Graham, 1907) still recounted the praises of the Porfiriato for the progress bequeathed upon the Mexican people.

[66]A good example of this growing opposition would be the Methodist pastor, José Rumbia Guzmán. He pastored a congregation in Río Blanco, composed largely of textile workers. He was supportive of them in their strike, which turned into violence. For a thorough examination of his involvement, see Jean Pierre Bastian, "Itinerario de un Intelectual Popular Protestante, Liberal y Francmasón en México: José Rumbia Guzmán, 1865-1913," Cristianismo y Sociedad 92 (1987): 91-108.

[67]From November 1909 on, the Presbyterian Moisés Sáenz was Chief Editor of the paper that Madero himself started, the Anti-Reeleccionista. Jean Pierre Bastian, Protestantismo y Sociedad, 109-15, provides many examples of such support. Cf. Deborah Jo Baldwin, Protestants and the Mexican Revolution.

[68]Although Madero was not a radical reformer, he did support the restoration of political democracy, an expanded program of public education, and partial restoration of lands confiscated during the Porfiriato. He described his program in the Plan de San Luis Potosí. This Plan can be found in Jesús Herzog, Breve Historia de la Revolución Mexicana: Los Antecedentes y la Etapa Maderista (Mexico City: Fondo de Cultura Económica, 1962), 133-42. The fact that he was not a devout Catholic (he was more of a mystic or spiritualist) also attracted Protestants to his cause.

[69]When Madero was imprisoned during the election campaign, Osuna had to leave the country for safety reasons. See Andrés Osuna, Por la Escuela y por la Patria (Mexico City: CUPSA, 1943) for one evangelical's autobiographical description of the revolution and his participation in it.

[70]The Catholic Church denied that it had abetted Huerta; Francis C. Kelley, Blood Drenched Altars 2d ed. rev. (Milwaukee: The Bruce Publishing Company, 1935), 469-75. But there is strong evidence to the contrary. For example, the National Catholic Party's defeated Vice-Presidential candidate Francisco De

Several revolutionary leaders such as Venustiano Carranza, Pancho Villa, Alvaro Obregón, Emiliano Zapata, and Pascual Orozco immediately rose up to challenge Huerta. The overwhelming majority of evangelicals who took up arms joined these revolutionaries.[71] Pascual Orozco himself was an active Congregationalist. Other Protestants aided the revolutionary cause with their pens. Otilio Montaño, a Methodist school teacher, helped write the Plan de Ayala for Zapata.[72] Many leading evangelicals used their influence to dissuade the United States from intervening in the war.[73] Huerta and his forces fell in July, 1914.

As the revolutionary fighting began to die down, the Protestants began to flourish in the country. They were able to have a larger influence in society than their numbers might suggest. Many evangelicals occupied key positions within the Carranza government.[74] Andrés Osuna was given a personal invitation by Carranza to head up the department of Education in Mexico City.[75]

The Constitution of 1917 was more radical than the First Chief Carranza

---

la Barra became a member of Huerta's cabinet.

[71]Bastian, Protestantismo y Sociedad, 146-47, gives a list of several pastors and laymen who held significant positions in the different revolutionary armies.

[72]Gonzalo Báez Camargo, "Los Protestantes en la Revolución Mexicana," Estudios Ecuménicos (November 1971): 14. Although the Plan de Ayala was written in November 1911, Montaño continued to participate actively in the Revolution. He was one of the Zapata representatives in the Soberana Convención Revolucionaria, a signer of the Ley Agraria (October 26, 1915) and a member of the cabinet of Francisco Lagos Cházaro, director of Public Instruction.

[73]When the United States took the port of Vera Cruz, Huerta issued a patriotic call for all Mexicans to defend their country. The Methodist Seminary in Puebla closed so that its students could join the revolutionary armies, but not Huerta's. The director of the school offered the facilities to be used as a hospital if necessary. See Bastian, Protestantismo y Sociedad, 137-41, and Robert E. Quirk, An Affair of Honor: Woodrow Wilson and the Occupation of Vera Cruz (New York: McGraw-Hill Book Company, 1964).

[74]Missionary Inman described Protestant participation in both the Revolutionary fighting and the Carranza government in the following terms, "When the Mexican Revolution began, the Protestant Churches became involved in it almost unanimously, because they believed that the revolutionary program contained the same content that they had been preaching for many years and that the triumph of the Revolution would signify the triumph of the Gospel (Protestant). There were entire congregations, that led by their pastors, enlisted voluntarily in the revolutionary army, and while the men went to the front of battle, the women helped them from their homes. Many Protestants now occupy (in 1919) positions of prominence in the Mexican government. The Mexican people have seen that the Protestants favored the Revolution and were willing to fight for its program." Quoted by Joaquín Cardoso, "La Historia del Protestantismo en México" in El Protestantismo en México, ed. José González B. and others (Mexico City: Buena Prensa, 1946), 18-19.

[75]For an inside account of Osuna's involvement see Osuna, Por la Patria y por la Escuela, 133-215.

had desired. It contained several anti-religious articles, which though mainly directed against the Catholic Church could also be applied to the Protestants. Article 3 prohibited churches from sponsoring schools and priests or pastors from being teachers. Article 5 forbade monastic orders. Article 24 granted religious freedom, but limited that freedom to religious services held indoors in government owned and regulated buildings. Article 27 stated that no church could acquire, own, or administer property.

Article 130 was the most radical of all. Some of its stipulations included the following:

> The law does not grant any legal standing to the religious associations known as churches.
>
> It is necessary to be a Mexican by birth in order to be a minister of any religious creed in Mexico.
>
> Ministers of religion may not, either in public or private meetings, or in acts of worship or religious propaganda, criticize the fundamental laws of the country, the authorities in particular, or the Government in general; they will have no vote, and may not assemble for political purposes.
>
> Studies carried on in institutions devoted to the professional training of ministers of religious sects may under no circumstances be officially recognized.
>
> Periodical publications which, either by reason of their program, title, or merely by their general tendencies are of a confessional character, may not comment upon any of the political affairs of the union, or publish any information regarding the acts of the authorities of the country or of private individuals, which have to with public affairs.
>
> The formation of any political associations whose name bears any word or indication relating to any religious belief is strictly prohibited. No meetings of a political character may be held within churches.
>
> The infraction of any of the preceding provisions will never be subjected to a trial by jury.

The new Constitution was completed in February, 1917. For the next nine years its harsh legislation was not enforced. Carranza and Obregón appreciated the support they had received during the war and therefore assured Protestants that these laws would not be enforced against them.[76]

---

[76]Not all revolutionary leaders thought so kindly of the Protestants. Penton, "Reformation," 126-27, describes that Ex-Secretary of Public Education Feliz Palavicini was a delegate to the Constitutional Congress and launched the following diatribe against the Protestants in a discussion concerning Article 3: "If the exploitation of our conscience must continue as before, it would be unjust and immoral to undermine the characteristics of our nationality by permitting the substitution of a national cult by that

Obregón was more anti-clerical that Carranza, but could not risk reopening a battle with the Catholic Church. When asked why he did not repress church-run schools, he replied,

> We are not unaware of the menace of these Catholic schools whose aim is to inculcate anti-government and anti-revolutionary propaganda. But at present there is not enough money nor facilities for the government to teach all Mexican children. It is preferable that they receive any instruction than grow illiterate.[77]

A decision made outside of Mexico during the Revolution greatly shaped Mexican Evangelicalism during the 1920's. For safety reasons most North American missionaries abandoned Mexico during the seven years of revolution and fighting. In 1914 representatives of several mission boards met in Cincinnati, Ohio to consider ways to encourage greater cooperation among the different denominations.[78] After much debate, stretching over the next three years, the representatives reached an agreement. The "Cincinnati Plan" consisted of dividing Mexico into eight different regions and assigning one of the eight participating

---

of a powerful and dominating neighbor. Our religion, Señores Deputies, has persisted among our people for centuries and centuries in spite of its dominating characteristics. The Committee wants those who teach classes in school to be sacristans, not clergymen. The Committee means well but it has not given thought to the lurking danger of Yankee conquest. The ingenuity of Protestant clergymen is admirable, The Protestant minister organizes sporting clubs that popularize English terminology; he has organized the Young Men's Christian Association, where music is played, where bad verse is recited, where the 'one-step' is danced, and where occasionally the Bible is opened and the Epistles of St. Paul are read. But the Protestant minister does not stop there, not being distinguishable from other men because he does not wear, I repeat, an episcopal ring, a bonnet, or a crown, he infiltrates in all official establishments disguised as a revolutionary radical. Taking advantage of the means that support Mexican Catholicism, he collects with his right hand the salary of a lay teacher, while with his left hand he receives the money of the Protestant missions of the North American Republic and is an aspect of conquest. I do not come here to argue with false testimony or with lies; I come to argue with facts. Do you think that we liberals would permit Señor Mora y del Río (the primate of Mexico) to act as the General Director of Education in Mexico City? Well, General Múgica, the General Director of Education in Mexico is an ex-Protestant minister. The director of a high school in Mexican is a Protestant minister. And various inspectors (of the Department of Education) are Protestant ministers. And do you know why, Señores Deputies? It is because of the admirable ingenuity of the Protestant ministers. Like parasites on the leaf of the tree, they take its color so that they will not be noticed. . . . I assure you that it is not the Mexican people who support the Protestant cult in the Republic. I assure you that the Protestant cult is financed with Yankee money." Although this quote reflects Palavicini's personal hurt at being removed from his post by Carranza, at the same time it shows the penetration of evangelicals in high educational circles.

[77]Ernest H. Gruening, Mexico and Its Heritage (New York: The Century Company, 1928), 220.

[78]This was not a totally new phenomenon. The desire for greater cooperation and even unification had been talked about at previous missionary congresses in Mexico and throughout Latin America.

denominations[79] to each region. The remaining denominations would stay out of each other's "turf." Mexico City, being a large city and the nation's capital, would be available for evangelization and church planting by any denomination. The participants would form one united seminary, one common publishing house, and combined interdenominational magazine.

This plan, although commendable in its desire for Christian unity, met with much opposition because the Mexican Church leaders were not involved in the decision making process. Although some Mexican leaders grudgingly went along with the plan, others refused from the very beginning. For example, the Presbyterian Church US mission had been working in northern Mexico for almost fifty years. The Cincinnati Plan stipulated that they pull up stakes and work in the states of Michoacán, Morelos, Guerrero, and part of the state of Mexico. The work in northern Mexico would be turned over to the Methodist Episcopal Church (South). The Mexican Presbyterian leaders refused to become Methodists and organized their own "Nacional Fronterizo" Presbytery, thus rejecting missionary personnel and funds.[80] The implementation of the plan created distrust and hard feelings between nationals and foreign missionaries which lasted several years.[81]

Although the common publishing house, Casa Unida de Publicaciones, has continued to publish books up unto the present, the other united ministries were short-lived. The interdenominational magazine, El Mundo Cristiano, circulated only from 1919 until 1929, as the denominations began to publish their own magazines

---

[79]The eight denominations were the Presbyterian Church US (South), the Presbyterian Church USA (North), the Church of Friends (Quakers), the Associate Reformed Presbyterian Church, the Methodist Episcopal Church, the Methodist Episcopal Church (South), the Congregational Church and the Disciples of Christ. The American Baptist Church (North) sent delegates to some of the meetings, but eventually decided not to participate.

[80]The creation of the Presbiterio Nacional Fronterizo forced those northern Presbyterians to become self-supporting, self-governing, and self-propagating. Their example has been cited frequently as a model for other Mexican Protestants to emulate. See Saul Tijerina G., Huellas Imborrables: Historia de la Iglesia Nacional Presbiteriana "El Buen Pastor," de Monterrey N.L. (Mexico City: El Faro, 1984), 37-40, and Eduardo Carrero, La Iglesia Presbiteriana en México: Sus Conquistas, Sus Problemas, Su Actitud, (Mexico City: CUPSA, 1927), 62-79.

[81]Eduardo Carrero, Iglesia Presbiteriana, 62-63, wrote a decade later, "The Missions have never revealed themselves so unknowledgeable of Mexican Presbyterianism as when they thought that through the articles of an irrational plan, thousands of borderland Presbyterians would consent to erase all of their history of struggles and sacrifices; to pluck from their minds the blessed memory of those who gave their lives in laying down the foundations of that work; to fold their hands out of fear of losing financial aid, and topping it all, to break ties with the Mexican Presbyterian Church. And to think that some Presbyterian missionaries approved such an absurdity!" Thirty years later, one of the first acts of the newly formed General Assembly of the Presbyterian Church was to declare the Cincinnati Plan null and void.

again.[82] The united seminary also disbanded.[83]

From 1926 to 1929 militant Catholics and government representatives were embroiled in the Cristero War.[84] President Elias Calles promised that he would implement the anti-religious elements of the 1917 Constitution, which Presidents Carranza and Obregón had not enforced. The Catholic Church, through its Archbishop Mora y del Río, announced on February 4, 1926 that it did not recognize the validity of Articles 3, 5, 27, and 130 of the Constitution and would fight against them.[85] The government understanding the Archbishop's statement to be seditious, ordered the arrest and deportation of all foreign priests on February 11. State governors were ordered to enforce Articles 3, 5, and 130 as soon as possible.[86] Strict and oppressive implementation brought forth many protests and riots. The Mexican Episcopacy made known their momentous response on July 25 in a pastoral letter signed by 8 archbishops and 29 bishops. They announced, "we order that after July 31 until we order otherwise all religious services requiring the intervention of priests shall be suspended in all the churches of the country." They considered this to be "the only way open to manifest nonconformance with the anti-religious laws of the Constitution."[87] Although the Catholic Church expected violent disturbances to break out, the government took control of the churches on August 1 without serious disorders. After further attempts to amend the Constitution failed, Catholics in Jalisco, Guerrero, Michoacán, Colima, Guanajuato, Querétaro, Puebla, and Vera Cruz, resorted to

---

[82]Carrero, Iglesia Presbiteriana, 42, affirmed that only 200 Presbyterians received El Mundo Cristiano in 1927, but 3,600 families received El Nuevo Faro, the official organ of the Presbyterian Synod.

[83]Another attempt at unifying the seminaries was tried in the 1970's and 1980's with similar results. See the section on the Comunidad Teológica in Chapter 4.

[84]For the most thorough study of the Cristero War, see Jean Meyer, La Cristiada 3 vol. (Mexico City: Siglo XXI, 1973); cf. Mecham, Church and State, 380-415.

[85]An interview with Archbishop Mora y del Río appeared in El Universal on February 4, 1926 with the following quote, "The doctrine of the Church is invariable, because it is the divinely revealed truth. The protest which we Mexican prelates formulated against the Constitution of 1917 respecting the articles which are opposed to religious liberty and dogmas is maintained firmly. It has not been modified but strengthened because it is derived from the doctrine of the Church. The information which El Universal published on January 27 to the effect that there would be inaugurated a campaign against the laws, unjust and contrary to natural right, is perfectly true. The Episcopacy, clergy, and Catholics do not recognize and combat Articles 3, 5, 27, and 130 of the existing constitution. This decision we cannot by any motive alter without being traitors to our faith and our religion."

[86]A description of the restrictive measures implemented by the government can be found in Mecham, Church and State, 393-95.

[87]El Universal, 25 July 1926.

armed violence. The armed conflict lasted in certain sections for three years. The government accused the clergy of having incited the violence. The priests denied it, but at the same time affirmed the right of the Catholic laity to protest.[88]

A tentative agreement to end the conflict and permit the priests to return to their parishes was worked out in 1928, but was then hampered by the assassination of President-elect Obregón by a religious fanatic. Emilio Portes Gil, upon assuming the presidency, announced on May 1, 1929,

> No religion will be persecuted, nor is the government guilty of any persecution of any sect. Liberty of conscience will be respected as heretofore. The Catholic clergy, when they wish, may renew the exercise of their rites with only one obligation, that they respect the laws of the land as the ministers of other denominations are doing.[89]

Further negotiations resulted in the priests celebrating masses again on June 27, 1929.[90]

One might expect that the Protestants would have benefited greatly during the War of the Cristeros. It is true that the Evangelicals, in general, submitted to the legislation contained in the Constitution and other decrees. Early on, President Calles had commended the Protestants for their submission to the government.[91] That submission bordered on "blind obedience" in certain cases. For their obedience, they were rewarded with enhanced legal status. In many states each denomination was permitted to have as many ministers as the Catholic church had priests.[92] Evangelicals felt they had Calles' personal support in addition to his official commitment to defend their constitutional rights.[93]

---

[88]Archbishop Mora y del Río told Minister Adalberto Tejeda, "We have aided no revolution. We have plotted no revolution, but we do claim that the Catholics of Mexico have the right to fight for their rights by peaceful means first and with arms in an extremity." Quoted in Mecham, Church and State, 400. The Archbishop and five other priests were immediately deported.

[89]New York Times, 2 May 1929.

[90]Many estimate that 1,200,000 lives were lost during the three years of the Cristero War; "Mexico" Cidoc Informa 2:5 (March 1965).

[91]"The law clearly states that all priests of all cults must be of Mexican nationality. Actually the Protestant ministers are working in Mexico without harming anyone for they have always adjusted themselves to the law." Excelsior, 10 August 1926. This quote by Calles is somewhat contradictory, because those "Protestant ministers" included many foreigners.

[92]Mecham, Church and State, 385.

[93]The official 1928 annual report of the Comité de Cooperación reported that, "It is reported that President Calles recently told a personal friend that he had prepared the way for the Evangelicals, but that they would have to do the rest, if they wanted to reap the harvest. The doors are certainly wide

Some numerical growth among Protestants can be attributed to the fact that the Catholic churches were closed for three years. But many Protestant churches experienced great difficulties during the Cristero rebellion. In the countryside, Protestants were frequently attacked by Cristeros, because of their presumed alliance with the government. Many evangelical Christians were killed.[94]

The great depression of 1929 affected Mexican Protestantism in many ways. Fewer funds meant fewer foreign missionaries and less money available for social ministries (schools, hospitals, medicines, etc.). Many teachers in the evangelical schools had to be let go and several classes were suspended. Relations between nationals and foreign missionaries again became strained as nationals wondered how "rich Americans" could suddenly become poor.[95] More emphasis was given to the concept of self-supporting churches. Greater independence and nationalism resulted.[96]

The Lázaro Cárdenas administration (1934-1940) has generally been considered as anti-religious. In the fall of 1934 a dramatic change took place in Article 3 of the Constitution. The clause stipulating "lay" education was changed to require "socialistic" education.[97] Its basic anti-religious characteristic can be seen in that "in addition to excluding all religious doctrine, it shall combat fanaticism and prejudice, and to this end the school shall organize its teachings and activities in a manner that will permit it to create in the youth an exact rational concept of the universe and of social life." Churches were not allowed to sponsor primary, secondary, or teacher training schools. Ministers and priests were not permitted to teach or serve in the administration of schools. Almost all of the Protestant schools were closed as a result of this legislation, never to be opened again.[98] Some Evangelical schools were bought by the government, while others were confiscated.

---

open for the National Protestant Churches of Mexico, and we ought to sympathize with them and help them with all possible means to fulfill their duty and to take advantage of these great opportunities." Quoted by Joaquín Cardoso, "Historia", 19.

[94]Alice McClelland. Mission to Mexico (Nashville: Board of World Missions, Presbyterian Church in the United States, 1960), 39-41.

[95]McClelland, Mission to Mexico, 46-47.

[96]Patterson, Century of Baptist Work, 123-52.

[97]Although Cárdenas had taken office, this legislation was pushed through Congress by ex-President Calles who still maintained extensive control over much of the government.

[98]Most Catholic schools were also closed, but re-opened later when the legislation was changed back to "lay education." Currently two million Mexican children are being educated in Catholic private schools, although this is technically illegal.

During the Cárdenas administration, the Protestants did find government protection and even encouragement for their ministry to native Mexican Indians. William "Cam" Townsend had done Bible translation and missionary work with an Indian group in Guatemala. The Presbyterian Moisés Sáenz, Sub-Secretary of Education with responsibility for rural schools, encouraged Townsend to come to Mexico and work with the indigenous population. Townsend came and brought many Bible translation missionaries with him. Thus, Wycliffe Bible Translators came into existence.[99] Over the years, Townsend and President Cárdenas became good friends. In 1938, when Cárdenas nationalized the oil industry (a very unpopular action in most business and government circles in the United States), Townsend wrote a book[100] and went on a speaking tour defending the Cárdenas policy.[101] Cárdenas responded in kind, granting properties and government contracts to Townsend.

The 1920's and 1930's saw significant movement in the theological composition of Mexican Protestantism. The historic denominations in the United States were undergoing the Fundamentalist-Modernist controversy.[102] Up until that time the vertical human-God dimension and the horizontal human-neighbor dimension of the Gospel had both been stressed. But as the debate deepened, the churches became more polarized. The theological liberals (modernists) emphasized "social" concerns whereas the theological conservatives

---

[99]Wycliffe is also known as the Summer Institute of Linguistics (el Instituto Lingüístico de Verano). The latter is the name by which Wycliffe has entered into educational and technical contracts with governments and universities throughout the world. In the decade of the 1980's, Wycliffe came under much criticism from anthropologists, Marxists, and the Catholic Church in many countries, including Mexico. Their self-defense can be found in Instituto Lingüístico de Verano: Conformado e Impulsado en México (Mexico City: Instituto Lingüístico de México, 1984). Strong criticism of Wycliffe can be found in David Stoll, Fishers of Men or Founders of Empire? (London: Zed Press, 1982) and in Dominación Ideológica y Ciencia Social: El Instituto Lingüístico de Verano en México (Mexico City: Nueva Lectura, 1979).

[100]Townsend, William. Lázaro Cárdenas: Mexican Democrat (Ann Arbor: George Wahr, 1952).

[101]Townsend was not the only one who defended the action taken by Cárdenas. The Mexican Catholic hierarchy also supported the President's policy, thus easing Catholic church-state tensions and leading into the more harmonious relationship initiated by President Avila Camacho.

[102]This controversy at the beginning of the century has had profound, global consequences up until the present day. For good historical treatments of Fundamentalism and its social implications see George Marsden, Fundamentalism and American Culture: The Shaping of Twentieth Century Evangelicalism, 1870-1925 (New York: Oxford University Press, 1980), David O. Moberg, The Great Reversal: Evangelism versus Social Concern (Philadelphia: Lippincott, 1972), Timothy P. Weber, Living in the Shadow of the Second Coming: American Premillennialism, 1875-1982 (Grand Rapids: Zondervan, 1983), and Ernest R. Sandeen, The Roots of Fundamentalism: British and American Millenarianism, 1800-1930 (Chicago: University of Chicago Press, 1970).

(fundamentalists) concentrated on "spiritual" aspects of the faith. The majority of foreign missionaries in Mexico during these two decades tended to be situated more towards the Fundamentalist end of the theological spectrum.[103] The Mexican churches, by and large, inherited and continued to defend a theologically conservative stance.[104] As a consequence, the theology of Mexican Protestants favored an "apolitical" posture, generally submissive to governmental action. In 1935 certain Presbyterian missionaries reflected upon the anti-religious educational legislation and concluded "we feel God has spoken, and we are satisfied."[105]

Another theological change came about through the Pentecostals. The 1920's and 1930's saw the birth and rapid growth of many Pentecostal groups in Mexico.[106] Frequently it was Mexican braceros, who embracing Pentecostalism in the United States, returned to their country spreading their new found faith. The "Iglesia Apostólica" was started in Chihuahua in 1914 and quickly spread to other parts of the country.[107] The "Asambleas de Dios" began work in Tamaulipas and Matamoros in 1916 and came to Mexico City in 1920.[108] The "Iglesia de Dios en la República Mexicana" was begun in Mexico City in 1920 by David Ruesga.[109] Valente Aponto González was a Baptist layman, who upon receiving the "Pentecostal" experience, began planting in 1930 a network of churches that later became known as the "Movimiento de Iglesias Evangélicas Pentecostales

---

[103]Missionary enterprise, understood as the conversion of individuals, could very easily identify with Fundamentalism. The concept of the Modernist "Social Gospel," although facilitated by circumstances in the United States, found little place in Mexico, as political restrictions and Catholic dominance permitted little social expression by the Protestants.

[104]Of all the historic churches in Mexico, only the Methodists belong to the liberal World Council of Churches, and many of them disapprove of such affiliation.

[105]McClelland, Mission to Mexico, 56. The attitude of resignation expressed in the identification of all events as the will of God is more common in Latin American Catholicism than it is in Protestantism. Yet that kind of resignation has become more pervasive within evangelical circles.

[106]For a good general introduction to Latin American Pentecostalism, see Pedro Wagner, Avance del Pentecostalismo en Latinoamérica, 2d ed., (Miami: Editorial Vida, 1987).

[107]For the most thorough treatment of the Apostolic Church in Mexico, see Manuel Gaxiola, La Serpiente y la Paloma: Análisis del Crecimiento de la Iglesia Apostólica de la Fe en Cristo Jesús de México (Pasadena: William Carey Library, 1970); also the Directorio Evangélico de la Ciudad de México, 1969-1970 (Mexico City: Federación Evangélica de México, 1969), 8, that Gaxiola edited.

[108]Gaxiola, Directorio, 9.

[109]David G. Ruesga, "Historia de Nuestras Iglesias" El Camino a La Vida (July-September 1987): 3-5; cf. Gaxiola, Directorio, 16.

Independientes."[110] The "Iglesia de Dios" (Evangelio Completo) was started in 1932 in the state of Sonora by María de los Angeles Rivero.[111] Other independent Pentecostal groups also began work in this period.

Although the historic denominations preceded these Pentecostal groups by fifty or sixty years, the Pentecostals soon caught up with and surpassed their non-Pentecostal brethren.[112] Latin American Pentecostals in general tend to be theologically conservative and politically withdrawn.[113] A strong emphasis on eschatological events leads them to be heavily other-worldly in focus. A spiritual-material dualism often pervades Pentecostal faith. These characteristics were not only true of Mexican Pentecostals,[114] but also influenced the non-Pentecostal groups who imitated some of their methods and practices.

As the first three decades of the Revolution came to a close, the social dimension of the Protestant church in Mexico had undergone a slow but radical change. It had entered this period as a small minority, but quite open to Mexican society. It wielded a considerable influence in the educational and medical spheres. During the revolutionary fighting, Protestants distinguished themselves both in military and non-military positions. But the great social upheavals of the 1920's and 1930's, together with theological changes and denominational relocation, moved the Mexican Protestant churches toward a more inward focus. Upward mobility had given many Protestants more economic influence but also tended to produce a more conservative mentality.[115] Some of the greater numerical growth of the latter years can be attributed to the positive social ministries of the earlier years which had given the Protestants greater acceptance. With the Church-State battles coming to an end, the Evangelicals entered the 1940's with a large evangelistic emphasis and limited socio-political involvement.

---

[110]This movement grew to 600 churches and congregations by 1969; cf. Gaxiola, Directorio, 23.

[111]Gaxiola, Directorio, 17.

[112]It is estimated that 60 to 70% of Mexican evangelicals today are Pentecostal.

[113]See Christian Lalive El Refugio de las Masas (Santiago: Editorial del Pacífico, 1970).

[114]Some new non-Pentecostal churches (eg. Nazarenes, 1926) with most of the same characteristics made their entry into Mexico during this period, and therefore added to the overall tendency of lesser social involvement.

[115]The International Missionary Council asked the Director of their Department of Social and Economic Research to do an in-depth study of the economic situation of evangelicals in Mexico. He did so in 1940 and discovered a strong economic base for future evangelical expansion and penetration into Mexican society. J. Merle Davis, The Economic Basis of the Evangelical Church in Mexico (New York: International Missionary Council, 1940).

<u>Growth and Stability (1940-1964)</u>

Shortly after being elected president in 1940, Manuel Avila Camacho was asked about his attitude toward the enforcement of the Constitution's anti-religious laws. He responded, "I am a believer." The major conflicts between the Mexican government and the Catholic Church were at an end. The Catholic Church soon took advantage of the new situation.[116] Schools were reopened, religious processions became commonplace, and priestly vestments reappeared on the streets. A pastoral letter from Mexico's archbishop, calling attention to the spread of Protestantism and urging Catholics to reject it,[117] brought forth a wave of persecution.[118] El Comité Evangélico de Defensa came into existence to defend evangelicals from attacks. Economic pressure was brought to bear upon some Catholics who befriended Protestants.[119]

Although Article 3 of the Constitution was modified again in 1945 removing the clause regarding "socialistic" education, few Protestant schools were reopened.[120] Evangelical Christians did not recover their outward educational influence. They concentrated more on internal Christian education.[121]

---

[116]See Soledad Loaeza, "Notas para el Estudio de la Iglesia en el México Contemporáneo" in <u>Religión y Política en México</u>, ed. Martín de la Rosa and Charles A. Reilly (Mexico: Siglo Veintiuno Editores, 1985), 42-58. Surprisingly, the Catholic Church became one of the government's most enthusiastic supporters. For example, in 1942 Monseñor Luis María Martínez urged Catholics to support the government's foreign policy "given that legally and morally the civil government is the only authority that can define such a policy" and "in case of doubt, according to Catholic doctrine, Catholics should align themselves with the government opinion."

[117]Many books and pamphlets were published to denounce and refute Protestantism. The publishing house "Buena Prensa" was most prolific in its publications including titles such as <u>Veinticinco Respuestas sin Replica a los Cien Disparates de los Protestantes</u>, <u>Los Principales Errores que se Difunden Actualmente en México</u>, <u>Los Errores del Protestantismo</u>, and <u>El Peligro Protestante</u>.

[118]Many incidents of persecution were published in the magazine <u>Tiempo</u>, 8 February 1952.

[119]Baptist missionary Reid, <u>Challenge of Mexico</u>, 84-85, describes a conversation he had with a printer in Guadalajara: I am a Mason and sympathize with the work you people do. However, the priest has five thousand papers a week printed in my shop, and you have one thousand a month. He tells me that if I keep on working for you, he will take his paper to another shop and also that his friends will stop giving me their business. That means that he threatens me with a general boycott. I am not a fanatic, but I have to live, so I cannot print your paper any more."

[120]The law still prohibited churches from sponsoring schools and ministers from teaching in them. Catholics got around this obstacle by creating "civic associations" to sponsor these schools. Only a few Protestant groups did the same (eg. the Instituto Juárez, a school founded in 1945 by Presbyterian laymen in Mexico City. McClelland, <u>Mission to Mexico</u>, 79.

[121]For example, the Presbyterians established a Bible School for Women in 1943 in the Mexico City suburb of Coycacán. During the later 1940's many of the older historic denominations spent much time

Protestants did get involved with students through the establishment of "internados," student boarding homes with a Christian environment, in strategic academic centers.[122] But these did little to integrate the Christian faith with the academic disciplines.

World War II had slight effect upon Mexican Protestantism. Mexico's relatively small involvement in the war did not produce much controversy in or participation by the churches. A larger influence was felt as the war drew to a close. As North American servicemen came home, many more missionaries were sent out to all the world, including Mexico. They were sent not only to the existing churches, but also to help establish many new denominations[123] and institutions.[124] The overwhelming majority of these new missionaries belonged to the Fundamentalist or Conservative Evangelical wing of North American Protestantism, and therefore had a lesser appreciation for social ministries.

Avila Camacho's pro-Catholic policy was expected to be modified by his successor, Miguel Alemán Valdés. Alemán was not affiliated with any church and his mother, Tomasa Valdez de Alemán, was an active member of the Presbyterian Church.[125] But Alemán continued the same religious stance of his predecessor, evidently desiring to maintain close and friendly relations with the Catholic Church. Catholics prospered and became more active socially and politically under his administration.[126]

Protestants felt that they labored under several legal restrictions. More than

---

on their "diamond" anniversary celebrations. The Presbyterians took advantage of their anniversary to create their General Assembly. These celebrations also contributed to the trend of becoming more ingrown in their ministries.

[122]McClelland, Mission to Mexico, 67-69, describes the "internados" that the Southern Presbyterian Mission opened in Toluca, Zitácuaro, Chilpancingo and Teloloapan.

[123]These were the offspring of new "faith missions" instead of historical denominations.

[124]Several theological institutions were formed during this period, frequently with North American support. The Instituto Evangelístico de México was initiated in the 1940's. Compañerismo Estudiantil was begun by Ed Pentecost in 1946. A dispensational seminary in Puebla was started at the same time. Although these organizations were interdenominational in character they all maintained a conservative theology.

[125]Protestants were disillusioned by the Alemán regime. When the corruption of his administration became quite evident, Protestants downplayed the religious affiliation of his mother, claiming that she was only a nominal Presbyterian. Lecture given by Presbyterian Pastor Pablo Pérez on March 4, 1991 in the Centro de Estudios Superiores de Integración Cristiana. Patterson, Century of Baptist Work, 154, claims that his mother was a Methodist.

[126]Records released in 1953 revealed the amazing growth and resurgence of the Catholic Church.

1000 applications for the opening of Protestant church buildings had been "shelved" during the administrations of Avila Camacho and Miguel Alemán. The Secretaría de Gobernación had done this on "orders from above." If the applications had been refused outright, the Evangelicals could have appealed to the Supreme Court for redress of grievances.[127]

Adolfo Ruiz Cortines, President from 1952 to 1958, resumed the Mexican liberal tradition of protecting the Protestant minority. An attack in 1953 against Protestants in Tepeji del Río, Hidalgo, met with swift government intervention. "Once government intervention came, it was quick and to the point. Seldom has official action to maintain the law and to insure their constitutional rights to Protestants been more prompt and determined."[128] Ruiz Cortines also terminated Gobernación's practice of shelving Protestant applications for opening new temples, and thus enabled Evangelicalism to flourish during his term.[129]

The presidency of Adolfo López Mateos was warmly welcomed by Mexican Protestants. Their expectations of continued favored political status and protection were fully met. In addition, the nation's First Lady, Eva Sámano de López Mateos, was an active Protestant. Protestants frequently asked for, and received, her intervention in political problems.[130]

Although statistics regarding Protestantism in Mexico can be misleading,[131] most researchers agree that Evangelicals experienced strong growth during the 1920's and slightly less in the 1930's. They obtained somewhat greater growth during the Avila Camacho and Alemán administrations, and a more rapid increase during the governments of Ruiz Cortines and López Mateos.[132]

---

[127]Gonzalo Báez-Camargo, "Punish Mob for Attack on Chapel," The Christian Century 70 (2 September 1953): 998.

[128]Ibid.

[129]Penton, "Reformation," 146. This new legal openness by the authorities was probably one of the important factors for the dramatic numerical increase of evangelicals from 1952 to 1957 when the total Protestant community tripled in size. See Clyde Taylor and Wade Coggins, ed. Protestant Missions in Latin America: A Statistical Survey. (Washington: Evangelical Foreign Mission Association, 1961).

[130]The most controversial exception to this policy was the case of Rubén Jaramillo. Many of Jaramillo's followers believe that his assassination was ordered by López Mateos; see Rubén Jaramillo, Autobiografía y Asesinato, 3d ed. (Mexico City: Ed. Nuestro Tiempo, 1978) and Raúl Macín, Un Profeta Olvidado (Montevideo: Tierra Nueva, 1970).

[131]Penton, "Reformation," 288-94, wrote an extensive appendix concerned solely with the difficulties involved in the statistics regarding Mexican Protestants.

[132]The 1930 census revealed that Protestants had grown by 76.23% during the 1920's. The 1940 census showed that this rate of growth had dropped to 36.55%. During the 1940's it rose again to 85.50%. Figures obtained from the denominations themselves vary somewhat from these "official"

One of the leading Catholic scholars on Mexican Protestantism, the Jesuit priest Pedro Rivera, saw Protestant growth posing an "extraordinary danger" that would account for 7.5% of the total population by 1970, and perhaps 16.5% by 1980.[133]

As the López Mateos administration came to an end, the future looked very bright for Mexican Protestants. Economically, many had become middle class, politically, they benefited from government protection and influence, and socially they had acquired much respectability with one of their members as the First Lady of the country. Yet much of their advance was due to earlier educational and social ministries. The loss of such ministries would prove to be debilitating later on.

---

figures.

[133]Pedro Rivera R., Protestantismo Mexicano: Su Desarrollo y Estado Actual, 3d ed., (Mexico City: Editorial Jus, 1961), p. 16, fn. 6.

CHAPTER 3

THE NATIONAL PRESBYTERIAN CHURCH OF MEXICO

Historical Background

The National Presbyterian Church of Mexico is one of the oldest Protestant denominations in the country.[1] Presbyterian roots go back to the mid-nineteenth century. Three pioneers stand out for the foundations they laid for the Presbyterian Church. Dr. Grayson "Julio" Mallet Prevost[2] was a medical doctor who accompanied the U.S. troops in the war of 1846-47. He decided to remain in Mexico to practice his medical profession as well as serve as American consul. He married the daughter of Severo Cosío, an influential Zacatecan.[3] Prevost's personal evangelistic work in Villa de Cos, Zacatecas prospered and led to the development of a vibrant congregation[4] that later became affiliated with the Presbyterian Church. It was Dr. Prevost that persuaded the Presbyterian Church in the United States of America (Northern Presbyterians) to send their first missionaries to Mexico in 1872.

Melinda Rankin[5] was a New Englander who moved to Brownsville, Texas to start a school for Mexican children. When the Civil War broke out, being a northern abolitionist, she crossed over into Matamoros, Mexico and began a school there. Later, she moved to Monterrey and began missionary evangelistic and

---

[1]The most important self descriptions of the Presbyterian Church can be found in Centenario 1872 - 1972 Iglesia Nacional Presbiteriana de México (Monterrey, Nuevo León: Comité Pro-Centenario, 1973), published to commemorate the centennial celebration in 1972; Gómez Pascóe, Nicanor Felipe, Fernando Padilla, and Nicanor Gómez R., eds. Libro Histórico de las Bodas de Oro del Sínodo General de la Iglesia Presbiteriana de México, Julio 6, 1901-1951 (Mexico City: El Faro, 1956); Primer Centenario de la Obra Femenil Presbiteriana en México, 1887-1987 (Mexico City: 1987); and El Faro, their official denominational magazine.

[2]Centenario, 43-44, 131-32, 143, Martínez Orígenes del Presbiterianismo, 43-87, and James Ervin Helms, "Origins and Growth of Protestantism in Mexico to 1920" (Ph.D. dissertation, The University of Texas, 1955), 11-13, 19, 224-26.

[3]Apolonio C. Vázquez, Los que Sembraron con Lágrimas: Apuntes Históricos del Presbiterianismo en México (Mexico City: El Faro, 1985), 322-26. Cosío served as governor of Zacatecas, then later as director of Hacienda.

[4]Ibid. The church had regional and national influence as well through its magazine La Antorcha Evangélica, first published in 1869.

[5]Rankin's own evaluation of her ministry in Mexico can be found in Twenty Years among the Mexicans. See also Centenario, 40-42, 130-31, Martínez, Orígenes, 9-41, and Helms, "Origins," 16-20, 229. A more critical analysis of Rankin's work, as well as that of other Presbyterian pioneers can be found in Daniel García Ibarra, Inicios de la Iglesia Presbiteriana en México (Mexico City: El Faro, 1986).

educational work. Recruiting Mexicans to be colporteurs and obtaining support from the U. S. Presbyterian Church, she spearheaded evangelistic ministry throughout much of northern Mexico. Churches were planted in Monterrey, San Francisco, Mezquital and Cadereyta. Education also received great emphasis in her work, including the founding of the important school for girls and young women in Saltillo.

Arcadio Morales[6] was the dominant Mexican Presbyterian of the nineteenth century. Born into a humble family,[7] his father died when he was but nine years old. He became converted in 1869 through the work of Sóstenes Juárez[8] in one of the schismatic churches of the "Padres Constitucionalistas." A year later, he was selling Bibles as a colporteur in Mexico City and Puebla as well as leading a Bible study group in the capital. When the Presbyterian missionaries arrived in Mexico City in 1872, Morales joined forces with them, bringing his congregations in Mexico City, Ozumba, Tizapán, San Pedro Mártir, and Veracruz into the Presbyterian fold. He was a noted evangelist[9] and pastor with great initiative. He founded the First Presbyterian Church of Mexico City, "El Divino Salvador," and pastored it for over fifty years until his death in 1922.

The arrival of missionaries from the Presbyterian Church U.S.A. (Northern) in 1872 and the Presbyterian Church U.S. (Southern) brought more structure to evangelical work already begun by these pioneers. Many churches and schools were started within the first few years. By the mid 1880's enough churches had been planted to form three different presbyteries (Zacatecas - 1883, Tamaulipas - 1884, and Mexico City - 1885).

Important educational institutions were also started early such as the Presbyterian School and Theological Seminary in Coyoacán (1882),[10] and another seminary and high school for men in Río Verde, San Luis Potosí in 1890. Numerous schools for women were established. Many of these were normal schools, to prepare teachers for the elementary schools associated with the churches. These teacher training colleges were established in Mexico City (1881), Matamoros (1883), Saltillo (1892), and Aguascalientes (1881). By 1906, the

---

[6]Centenario, pp. 59-65, 131. See also Martínez, Orígenes del Presbiterianismo, 89-157; Vázquez, Sembraron, 128-34; Westrup Paladines del Evangelio, 37-56; and Bastian Los Disidentes, 40, 43, 57.

[7]Hazael T. Marroquín, "Circulación e Influencia de la Biblia en México: 'La Fe es por el Oir'," El Faro 79 (April 1964): 12-13, describes the poverty of Arcadio's family. His mother was Indian and came from a very humble background.

[8]It is not clear whether Sóstenes Juárez was a nephew or a cousin of President Benito Juárez.

[9]He was known as the "Moody of Mexico" due to his powerful, evangelistic preaching; Helms, "Origins," 240.

[10]Centenario, 355-84, and Vázquez, Sembraron, 336-42.

Northern Presbyterian mission had a total of 32 schools functioning.[11] The quantity and quality of these schools made important inroads into the Catholic population, thus provoking strong criticism by the clergy.[12]

Although the educational ministry of the Presbyterians was very strong during this period, little was done in the area of medical care. A limited medical ministry was started in northern Mexico in 1881 by the American doctor Walton Graybill.

Presbyterians played an active role during the Mexican Revolution.[13] At least three pastors, Eliezer Moreno, Miguel Peralta, and Ponciano Medina, left their flocks (or perhaps led their congregations into battle) to occupy mid-level leadership positions in the revolutionary armies.[14] Presbyterian laity[15] entered the ranks of the revolutionary forces in great numbers. Aarón Sáenz rose to the position of Jefe del Estado Mayor in Obregón's army. At the other end of the country, General Ignacio Gutiérrez was a leading force in the Madero Revolution in Tabasco.[16] In the port of Veracruz the important Oficina de Información y Propaganda Revolucionaria was directed by Gregorio A. Velásquez, an ordained Presbyterian minister.[17]

---

[11]Centenario, 334.

[12]Vázquez, Sembraron, 336, cites Agustín de la Rosa, a Catholic priest, who lamented in the newspaper El Tiempo of February 23, 1889, "Take a look at all the Republic; wherever the Protestants have invaded you can find the schools they have established."

[13]Deborah Jo Baldwin, "Variation within the Vanguard, Protestants and the Mexican Revolution" (Ph.D. dissertation, University of Chicago, 1979); "Broken Traditions: Mexican Revolutionaries and Protestant Allegiances," The Americas 40 (1983): 229-258; and Protestants and the Mexican Revolution: Missionaries, Ministers, and Social Change has written extensively on the subject of Protestant participation in the Mexican Revolution. For the most complete study of growing Evangelical opposition to Porfirio Diaz's regime, see Bastian, Los Disidentes and "Sociedades Protestantes en México." Both authors dedicate much space to the Presbyterians.

[14]Bastian, Protestantismo y Sociedad, 146-47.

[15]The term "laity" is not very helpful, since it gives the impression of a sharp clergy/non-clergy distinction. Such a distinction was not emphasized in early Mexican Protestantism, and even less in New Testament Christianity. Even so, the term "laity" will be used, albeit with reservations.

[16]A fairly complete description of Gutiérrez's participation can be found in José Coffin S. El General Gutiérrez: Héroe Presbiteriano de la Revolución Maderista en Tabasco 3rd ed. (Mexico City: El Faro, 1988).

[17]This center, under the jurisdiction of the Departamento de Instrucción Pública, was used to promote the Carrancista revolutionary movement through literature and speakers. According to missionary Wallace this was a "totally Protestant center", as Velásquez recruited a large number of evangelicals, including Presbyterians Pedro Navarro, Conrado Morales, Jacinto Támez, Moisés Sáenz, and Lisandro

Many Presbyterian pastors used the power of the pen to influence events during the war. Several protested the U.S. invasion of Veracruz, and they urged their American counterparts to use their political influence to deter greater U.S. involvement in Mexico.[18] Although some Presbyterians received certain privileges for their support of the Constitutionalist forces,[19] others paid for their participation in the revolution with harassment, forced conscription into Huerta's army, and even death.[20] A dormitory and a mission residence at the Presbyterian Seminary in Coyoacán were destroyed by fire in 1914.[21]

As a result of their extensive participation in the revolution, Mexican Presbyterians (and Protestants in general) received many opportunities in the post-war governments.[22] Obregón promoted Aarón Sáenz to mayor of the Federal

---

Cámara (one of the founders of the Presbiterio del Golfo in 1896) to carry out the center's program. Velásquez was a Carrancista delegate to the Aguascalientes Convention. Deborah Baldwin, "Diplomacia Cultural: Escuelas Misionales Protestantes en México," Historia Mexicana 36.2 (1986): 297-98.

[18]W. Reginald Wheeler, Dwight H. Day, and James B. Rodgers, Modern Missions in Mexico (Philadelphia: The Westminster Press, 1925), 98, include a letter written by a pastor from Tabasco, "Very dear Brethren in the Lord: I am sure that no true Christian in your nation desires war with Mexico, because such desires would be the denial of his Christian sentiments. May the thousands which make up our denomination in the United States express frankly and openly their attitude opposed to the terrible struggle, foreign to Christianity and civilization, and clearly against the culture of that great American people. Our church should be the first to raise its Christian voice in authority against the savage struggle which may take both peoples no telling whither, covering them with desolation, ruin, and ignominy, because the struggle would be terribly costly and long drawn out and one in which the blind fury of hate would let loose the most horrible deeds imaginable for the misfortune of both nations. Brethren, very beloved, it is urgent that you, in these moments, make your Christian influence felt so that the evil should not advance, but that on the contrary it may be clearly seen that the great spirit of Christ which abounds in you has dominated the blind passions of men." The authors note, ibid., 107, that not all American missionaries shared this pastor's sentiments. Rev. N. J. Elliott was imprisoned for two weeks. Later he made his way to Veracruz and wrote, "When we saw the American soldiers and marines in abundance on the streets and American battleships in the harbor, it was a sight to cheer a weary soul. When I saw 'Old Glory' waving from the flagstaff, I reverently took off my hat and thanked God that though I was not yet in my own land, I was safe under my own flag."

[19]Helms, "Origins," 313, notes that after the Carranza forces captured Matamoros on June 3, 1913, only the Protestant churches and schools were allowed to remain open. Constitutionalist soldiers attended Presbyterian church services and school exercises.

[20]Ibid., 99-107.

[21]It was thought that anti-American and anti-Protestant sentiment (both stirred up by Huerta) were the causes behind the arson.

[22]The Catholic priest, Francis Kelly, Blood Drenched Altars, 312, calculated that 50 percent of those that occupied positions of importance in the Carranza regime had studied in Protestant schools in Mexico or in the United States.

District and later to governor of the state of Nuevo León.[23] His brother Moisés Sáenz succeeded Vasconcelos as director of Public Education.[24] Celia García de Alarcón helped Moisés Sáenz found the program of secondary education, and later she became the director of the secondary schools in the Federal District.[25] Pastor Alfonso Herrera became director of the Universidad de México during the Carranza government, and later, director of the Escuela Técnica Nacional de México.[26]

Although several Presbyterian individuals held key government positions and influence, the Presbyterian Church, at a congregational and denominational level, was weaker due to several factors. The Revolution had taken its toll upon the local churches. The churches affiliated with the Presbyterian Church U.S.A. (Northern) recorded 1,845 communicants in 1919, which was quite down from 4,744 communicants in 1912 and 5,014 in 1906. This decline in membership paralleled a decline in the number of schools sponsored, down from thirty-eight in 1906 to eleven in 1919.[27] In the decade of the 1920's the Presbyterians were able to establish a few quality schools,[28] but regained neither the quantity of schools nor the influence that they had achieved in the educational field prior to the Revolution.

The implementation of the Plan of Cincinnati[29] caused further weakness in the Presbyterian Church due to the relocation of personnel and reorganization

---

[23]Aarón Sáenz later abandoned his ties with the evangelical faith. Since he was a well known figure, his "apostasy" probably contributed to the later Protestant belief that politics were spiritually dangerous and therefore, an unsuitable profession for an evangelical believer.

[24]For this key figure Bastian dedicates an entire chapter "El Protestantismo de Moisés Sáenz, o Etica Protestante, Fundamento de la Escuela Activa en México," in Protestantismo y Sociedad, 153-67. See also Edwin H. Rosser, "Beyond Revolution: The Social Concern of Moisés Sáenz, Mexican Educator" (Ph.D. dissertation, The American University, 1970) and Francisco Javier Guerrero, "Moisés Sáenz, el Precursor Olvidado," Nueva Antropología 1 (1975): 31-55.

[25]"Jubileo de Oro de la Maestra Celia García de Alarcón," El Faro (May 1964): 6.

[26]Herrera was a graduate, together with Moisés Sáenz, of the Presbyterian school in Coyoacán. He was an ordained Presbyterian pastor for 17 years before switching to the Methodist denomination in 1912. See Baldwin, "Diplomacia Cultural," 295, and Gómez, Libro Histórico, 55.

[27]Helms, Origins, 247-66, 297-313, describes with great detail and numerous statistics the educational work of the Presbyterian Church up until 1920. He notes that the southern Presbyterians ceased giving mission money for day schools after 1917. This was due to the prohibition of religious education in private schools stipulated by the Constitution.

[28]The Turner-Hodge School for Girls opened in Mérida, Yucatán in 1918. Other day schools were established in Morelia and Toluca, and an agricultural school in Teloloapan, Guerrero.

[29]The Plan of Cincinnati is discussed at greater length in Chapter 2.

of structures involved. The missionaries of the Presbyterian Church U.S. (Southern) had to pull up stakes and move from the states of Tamaulipas and Núevo León to their new assigned territory in the states of Morelos, México, Guerrero, and Michoacán. The new work in these states took many years to become established.

It was assumed that the Presbyterian churches in northern Mexico would become affiliated with the Methodist Church assigned to that territory. The Presbyterian congregations refused to do so, and formed their own Presbiterio Nacional Fronterizo. Consequently, they lost access to missionary personnel and subsidies. In spite of sacrificial giving by the Mexican churches in the Presbiterio Nacional Fronterizo,[30] the loss of missionary funds and teachers forced the presbytery to close many of its schools.

The missionaries with the Presbyterian Church U.S.A. (Northern) experienced less relocation as they retained their fields in Chiapas, Tabasco, and Yucatán. Even so, they had to abandon their work in the states of Coahuila, Hidalgo, Nuevo León, San Luis Potosí, and Zacatecas.

The Plan of Cincinnati became divisive in additional ways. The Methodists turned over many church buildings to the Presbyterians in the areas the missionaries vacated such as in the states of (?) Michoacán and México. The Presbyterians in the Presbiterio Nacional Fronterizo refused to do likewise since they continued to use their buildings. This caused hard feelings between the two denominations.

There was even more bitter strife within the Presbyterian fold. For over two decades lines were drawn between the "cooperacionistas" who favored working ecumenically with other denominations on joint ventures such as the Seminario Unido and the Casa Unida de Publicaciones and the "nacionalistas" who not only refused to participate with other denominations but also denied their Presbyterian brothers and sisters the right to do so.[31] Other issues became a part of this controversy, including the fundamentalist/modernist theological issue. To defend themselves against these "modernist" or "liberal" charges, the ecumenically minded "cooperacionistas" also adopted a fundamentalist theology, which explains, in part,

---

[30]Wheeler, Day, and Rodgers, Modern Missions in Mexico, 11/ comment that, in 1921, the membership of this presbytery gave 50,000 pesos in offerings, out of a total of 80,000 pesos given by all Mexican Presbyterians!

[31]It is amazing that year after year this debate raged on, at the expense of other issues. In the official Libro Histórico it is clearly seen that this debate was a major issue for the Presbyterians during the 1920's and 1930's. What is surprising is that there is not even one mention of the Cristero War nor the 1934 change in Article 3 to "socialist education."

why most Presbyterians shy away from too much prophetic involvement in society.[32]

During the War of the Cristeros, the Presbyterians were overwhelmingly supportive of the government. The missionaries went out of their way to declare their obedience to the Calles administration.[33]

The change in Article 3 of the Constitution in 1934 closed down the majority of the Presbyterian schools. The (Northern) Presbyterian schools in Coyoacán and San Angel were confiscated by the government, whereas the Cárdenas administration bought out the (Southern) Presbyterian schools.[34] Many of the teachers from these Presbyterian schools, both foreign missionaries as well as national workers, were reassigned to do Christian Education within the churches. Cadres of Christian teachers held Vacation Bible schools, Bible institutes, camps, retreats, conferences, lay seminars and did home visitation to strengthen the local churches. Many congregations saw a marked increase in conversions, baptisms, and new members.[35]

Although Lázaro Cárdenas was thought to be anti-religious, Mexican Presbyterians were fairly enthusiastic about his administration. Early on, Cárdenas encouraged Townsend to begin the ministry of Wycliffe Bible Translators with several Indian groups. Presbyterian Moisés Sáenz brought Townsend and Cárdenas together, who then became good friends.[36] Since much of the work of the Wycliffe Bible Translators was with ethnic groups in southern Mexico (ie. Presbyterian territory), most of the converts from these Indian groups became members of Presbyterian churches.

Hazael T. Marroquín, director of the Agencia Bíblica, had a personal interview with President Cárdenas on February 26, 1938, to solicit an exemption from import duties on Bibles imported into Mexico. On June 30 of the same year, by executive decree, all books were declared exempt from duties. Marroquín and

---

[32]Presbyterian leaders Abel Clemente, interview by author, 22 May 1991, Mexico City, and Saúl Tijerina, interview by author, 5 July 1991, Mexico City, both confirmed that this movement toward a more conservative posture was indeed the case. It happened again in the mid 1950's when the El Divino Salvador church and other like minded congregations seceded from the General Assembly.

[33]Alice McClelland, Mission to Mexico, 40, 49, long-time Presbyterian missionary wrote that "scrupulous care was taken to meet every legal requirement for both churches and schools" and that "every care was taken to comply with existing regulations and possible future ones."

[34]Ibid., 50.

[35]. The Southern Presbyterians showed almost a 100% increase in new church members in 1935. That higher annual increase was maintained for several years.

[36]See chapter 2 for a more thorough treatment of the friendship between Cárdenas and Townsend.

other Presbyterians saw President Cárdenas as a tool in God's hand.[37]

During President Avila Camacho's administration, Article 3 of the Constitution was changed back to read "lay education" instead of "socialistic" education. Although this legislation did not take place until 1945, the old law had not been enforced during most of his administration. Presbyterians in Mexico City had anticipated this new legislation and opened the Instituto Juárez on February 1, 1945.[38] Strong economic backing was given by General Aarón Sáenz, Ambassador Leandro Garza Leal, and Presbyterian businessman Fernando R. Rodríguez. The Junior High School was founded in 1950 and the High School in 1959.

The Presbyterian Church in Mexico City re-entered the medical field in 1945 by opening the Sanatorio La Salud, as well as a school for nurses.[39] The Christian Medical Association of Mexico City also became quite active during the 1940's with brigades to isolated parts of the country. Presbyterians doctors also rushed to help out during disasters, such as various earthquakes that shook Vera Cruz, Oaxaca and Guerrero.[40]

The internal conflict between cooperacionistas and anti-cooperacionistas took a dramatic turn in the 1950's when the Divino Salvador Church came under the influence of separationist Carl McIntire. The church broke away from the denomination and took other churches with it.[41] They created a new presbytery,

---

[37]Hazael T. Marroquín, "Circulación e Influencia de la Biblia en México: Dos Eventos Trascendentes," El Faro (June 1964): 15. Dr. Elías Mercado Hurtado, interview by author, 15 April 1991, Mexico City, stated that he and most of the Presbyterians had great admiration for President Cárdenas due to his concern for the campesinos. This admiration continued for many years after his presidency ended.

[38]Flora R. de Garza Leal, "XXV Aniversario de la Fundación de los Departamentos de Primaria y Jardín de Niños del Instituto Juárez," El Faro (August 1970): 16-17. The Divino Salvador Church was the main church behind this project.

[39]Dr. Elias Mercado Hurtado, interview by author, 15 April 1991, Mexico City. The doctors who participated the most in La Salud were Rafael Marroquín, Moisés López, David Macías, and Elias Mercado.

[40]Ibid.

[41]This division created deep emotional wounds within the denomination. For many years the Divino Salvador Church defended its actions and accused the other Presbyterians of being "modernists". For example, in the official magazine of the church, Elia Ruth Maldonado de Castellanos, "Eminente Posición Espiritual de la Iglesia Nacional Presbiteriana," Curriculum Vitae (November 1961): 15, affirmed that "we will continue fighting against the modernism that has caused so much damage to the pure customs of Christian conduct, and we will in no way participate in the so-called "ecumenical movement" that so grieves the Holy Spirit, because we are fully aware that this offends the Lord and we know that darkness cannot be united with light." A defense of the Divino Salvador position can be found in Alberto Rosales P., Estado e Iglesia en México: Legislación Religiosa (Mexico City: n.p., 1990), 10-21. He explains how government courts were forced to intervene to order to resolve the disputes concerning church properties.

the "Presbiterio Nacional de la Ciudad de México," which included "the totality of the adherents of the genuine, national Presbyterian Church."[42] In their creed, they stated that "we BELIEVE that the essential and only function of the Christian Church is the proclamation of the gospel and its own edification, as the Body of Christ."[43] Some members who were not satisfied with this decision split off to form the Príncipe de Paz Church that did stay within the Presbyterian fold. Years later, the Divino Salvador Church rejoined the Presbyterian denomination, and hosted the centennial celebration in 1972.[44]

The Student Movement of 1968

The Presbyterians entered the Díaz Ordaz presidency (1964-1970) with a greater social presence than either the Baptists or the Church of God (Iglesia de Dios en la República Mexicana). They were involved in social ministries at different levels (personal, local church, presbytery, and general assembly). To be sure, participation varied from region to region and even between local churches within the same presbytery, but overall, the Presbyterians affirmed that Christians should be active in society. In a key article in El Faro entitled "La Vida Cívica del Creyente," author José Hernández stated very succinctly:

> In what pertains to the Christian believer, he cannot isolate himself from civic life, neither do his convictions permit him to be indifferent to the struggles for social and political progress in his country. That is to say, we are not commenting about a sympathetic sentiment of the Christian toward the social struggles for freedom of people, but rather we are speaking about the participation of the believer in those struggles.[45]

Hernández went on to mention a long list of Mexican evangelicals and foreign missionaries who contributed to "the wholistic progress of their communities" through their participation in the Mexican Revolution and in "school boards, hospitals, benevolence institutions, libraries, and literary, temperance, and

---

[42]Maggie Coffin de Ruiz, "El Mensaje Mundial del Pbro. Eleazar Z. Pérez," Curriculum Vitae (November 1961): 22.

[43]Maldonado, "Eminente Posición," 16. Here, "proclamation" means verbal proclamation only. Social ministries are excluded.

[44]Some of the churches that were started by El Divino Salvador Church came back into the denomination in 1965. Many formed the conservative "Lluvias de Gracia" Presbytery. Some of the more well-known leaders of this group were Marcelino Ortiz and Vidal Valencia. The Divino Salvador Church itself came back into the General Assembly on January 16, 1969.

[45]José Hernández J., "La Vida Cívica del Creyente," El Faro (September 1964): 4.

morality campaigns."[46] Evangelical institutions are patriotic and give their support to progressive governments. The author ended his article by claiming that "a good evangelical Christian is always a good citizen. To Caesar, that which belongs to Caesar."[47]

Presbyterians took pride in their political connections and were generally quite supportive of each president in turn. Presbyterian Hazael T. Marroquín could boast that, while he was director of the Agencia Bíblica in Mexico, he had personally presented Bibles to five different presidents who expressed deep gratitude for the Scriptures.[48] Presbyterians were especially proud and supportive of President Adolfo López Mateos because his wife, Eva Sámano de López Mateos, was an active Presbyterian.[49] Many uncritically applauded the achievements of his entire administration. This can be seen in the lead article of El Faro of October 1964:

> It is necessary that we evangelicals of this country proclaim--and that we state it in a religious publication such as El Faro--that our patriotic sentiment impels us to render hearty applause to the President and his co-laborers, for the magnificent advances that our country has achieved under his administration.[50]

The First Lady was praised for her own accomplishments, especially for founding the Instituto Nacional de Protección a la Infancia (INPI), which among its many services provided three million breakfasts daily to school children.[51]

---

[46]Ibid., 5.

[47]Ibid. Hernández commits a subtle, but substantial, error in equating evangelical participation in the Mexican Revolution with evangelical socio-political participation in the 1940's, 1950's and 1960's. In both situations the participation was public and visible. The author does not appear to notice the difference between radical changes (such as those implemented by Osuna and Sáenz), more gentle reforms, and actions which defended the status quo. Although Hernández affirms that the Christian believer should be active in social and political struggles for freedom, in fact, Presbyterians in Mexico did not participate in such struggles if the ruling PRI party were the supposed oppressor.

[48]Hazael T. Marroquín, "Circulación e Influencia de la Biblia en México: Biblias Obsequiadas a Presidentes de la República," El Faro (August 1964): 17. Those five presidents were Plutarco Elías Calles in 1927, Lázaro Cárdenas in 1934, Manuel Avila Camacho in 1943, Miguel Alemán in 1948, and Adolfo Ruiz Cortines in 1952.

[49]This is quite ironic because Mexican Presbyterians are very opposed to "mixed marriages" (ie. an evangelical marrying someone who is not an evangelical). It seems that when the "pagan" spouse is the President of the Republic, there is an exception to the rule.

[50]José Hernández Jiménez, "Un Hombre y una Dama ante la Historia," El Faro (October 1964): 2-3.

[51]Ibid., 3. See also Ma. del Rosario Dávalos de Cabello, "La Labor de la Esposa de un Presidente," El Faro (October 1964): 4-5.

Presbyterians continued to emphasize their contributions and responsibilities in the educational arena. In the lead article of El Faro of February 1964 entitled "El Aporte Evangélico a la Educación," the author not only presented a historical survey of evangelical contributions to education, he also exhorted Mexican Presbyterians to fulfill their calling in this area by founding new schools.[52] Presbyterians still exercised control over some important primary and secondary schools. The Instituto Juárez in Mexico City and the Colegio Americano in Mérida, although having lost some of their prestige and reputation, were still strong academic institutions.[53] Presbyterian laity had also established the Instituto Juárez in Morelia and the Instituto Lázaro Cárdenas in Cuernavaca.[54] The Fernando R. Rodríguez School, begun in 1958, had grown and prospered. On February 28, 1964 it inaugurated its current spacious facilities on Arenal street in San Angel, Mexico City.[55]

To meet the needs of college students, the Presbyterian church responded in different ways. Dr. Gaspar Langella was appointed director of Student Ministries and was headquartered in Mexico City.[56] A student center, the Asociación Cultural Estudiantil A.C., was established near the large Universidad Nacional Autónoma de México, including a dormitory for university students who came from outside of Mexico City. Many Presbyterian churches had strong groups of Esfuerzo Cristiano (Christian Endeavor). Especially in Mexico City, these groups

---

[52]"El Aporte Evangélico a la Educación," El Faro (February 1964): 4-6. In addition to the exhortation to establish evangelical schools, Presbyterians were also encouraged to have a profound participation in the public schools. See Susana Arjona, "La Escuela Pública de México," El Faro (January 1969): 18-19. That same call to participate in the education in Mexico was sounded again in "La Educación y las Iglesias Reformadas en México," El Faro (January 1970): 12-15. The author also issued a call to establish a Protestant university.

[53]During the early 1960's the Colegio Americano underwent several problems, including four different directors in a two year period. Apparently the school regained much of its earlier prestige and several problems began to be resolved when Juan Leandro Garza Marroquín became the director in April, 1963. It is revealing to note that one of the difficulties he faced was an active group of Communist students living in the "Internado". He quickly got rid of them. See Juan Leandro Garza Marroquín, "Colegio Americano," El Faro (May 1964): 16-19. By 1969, the Instituto Juárez, although academically strong, had only 55% evangelicals among its faculty; "La Educación y las Iglesias Reformadas en México," El Faro (January 1970): 14.

[54]McClelland, Mission to Mexico, 79.

[55]Elena G. Meléndez, "Escuela 'Fernando R. Rodríguez'," El Faro (April 1964): 8-10.

[56]He immediately organized certain courses to help the youth respond "Christianly" to the academic world.

tended to have many college students in their ranks.[57] The Presbyterian Seminary, although primarily involved in training students for the pastoral ministry, was not totally isolated from secular education. Many seminarians, upon completion of their theological studies, were given scholarships to study at the National University.[58]

The remarkable events of the 1968 student movement took the Mexican Presbyterian Church, as well as many other institutions, by surprise. Few churches were able to understand the goals of and the forces within the student movement and therefore did not know how to respond to the large scale protests. During the summer months, the only official comment came through the magazine El Faro.[59] Eduardo Fernández Carrero commented on the student disturbances:

> After looking through a turbulent sea of data, it is becoming increasingly clear, that elements foreign to the student body have used the students to cause the disturbances. These inciters, enemies of the Mexican cause, infiltrated student ranks, and caused great damage, whose magnitude still cannot be calculated. Students have the responsibility to be alert vigils and make sure that their ranks are not contaminated by the intromission of spurious and worn-out elements.[60]

It is probable that this commentary referred to the events of July and August, although they did not appear until the October issue. These comments reached their Presbyterian audience just after the October 2 massacre had occurred. This

---

[57]The Mexican Presbyterian Church, being one of the oldest Protestant churches in Mexico, included many second, third, and fourth generation evangelicals who had moved up the social ladder. Their emphasis on reading the Bible had led to an encouragement of education in general. Presbyterians in Mexico City placed a high value upon a college education.

[58]Professor Eliseo Pérez of the Seminario Teológico Presbiteriano de México, interview by author, 14 May 1990, Mexico City.

[59]Since El Faro was published only on a monthly basis, it was not to be expected that it could respond quickly to the events of the student movement. Nevertheless, there was a regular column entitled "Comentando las Noticias" by Eduardo Fernández Carrero that was quite appropriate for commenting national events. Even so, a lapse of at least one month was normal. For example, an article on student protests in Eastern Europe from the daily Excelsior of June 4 made the July issue of El Faro. Other articles from late June of the Excelsior were mentioned in the August issue of El Faro.

[60]Eduardo Fernández Carrero, "Comentando las Noticias," El Faro (October 1964): 20-21. In the same article he exhorts all Mexicans to do their very best to make the Olympics a success. "We cannot let this precious opportunity to promote our beloved country go by the wayside." At the end of the article, he sarcastically criticizes the Catholic Church for an agrarian reform program that would supposedly benefit the poor. He agrees that the church should intervene in the social sphere, "but not to impede progress, and not as an initiator of social reforms; a task which belongs to the civil government. Let us remember: 'Give unto Caesar that which belongs to Caesar and give unto God that which belongs to God.'"

interpretation of "outsider influence" circulated widely in Presbyterian circles and probably was a factor for the lack of protest among Presbyterians.

The only other mention of the student movement in El Faro of 1968 was made by the same author in the December issue:

> Student Restlessness: It has already been said that inciters infiltrated the student ranks, with totally negative purposes, and distorted the movement. People from within and outside the nation, adventurers unconcerned about our national prestige, took advantage of the youth's good will, to such an extent, that they have produced a snarled entanglement, in which everyone gives whatever opinion that comes into their mind. There exists no cause, as great as it might be, that should be used by anyone to divide the Mexican family. We trust that the situation will soon clear up and that tranquility will return, based upon mutual respect and complete justice.[61]

On the same page he praised the Olympics and hoped that they had "been able to raise the name of Mexico in every positive aspect."[62] Over the next few months Presbyterian publications made only oblique references to the massacre of October 2. For example, Manolo Martín in his review of 1968 comments that "the year that is ending has bequeathed us somber times, gloomy nights, bitter hours, tears that have not been wiped away and wounds that have not healed."[63]

The main Presbyterian Churches in Mexico City at the time were El Divino Salvador and Príncipe de Paz in the downtown area, Gethsemaní in Coyoacán, San Pablo in the Niños Héroes district and another congregation in the Alamos neighborhood.

The Divino Salvador church, due to its downtown location, had the greatest contact with the student movement. On July 30, the soldiers moved against the students in the National Preparatory School #1 and blew down the three hundred year old colonial door with bazooka fire. As students fled, they were mowed down by police gunfire. The Divino Salvador congregation was in the midst of a Bible study/prayer meeting.[64] Upon hearing the shots, they went up on the rooftop. When they saw the students being hit, they brought dozens into the safety of their church building. They were protected until the danger was over, and then they were escorted out secretly through a back door.

The church leadership of the Divino Salvador church was not aware of participation by its youth in the student movement. Nor did it provide formal

---

[61]Eduardo Fernández Carrero, "Comentando las Noticias," El Faro (December 1968): 12.

[62]Ibid.

[63]Manolo Martín, "Y . . . Llega Otro Año," El Faro (January 1969): 4.

[64]Pastor Pablo Pérez, interview by author, 23 May 1990, Mexico City.

guidance for the youth. Government surveillance of and legal limitations placed upon church services made public protest a risky venture. Neither El Divino Salvador nor any other Presbyterian church officially protested against the violence used by the police, not even after the massacre at Tlatelolco.

Two Presbyterian university students of the Gethsemaní Church (Coyoacán), Carmen Pérez and Teodoro Gómez, did participate actively in the student movement.[65] They were told by fellow Christians not to get involved in such actions, because "evangelicals do not participate in politics." Their involvement in the student movement did not cause the Gethsemaní church to take a stand during 1968,[66] but their participation was felt later on.[67]

The Presbyterian Church in the Alamos neighborhood had lost some of their adults and students prior to the 1968 movement. In 1966 some of their key personnel decided to leave the church to dedicate themselves to the evangelistic priorities of Campus Crusade for Christ.[68] This exodus of those most interested in student ministry left the Alamos church with few resources to respond to the student movement. Of the three denominations studied, the Presbyterians were

---

[65]Carmen Pérez de Camargo, interview by author, 5 October 1990, Mexico City.

[66]Dr. Elias Mercado, interview by author, 15 April 1991, Mexico City, affirmed that he had given his sons in college freedom to participate in the movement, but urged them to use much prudence and in general recommended that they not get involved. Other leaders at Gethsemaní gave similar advice. Some sympathy for the movement existed in this church due to the fact that there were many public school teachers in the congregation.

[67]Carmen Pérez later became a staff worker with Compañerismo Estudiantil (IFES). Her participation in the 1968 movement gave Compañerismo Estudiantil a political awareness and activism that was lacking in other student ministries such as Campus Crusade for Christ.

[68]Eduardo Dueñas, interview by author, 11 October 1990, Mexico City. During the 1960's and 1970's many evangelical youth and some adults chose to participate heavily in the ministry of Campus Crusade for Christ, and thus limit or abandon their involvement in their local churches. This led many churches to reject the student ministry of Campus Crusade, especially in the early 1970's. Many of those involved in Campus Crusade complained that the churches were out of touch with their students. A reconciliation of sorts was begun in 1978 with Campus Crusade launched their "Vida para Todos" program (Here's Life, Mexico) which focused on evangelism through the local church. Much of this distrust of Protestant student ministries also applied to other student ministries such as Compañerismo Estudiantil and the Navigators, although Compañerismo Estudiantil enjoyed somewhat better relations with the local churches. Most Presbyterian churches had already rejected the ministry of MEC (Movimiento Estudiantil Cristiano), affiliated with the World Council of Churches, due to its theological (and social) liberalism. See Hugo Magaña Aguilar, "Una Reflexión Pastoral sobre el Ecumenismo: El Movimiento Estudiantil Cristiano en América Latina y el Caribe, 1951-1986" Licenciatura thesis, Instituto Internacional de Estudios Superiores, 1987.

the most affected by Campus Crusade for Christ.[69] The political posture of Campus Crusade in the United States (and throughout the world) was and continues to be politically conservative.[70] Campus Crusade has consistently characterized the Mexican student movement of 1968 as "communist," "leftist," and "revolutionary."[71] Consequently, students were not encouraged to participate in the activities of the student movement.

Occasionally, Campus Crusade staff would accompany some of their students to the protest rallies to hear the speakers, and later, would point out the "weaknesses and errors" of the student movement's ideology.[72] Even after the massacre in Tlatelolco, Campus Crusade did not protest the action of the government or of the police. Since Campus Crusade students and staff were one of the major links between the churches and the universities, their perspective on the student movement gained a large hearing among the Presbyterian churches.

An interesting incident involved Pablo Carrillo, a Polytechnic student who was present at the manifestation in Tlatelolco on October 2. When the soldiers started shooting, Pablo was able to escape without harm. Later that evening he attended an evangelistic campaign in a Presbyterian church with evangelist Juan M. Isáis preaching. According to his own description, the violence of Tlatelolco was a decisive factor in his conversion that night. His concern for evangelism and social concern later became manifest in Operación Movilización, Compañerismo Estudiantil, and Proyecto Magreb.[73]

As a result of the 1968 student movement there was a widespread political awakening among Mexican youth in general, and especially among those who lived in Mexico City. Presbyterian youth reflected this growing political awareness more than most other Protestants. Carmen Pérez from the Alamos Presbyterian

---

[69]The Baptists generally do not participate in interdenominational activities, due in great part to their emphasis on believer baptism, a doctrine not shared by many historical denominations. Thus, they have provided their own campus ministry (Centro Estudiantil Bautista = Baptist Student Union) in the key university cities of the country. The Iglesia de Dios en la República Mexicana also tends to avoid participation with historical denominations due to differences regarding the charismatic gifts and the "pentecostal experience."

[70]Jack Voelkel, Student Evangelism in a World of Revolution (Grand Rapids: Zondervan, 1974), compares and contrasts the student ministry in Latin America of Campus Crusade for Christ, International Fellowship of Evangelical Students, the Navigators, and the Southern Baptist Convention. One of Campus Crusade's weaknesses is their lack of theological reflection on the issues students face. Voelkel laments that "up until now, little emphasis has been placed on dealing with the deep and vital questions all students face in the university."

[71]"Nationals are the Key," Here's Life World Report 2.3 (June-July 1984): 3-5.

[72]Eduardo Dueñas, interview by author, 11 October 1990, Mexico City.

[73]Pablo Carrillo, interview by author, 28 June 1991.

Church and Sergio Sánchez[74] from a Presbyterian church in Oaxaca became staff workers for Compañerismo Estudiantil (affiliated with the International Fellowship of Evangelical Students). Their several years of campus ministry raised the social and political consciousness of Protestant students in general and Presbyterians in particular. International staff workers for the IFES such as Samuel Escobar, René Padilla, and Pedro Arana contributed to an increasing social and political awareness among Mexican evangelicals through their visits and writings.[75]

As a direct consequence of the student movement the Department of Christian Education of the National Presbyterian Church[76] organized a national student congress in 1970 in San Luis Potosí. The purpose of the congress was "to study the Christian faith, the problems of contemporary society and the participation of Christian students in this society."[77] Five areas were studied: (1) God, Faith and Humanity in the University Reality; (2) Culture and Humanities; (3) Socio-Political and Economic Problems; (4) The Arts and Recreation; and (5) Dating, Sexuality and Human Relations. The students manifested their "inconformity, uneasiness, and concern"[78] regarding both the Mexican reality and the Protestant support of the status quo. They recognized with shame their own

---

[74]Sergio Sánchez, interview by author, 15 April 1991, Mexico City. In 1968 Sánchez was a high school student at the University of Chapingo, an agricultural school just east of Mexico City. He lamented the fact that during the movement, the Protestants tried to maintain an apolitical stance, or at most a "hushed solidarity" (solidaridad callada) with the movement. The heightened political activity of his generation moved him to study both Marxist economists such as Gunder Frank and evangelical writers such as René Padilla, Samuel Escobar, and John Howard Yoder.

[75]Some of their most widely read books in Mexico include Samuel Escobar, Diálogo entre Cristo y Marx y Otros Ensayos (Lima: AGEUP, 1969), C. René Padilla, comp., Fe Cristiana y Latinoamérica Hoy (Buenos Aires: Ediciones Certeza, 1974), C. René Padilla, El Evangelio Hoy (Buenos Aires: Ediciones Certeza, 1975), and Pedro Arana Quiroz, Providencia y Revolución (Lima: Estandarte de la Verdad, 1970). Escobar's major address at the first Congreso Latinoamericano de Evangelización in Cochabamba, Bolivia in 1968 was a major turning point for Latin American evangelicals. His articulation of the social and political responsibilities of evangelicals broke with a long standing taboo. Theologically conservative evangelicals began (again) to wrestle with the socio-political problems of Latin America. Padilla and Escobar became quite well-known in evangelical circles after their major addresses at the Lausanne Congress on World Evangelization in 1974. See Voelkel, Student Evangelism, 104-10 for a succinct description of IFES ministry in Latin America.

[76]To be precise it was the Departamento de Labor Juvenil-Estudiantil de la Secretaría de Educación Cristiana. Official report of the Primer Congreso Estudiantil Presbiteriano, Section 1.1. It was co-sponsored by the Sociedad Bíblica, whose campus ministry director was Abel Clemente, a prominent Presbyterian leader.

[77]Ibid., Section 1.1.

[78]Ibid., Section 2.1.

indifference to "all positive, revolutionary ferment." They would no longer passively accept dogmatism nor restrictive ecclesiastical structures. They committed themselves to changing the church, making it more responsive to the needs of society, and thus, following more closely the "incarnational model of the Lord."

Several criticisms and proposals for change were articulated at the conference. Political apathy, so characteristic of Evangelicalism in Mexico (and the United States[79]) from the 1930's onward was acknowledged. Although easy answers for political problems were not proposed, there was an exhortation to permeate society with the Christian principles of freedom, justice, mercy and love. It was admitted that Christian youth were not equipped to integrate their faith with the demands of university life. The church was urged to provide a more adequate ministry for their students. The dominating influence of the United States was acknowledged and a call was extended to develop a more Mexican style of Christianity.

The congress was so threatening to the Presbyterian establishment that Daniel García, the national director of Christian Education, was removed from office.[80] This was evidence of a greater polarization taking place within the Presbyterian Church. The majority of Presbyterian leaders stayed away from involvement in political affairs and criticized those who did participate. The accepted "official" interpretation of the student movement among Presbyterians was that the students of the National University and the Polytechnic Institute were

---

[79]Political apathy among evangelicals in the United States is largely attributable to the Fundamentalist/Modernist controversy at the beginning of the century. For thorough treatments of this debate and its consequences see Marsden, Fundamentalism and American Culture and Moberg, Great Reversal. The Fundamentalist version of Christianity has been the dominant variety within Mexican Protestantism, having entered through missionaries, literature and Mexicans who studied in seminaries and Bible institutes in the United States. Whereas evangelicals in the United States have recently entered the political arena with vigor (eg. abortion, presidential elections, etc.), Mexican Protestants generally do not wield much political clout nor have demonstrated much interest in political affairs. This apathy towards political issues is beginning to change. Some of these more recent changes are examined in chapter 6.

[80]Pastor Daniel García Ibarra, interview by author, 26 October 1989, Mexico City. He feels that the student congress was the dominant factor in his removal. The evidence seems to substantiate his claim. Whereas El Faro heavily promoted the conference before it took place in the January, May, and July 1970 issues, it made no mention of the conference after the fact. Twenty years later the National Presbyterian Church had become more receptive to Garcia's views and appointed him to be the dean of their national seminary. Pastor Saul Tijerina, interview by author, 5 July 1991, Mexico City, affirmed that although his students who attended the conference returned to their Monterrey church with very positive comments about the conference, some of the influential, older leaders (eg. Lango, López, etc.) in the denomination were quite upset by several aspects of the conference.

confused, disoriented, and used by others.[81] This interpretation permitted certain leaders to justify their own lack of political involvement as well as their failure in providing orientation for the students. But the questioning spirit among some Mexican Presbyterians was spreading. Pastor Samuel Trujillo criticized the social and political apathy of the church and advocated: "We must leave our cloister and face the reality of the world."[82] A few months later, he used more "radical" language, stating, "I solicit a revolution because the epoch in which we live is full of great social, political and spiritual uneasiness. The Church must erupt within the world. . . ."[83] Raquel Lloreda affirmed:

> But the Gospel has the ferment that we need to change things now in the world in which we live. The needs have changed but the motivation is still the same: Christ the great agitator.[84]

The Christian Education Department produced new materials to be used in the churches. A more wholistic tone could be observed:

> The gospel interpreted in its best sense, embraces all that is integral to a human being, not just the soul, but also the body; not just spiritual well-being, but material well-being as well. The church has a gospel that penetrates all of the social structures. Therefore, it cannot remain silent when people suffer in their relationship with God, and in their relationship with each other.[85]

The Student Movement's long-term impact upon the Presbyterian Church can be seen by something that happened at the National Presbyterian Seminary. Student grievances in 1971 and 1972 (regarding courses, professors, lack of

---

[81]Ariel Zambrano, "Problemas Contemporáneos en los Paises Latinoamericanos," El Faro (February 1970): 19, described the student world as follows: "The university revolution continues its march in the two large centers of higher education in Mexico City, the National University (founded in 1551) and the Polytechnic Institute. Given the bloody encounters between the police, the army and the students, the Olympic Games were about to be suspended. The students formulated a petition for the authorities that contained six points having nothing to do with university life. These points surfaced as a result of the struggle, but not as its foundation or starting point. We are not trying to blame anyone, we only desire to point out a fact. The youth are disoriented. They are looking for something that they have not been able to find and they are using their energy in a movement like this." Zambrano's comment reveals the deep compartmentalization that characterizes much of Mexican Protestant thought. Just as "university life" (supposedly) did not have anything to do with national political issues, so "religious life" was also totally separate from socio-political issues.

[82]Samuel Trujillo, "Renovemos Nuestro Espíritu," El Faro (July 1969): 3.

[83]Samuel Trujillo, "Solicito una Revolución," El Faro (October 1969): 3. In a direct self-criticism he exclaimed, "I solicit a revolution because I see a Church that is slowly dying."

[84]Raquel Lloreda, "Campamento Juvenil," El Faro (August 1969): 13.

[85]Daniel García, "La Iglesia," El Faro (October 1969): 13.

communication, etc.) were not solved according to the students' expectations. The student leaders went over the head of the Seminary Council and sent a "Manifiesto" to every local church. They took their case to the General Assembly. Not receiving satisfaction, students went on strike and some graduating seniors boycotted the graduation ceremonies.[86] As a result, the seminary rector was replaced.

1972 was a crucial year for the Mexican Presbyterian Church. It celebrated one hundred years of life and ministry in Mexico in many diverse ways.[87] Its official membership had grown to over 65,000 communicants. As part of its coming of age, it declared a moratorium on foreign missionaries and funding.[88] Sixty missionaries returned to the United States. Funding, consisting of over half a million dollars, was also eliminated in order to implement the goal of becoming a self-supporting church. Several social ministries had to be curtailed and some were completely eliminated due to a lack of funds and personnel.

The moratorium on missionaries had theological and social underpinnings. Although there was a general acceptance and appreciation of the American missionaries working in Mexico at that time, there was great dismay over what the Mexicans saw as a profound shift taking place in the Presbyterian Churches in the United States. The Mexican Presbyterians rejected the theological liberalism which was being taught in most of the Presbyterian seminaries north of the border. The Mexicans also strongly disagreed with the U.S. position on the ecumenical movement. They could not understand why there was such effort placed upon the unification of the Protestant churches when that attempt had failed in Mexico half a century before.[89] Even more disconcerting were the ecumenical overtures made to the Roman Catholic Church, given the fact that Mexican Presbyterians

---

[86]David Legters, interview by author, 20 May 1991, Mexico City. Of course, those seniors did not receive their diploma. Some were able to receive their degree a year later.

[87]The most complete description of the centennial activities can be found in Centenario.

[88]Key insights regarding the aspirations and effects of the missionary moratorium can be found in two interviews with Pastor Saul Tijerina, one of the key national leaders within the Mexican Presbyterian Church. The first interview took place in 1971 and shows what were some of the expectations of the moratorium. The second interview, made in 1975, reveals some of the consequences of that decision. Saul Tijerina González, "Mexican Presbyterians' Adventure of Faith: A Case of Moratorium–Two Interviews," interview by J. Gary Campbell, International Review of Mission 64:254 (April 1975): 200-09.

[89]The Presbyterians in the United States were urging their Mexican brothers and sisters to place their seminary within the Comunidad Teológica that was in the process of formation. Many of the older Presbyterian leaders had lived through the united seminary experiment of the 1920's and could not understand why they were being urged to repeat that "mistake." David Legters, interview by author, 20 May, 1991, Mexico City, and Saúl Tijerina, interview by author, 5 July 1991, Mexico City.

had been repeatedly persecuted by Catholics for close to a hundred years.[90] The social agenda of the Presbyterian Churches in the U.S. also caused great alarm among Mexican Presbyterians. Financial support for armed revolution (sometimes associated with communist causes) did not fit into categories with which Mexican Presbyterians were comfortable.[91]

During the seventies and eighties liberation theology became a vital force within Latin American Catholicism. Although its impact upon Mexican Protestantism was somewhat limited,[92] Presbyterians attempted to respond to certain of the problems that were raised. A growing number of Presbyterian pastors and laity studied the social sciences.[93] As a consequence, simplistic analyses of social problems and their possible solutions gave way to more thorough analyses that considered a wider range of factors, causes, and interrelationships.

Certain Presbyterian laity created organizations to respond to the pressing social needs. Agronomist Sergio Sánchez formed the Asociación Mexicana de

---

[90]Saúl Tijerina, "Presbyterians' Adventure of Faith," 201. The Mexican Presbyterian Moderator at that time, Saúl Tijerina, stated ". . . our church does not view ecumenism and certain theological concepts in exactly the same way as the cooperating churches and we have a distinctive way of interpreting the program of the church." That same sentiment was repeated and those "theological concepts" were identified by several Presbyterian leaders in private interviews.

[91]Some of the concerns of Mexican Presbyterians can be seen in questions asked of Edesio Sánchez in 1975 when he was interviewed for a teaching position at the Presbyterian seminary. He was asked his opinion regarding liberation theology, modernism, the ecumenical movement, the charismatic movement, and two questions regarding higher criticism of the Bible (ie. Mosaic authorship of the Pentateuch and the unity of Isaiah). At least some of the members of the seminary board desired a conservative, traditional response for each topic. Although Sánchez did not fully satisfy their expectations, he did become a faculty member. Edesio Sánchez, Question-answer period following paper presented at the Primer Simposio Bíblico-Teológico of the Iglesia Nacional Presbiteriana, Mexico City, 5 July 1991.

[92]Liberation theology's greatest influence in Mexico City was felt at the Comunidad Teológica (a consortium of Protestant seminaries), especially at the Baptist (northern) seminary. The Presbyterians had little participation in the Theological Community, and in general were not very open to liberation theology. Even so, part of the Presbyterians' growing social and political awareness was due to the changing theological climate throughout Latin America.

[93]For example, Abner López, the current rector of the Presbyterian seminary studied sociology at the Comunidad Teológica in addition to his ministerial preparation at the Presbyterian seminary. Sergio Deras, an elder at the Berith Presbyterian Church and Program Supervisor of World Vision of Mexico, received his degree in Political Science at the National University.

Transformación Rural y Urbana, A.C. (AMEXTRA) in 1983 to meet those needs.[94] Although AMEXTRA is an interdenominational ministry, it works most closely with the Presbyterian church.

The Earthquakes of 1985

The earthquakes of 1985 caused many deaths and great destruction. Presbyterians in Mexico City, accustomed to earthquakes,[95] responded to the disaster at different levels and in different ways. On an individual level, Presbyterians immediately provided food, blankets, and counseling. The Presbyterian Seminary, whose facilities were unaffected by the tremors, canceled classes for several days and channeled their students and professors to help in rescue and relief work in diverse sections of the city.[96]

The Presbyterians quickly formed a special committee, the Comité Presbiteriano de Emergencia y Rehabilitación (COPER), to respond to the disaster. Its purpose was to help physically, morally and spiritually those persons most affected by the earthquakes. In the first months following the disaster, some Presbyterians got involved through COPER and provided food, clothes, and counseling for about one thousand persons housed in temporary shelters.[97] Presbyterian churches from other countries channeled funds to the earthquake victims through COPER, but most Mexican churches did not contribute to

---

[94]Sergio Sánchez, "Working Together Towards a Holistic Transformation: The Case of the Mexican Association for Rural and Urban Transformation (AMEXTRA, A.C.)," Working paper (Cuernavaca: AMEXTRA, 1990). Sánchez affirmed that the student movement of 1968 had a great impact upon him and his generation. The IFES authors provided some Christian alternatives for him. Sergio Sánchez, interview by author, 15 April 1991, Mexico City.

[95]Presbyterians had responded to earthquake disasters in other countries such as Perú (1970), Guatemala, and Nicaragua. Cf. Gamaliel Adame Brito, "Llamado Urgente a los Esforzadores Presbiterianos de México," El Faro (July 1970): 19.

[96]Abel Clemente, interview by author, 22 May 1991, Mexico City, affirmed that the seminary participation in rescue work was a key factor producing greater involvement by Presbyterian churches in Mexico City. Clemente was the Moderator of the Generai Assembly at the time. Pastor Saúl Tijerina, interview by author, 5 July 1991, Mexico City, informed that many Mexican Presbyterian churches outside of Mexico City sent food, blankets, money, medicines, etc. and channeled them through the seminary.

[97]Comité Presbiteriano de Emergencia y Rehabilitación, Informe que Presenta el Comité Presbiteriano de Emergencia y Rehabilitación (COPER) ante la XIX Reunión Ordinaria de la R. Asamblea General que se Realiza del 13 al 20 de Julio de 1988 en el Seno de la Iglesia "Ebenezer" de Cozumel, Quintana Roo. Mexico City: COPER, 1988.

COPER.[98] Later on, COPER became involved in projects to provide housing for seventy-five families which lost their homes.[99] Charges of mismanagement of funds were later raised against the administrators of COPER.[100] Although the charges were never proven, COPER's reputation did not fully overcome the damage that was caused.[101] Six years later, the organization still exists and has responded to human need in diverse disasters such as hurricanes,[102] drownings,[103] general poverty,[104] and an earthquake in El Salvador.[105]

A few Presbyterians from the affluent Puerta de Salvación Church in the

---

[98]Abel Clemente, interview by author, 22 May, Mexico City. Clemente served as COPER's president for the first few years. Some of COPER's early funding came through the Comité Ecuménico Mexicano de Ayuda a los Damnificados (CEMAD), but funding from that source was later terminated.

[99]Comité Presbiteriano de Emergencia y Rehabilitación, Boletín Informativo, Septiembre de 1987. Mexico City: COPER, 1987.

[100]Charges of mismanagement of funds have been raised against several organizations, both religious and secular, in the recent past. According to many of the interviewees, this has led to a general lack of trust in centralized organizations. COPER defended its own financial integrity. In an action not common among Mexican Protestants, COPER accused certain government officials of "threats, offenses, and other forms of pressure" and refusing to repay loans made to victims who received homes. It is unclear how public and forceful these accusations became. Comité Presbiteriano de Emergencia y Rehabilitación, Informe de Actividades ante la R. Asamblea General de la Iglesia Nacional Presbiteriana en su XX Reunión Ordinaria, que Tiene Lugar en la Iglesia "El Divino Redentor" Toluca, Edo. de Mexico, Período en Gestión: Julio 1988 - Junio 1990 (Mexico City: COPER, 1990), 3.

[101]Other factors contributed to this lack of trust in COPER. There is a great amount of distrust of many organizations with centralized funding, especially by provincial people of organizations headquartered in Mexico City.

[102]Comité Presbiteriano de Emergencia y Rehabilitación, Aid Plan for Victims of the Hurricanes that Devastated the State of Quintana Roo, Mexico, on September 14 and November 20, 1988 (Mexico City: COPER, 1988). Some leaders expressed dissatisfaction with the distribution of funds in this and other disaster relief projects. Regional rivalries seem to play an important role in these disputes.

[103]Comité Presbiteriano de Emergencia y Rehabilitación, Informe de la Visita para Llevar Ayuda a los Deudos de los Hermanos Presbiterianos Fallecidos el Día 3 de Diciembre de 1987 en el Río Tulija, Estado de Chiapas, México. Mexico City: COPER, 1987.

[104]Comité Presbiteriano de Emergencia y Rehabilitación, Report on the Visit to the Amuzgo Brethren in the Sierra of the State of Guerrero, Mexico. Mexico City: COPER, 1986.

[105]Comité Presbiteriano de Emergencia y Rehabilitación. Report Presented by the Commission Appointed by this Committee in Joint Meeting with the Officers of the General Assembly of the Presbyterian Church of Mexico, to Take Aid to Victims of the Earthquake in the City of San Salvador, El Salvador, Central America. Mexico City: COPER, 1986.

southern end of the city became quite involved in relief work.[106] Some of their youth helped out in the early days following the quakes with food distribution through the Dr. Vértiz Presbyterian Church. Later, three couples started to help out at the shelter established by the government in the Magdalena Contreras district.[107] As these families became more involved with the affected families, their participation became greater. Funds were raised to build homes and help the victims relocate to the town of Huehuetoca, north of Mexico City.[108] Much governmental "red-tape" had to be cut through. A young pentecostal Assembly of God pastor, Gabriel Aguirre, was willing to relocate with these families and accompany them in the process of reconstruction of homes and lives.[109] Due to their close contact with the victims, the social consciousness of the three couples increased.[110] Their local congregation did not commit itself to a long term involvement in the relief project. All three couples have since left that Presbyterian church and are now involved in churches with greater social consciousness.

<u>The Election of 1988</u>

The national election of 1988 was the most hotly debated election in recent history. Although the PRI candidate Carlos Salinas de Gortari officially received 50.3% of the total vote, many independent observers as well as much of the general populace believe that Salinas, in fact, lost the election to Cuauhtémoc

---

[106]Pastor Abram Pech, interview by author, 1 December 1989, Marilyn Stewart, interview by author, 19 June 1990, and Douglas Stewart, interview by author, 9 May 1991.

[107]A fairly complete description of the people sheltered in the Magdalena Contreras Casa Popular shelter can be found in the report of Pedro Gatica Sosa and Dr. Roberto García González, "Actividades Realizadas por el Personal Médico y Paramédico de la Delegación Magdalena Contreras, S.S.A., y U.N.A.M., en el albergue de Casa Popular" (Mexico City: Delegación Magdalena Contreras, 1985).

[108]Jim Cole, "Earthquake Victims Starting Over in Huehuetoca," <u>The Mexico City News</u>, 1 March 1986, 21.

[109]This created some controversy because Presbyterians do not usually work very closely with pentecostal groups. Five years later an established Assembly of God church has been formed in Huehuetoca with many of the relocated families as members. Aguirre continues to be the pastor.

[110]These families affirm that their involvement in this relief ministry was based upon their Christian convictions and their reading of the Bible. They have also participated in and been influenced by the ministry of Compañerismo Estudiantil and the Centro de Estudios Superiores de Integración Cristiana (CESIC). The writings of Escobar, Padilla, and others associated with the Lausanne movement have also influenced their participation. One of the men involved described the progression of their involvement as follows, ". . . it is amazing how God has initiated and sustained this project. We got into it simply as an initial response of Christian compassion and concern. But as often happens, one step leads to another and God continues to open doors that you never imagined He would, and so you keep following His leading." Doug Stewart, Mexico City, to Dick Dye, photocopy.

Cárdenas. In Mexico City, Cárdenas officially did receive more votes than Salinas. The Partido Acción Nacional candidate Manuel Clouthier came in a close third.

Interviews and conversations with over seventy Presbyterian pastors and laity reveal that the basic message (if any) proclaimed from the Presbyterian pulpits was that voting was a Christian duty. It appears that no church provided criteria or other guidelines by which political parties or candidates could be evaluated. Some of those interviewed felt that the church leadership failed its members in not providing some guidelines, although the majority believed that the church should not attempt to shape its members' voting habits. Both religious and legal factors were cited. Most interviewees agreed that social and economic factors were far more influential than evangelical beliefs in helping Presbyterians decide for whom to cast their ballots.

The results of the political surveys reveal that the Presbyterian alliance with the Partido Revolucionario Institucional still has some strength, but slipped considerably in the elections of 1988. The majority of Presbyterian votes in Mexico City were divided between Cárdenas (36.5%) and Salinas (33.3%) with a large degree of abstention (25.4%).[111] Few Presbyterians voted for Clouthier of the Acción Nacional Party (4.7%). Most Presbyterian leaders interviewed believed that the PAN's supposed or real ties with the Roman Catholic hierarchy dissuaded most Presbyterians from even considering the PAN as an option.[112]

In the years immediately following the elections there has been a growing interest and involvement by Presbyterians in political affairs. Much of this can be attributed to a general political awakening among much of the population. Another important factor was the visit made to Mexico by the Pope in May 1990. President Salinas, breaking with the liberal tradition, made overtures to the Catholic Church reminiscent of the later Porfiriato.[113] The Catholic hierarchy in Mexico formally

---

[111]Two thirds of Presbyterians voted against the PRI, if abstentions are counted as anti-PRI. Even those who voted for the PRI are not very enthusiastic. Sergio Sánchez, interview by author, 15 April 1991, Mexico City, attributes this to the fact that Presbyterians are tired of just receiving "crumbs" (migajas) from the PRI.

[112]According to Presbyterians in other regions of the country, the Acción Nacional Party did represent a viable option. Leaders from Mérida, Yucatán estimated that upwards of 60% of Presbyterians voted for the PAN; Germán Celis, interview by author, 24 May, 1991, Mexico City and David Legters, interview by author, 20 May, 1991, Mexico City. It seems that Presbyterians in certain industrial centers in the north, also voted for the PAN in large numbers. The historical ties between the Catholic clergy and the PAN are sketched by Octavio Rodríguez Araujo, "Iglesia, Partidos y Lucha de Clases en México," in Religión y Política en México, ed. Martín de la Rosa and Charles A. Reilly (Mexico City: Siglo Veintiuno Editores, 1970), 260-67.

[113]He invited several members of the Catholic hierarchy to accompany him at his inauguration on December 1, 1988. Although formal relations with the Vatican have not yet been restored, President Salinas did appoint Agustín Téllez Cruces in February 1990 to be his private ambassador to the Pope. See "Téllez Cruces: Niño Aplicado, Juez Obsecuente, Gobernador de Paso, Católico Vergonzante," Proceso

proposed changes in five articles of the Constitution.[114] The Presbyterian National Assembly convoked their own working conference during the Pope's stay in Mexico to analyze the Constitution and propose their own modifications.[115] The Berith Presbyterian Church sponsored a week long forum on the political responsibilities of Christians. This forum was sufficiently successful to warrant a second one a year later with PRI and PAN elected officials, as well as leftist presidential candidate Rosario Ibarra de Piedra as main speakers. On March 6, 1990, the Moderator of the Presbyterian General Assembly, Ignacio Castañeda Baños, together with two Presbyterian laity and representatives of the Baptists and Methodists, met with President Salinas. They manifested their concern that legislation protecting the freedom of religion and the separation of church and state be maintained.

Analysis

The Mexican Presbyterian Church entered the period under study with a socio-political involvement greater than the majority of Protestant churches in Mexico. Yet, Presbyterians participated very little in the student movement of 1968. Even after the massacre of October 2, there was no official protest or comment. There was greater involvement in the relief work and reconstruction following the 1985 earthquakes, but a relatively small percentage of churches and individuals stayed involved over a long period. The 1988 elections produced very little official comment by Presbyterian leaders. It is readily observed that the Presbyterian Church in Mexico did not publicly challenge the government's actions in any of the three events studied. Yet, there was a substantial response to immediate human need (eg. the Divino Salvador Church's rescue of dozens of fleeing students and various Presbyterians' relief work on behalf of the earthquake victims). What are the factors that help to explain why Mexican Presbyterians did participate socially in certain moments of extreme need or crisis, but did not raise a prophetic voice in the political sphere?

Certain historical factors must be kept in mind. The Constitution of 1917 prohibits pastors and churches from getting involved in politics. When the Roman Catholic Church challenged the offensive articles of the Constitution in 1926, the

---

694 (19 February 1990): 10-13. The ambassador's niece, Patricia Martínez Téllez, is the first candidate for public office of the new Partido Demócrata Cristiano (PDC).

[114]"Conferencia del Episcopado Mexicano to Señor Licenciado Carlos Salinas de Gortari," Open letter, 5 June 1989, Servicios Informativos Procesados, A.C., Mexico City.

[115]See papers presented at the Primera Consulta sobre Relaciones Iglesia-Estado: Problemática Actual de la Iglesia en México, Mexico City, 4-5 May 1990. Although no specific proposals were agreed upon, much interest was raised and the different presbyteries represented committed themselves to further study.

bloody Cristero War ensued with the consequent loss of Catholic power and influence. This provided a visual object lesson for Presbyterians (and all Protestants) not to challenge the government.

Article 3 of the Constitution was changed in 1934 to demand socialistic education in all schools, both public and private. Although that law was later modified in 1945 to read "lay education," Presbyterians had, by then, closed most of their schools. In the following years very few schools were opened, and these were operated strictly according to the law.

Presbyterians had been allies of the ruling political party (PRI) since the Revolution. Presbyterians, such as Moisés Sáenz and Leandro Garza, held key positions in several administrations. The fact that President Miguel Alemán's mother and President López Mateos' wife were both Presbyterians added to the Presbyterians' ties with the PRI. Although that original alliance has gone through times of stress and currently appears weak and strained, Presbyterians have not totally abandoned their former ally. They have not publicly challenged or criticized the government on any major issue.

In 1962 it was decided that all foreign missionaries serving the Presbyterian Church in Mexico would leave in 1972. The official reason given was that after one hundred years of foreign missionary help, it was time for Mexican Presbyterians to cut the umbilical cord. But some of the serious underlying factors were the theological and social disagreements over the mission of the church and the political and social implications of that mission. Whereas the Presbyterian Churches in the United States, and especially their Boards of Foreign Missions, saw a prophetic political and social ministry as essential to the Christian mission, Mexican Presbyterians did not.

It must also be remembered that the Presbyterians had special plans for the Olympics held in Mexico in October 1968. The General Assembly's Evangelism Commission had agreed to participate actively in the distribution of evangelistic literature. Saúl Cantú Saldaña, President of the Unión Nacional de Esfuerzo Cristiano, promised the participation of 5,000 youth for this evangelistic effort.[116] In their view, in light of the eternal gains of salvation to be achieved during the Olympics, a prophetic ministry within a questionable student movement paled in importance.

Doctrinally, Mexican Presbyterians have tended to see their relation to the government as being one of strict obedience. A certain interpretation of Romans 13:1-7 has dominated Presbyterian thought and practice. In that interpretation the phrase "submit (upotassesthai) to the governing authorities" is understood as meaning total obedience. Many commentators give a different interpretation to the

---

[116]"Olimpiada en México," El Faro (May 1968): 31. See also "Las Olimpiadas," El Faro (July 1968): 4-5, and "Un Programa de Hospitalidad y Orientación en A.C.E. para los Visitantes Mundiales a las Olimpiadas," El Faro (October 1968): 16.

passage, seeing the passive "upotassesthai" as a qualified obedience or respect. Such obedience is to be granted only in those circumstances when the specific criteria mentioned in verses 3 and 4 are met.

Vidal Valencia, one of the "successful" conservative Presbyterian pastors whose San Pablo Church[117] has grown greatly over the last forty years expresses a dominant theological position:

> According to the Bible, we see that the Lord Jesus Christ made a separation between the Church and the State. He said, "my kingdom is not of this world," and he did not dedicate his time to solving social or political problems. The Church has the task of multiplying in numbers and growing in the knowledge of the Lord, and that task is so large that the church does not have time to attend to political problems.[118]

During this century, dispensational theology has had a wide following among Presbyterians.[119] Dispensationalism teaches that the church age is the dispensation of grace and is incompatible with the covenant of "good works" found in the Old Testament. Therefore, even the concept of "good works" understood not as salvific but only as an expression of gratitude received little attention among the Presbyterian Dispensationalists (also known as Bible Presbyterians)[120]. Classical dispensationalism teaches that during the church age the world will become worse and worse, and consequently the church should withdraw from political involvement in order to remain pure and wait for the Lord's second coming. All attempts to improve the world are in vain and consequently a waste of time and resources. In contrast, Reformed theology sees more continuity

---

[117]A succinct history of the San Pablo Church can be found in Enrique Danwing, "Iglesia Presbiteriana San Pablo," in México Hoy y Mañana: Documento No. 2 "Estudio de Casos del Crecimiento de la Iglesia Evangélica en la Gran Ciudad de México" (Mexico City: Visión Evangelizadora Latinoamericana and Programa Latinoamericano de Estudios Socio-Religiosos, 1989), 99-107. Pastor Valencia has a wide following through both his preaching and writings ministries;

[118]"¿Qué Dicen los Líderes Evangélicos?" Gracia 70 (May 1990): 12.

[119]C. M. Cabrera, "Los Dos Pactos: Las Dispensaciones," El Faro (June 1968): 19-21, defends a traditional view of dispensationalism, divided into seven dispensations. Saul Tijerina, interview by author, 5 July 1991, confirmed that many Presbyterian pastors and seminary professors during the 1940's and 1950's held to dispensational theology. To this day, dispensationalism has many followers in certain regions of the country (eg. Tabasco).

[120]As a consequence, most of the positive examples in the Old Testament of believers who contributed to the social and political spheres of Israel or the surrounding nations are ignored in Dispensationalism. Sometimes these examples are even treated as "worldly" sub-Christian attempts at "works-righteousness" and therefore to be rejected.

between the Old and New Testaments[121] and tends to lay more emphasis upon the Lordship of Jesus Christ in all areas of life.[122] A return to a more Reformed theology and practice would lead to greater involvement in Mexican society.

[121]C. M. Cabrera, "Los Dos Pactos: Transición," El Faro (August 1968): 17, one of the major proponents of Dispensationalism among Mexican Presbyterians, claimed that "those who make an amalgam of these two covenants with the tendency to fuse them into one, try in vain to establish a continuity that does not exist. And that continuity does not exist, because God wanted the disparity to exist between the one and the other, so that the goodness of the one would shine brightly compared with the inefficacy of the other."

[122]H. Richard Niebuhr, Christ and Culture, 43, places John Calvin as the first explicit exponent of the paradigm of "Christ the Transformer of Culture.

CHAPTER 4

THE NATIONAL BAPTIST CONVENTION OF MEXICO

Historical Background

The National Baptist Convention represents one of the oldest Protestant groups in Mexico.[1] James (Diego) Thomson, the representative of the British and Foreign Bible Society who distributed Bibles throughout Mexico from 1827 to 1830, and again from 1842 to 1843, was a Baptist. Although no Baptist church was founded at this time, his ministry had long-lasting effects upon Dr. José María Luis Mora and other liberals during this period.[2]

James (Santiago) Hickey, an Irishman representing the American Bible Society, began preaching and selling Bibles to Mexicans in Brownsville, Texas and Matamoros, Mexico about 1860. Due to his abolitionist convictions and his colportage activities, Hickey moved to Monterrey in November 1862. He had also received an invitation from Thomas Westrup, an Englishman residing in Monterrey, who wanted to know more about the Christian faith. He soon began Bible studies and preaching services in both English and Spanish. On January 30, 1864 (others say Jan 1, 1863 and according to one report of Westrup Jan 24, 1864) he baptized his first three converts. As a representative of an interdenominational organization, he was not permitted to pastor a local church. Therefore, after baptizing Westrup, Hickey ordained him to be the pastor of the new church. The church identified itself before the government as "la Iglesia Cristiana de Monterrey," but doctrinally it was a "closed communion Baptist" congregation.[3] Hickey also established the first evangelical day school inside Mexico, at Monterrey on November 30, 1863.[4] Five other schools were soon started in nearby towns.

When Hickey died in 1866, Westrup carried on the work both within the Baptist church as well as succeeding him as representative of the American Bible Society. A schism developed within the church as some followed Melinda Rankin,

---

[1]The most important self-description of the National Baptist Convention can be found in La Luz Bautista, the official denominational magazine. Some key national leaders have written histories of the movement such as Alejandro Treviño, Historia de los Trabajos Bautistas en México (El Paso: Casa Bautista de Publicaciones, 1939). A more recent treatment of Baptist history, viewed from a North American missionary perspective, is Frank W. Patterson, A Century of Baptist Work in Mexico (El Paso: Baptist Spanish Publishing House, 1979).

[2]For more information about Thomson and his work see chapter 2.

[3]Enrique Tomás Westrup, ed., Principios: Relato de la Introducción del Evangelio en México. Escritos del Protagonista Principal en Dicha Obra: Tomás Martín Westrup (Monterrey: n.p., 1948), 31.

[4]Patterson, Century of Baptist Work, 27.

a Presbyterian, while others stayed with Westrup.[5] Westrup made contact with the American Baptist Home Mission Society (Northern) in 1868. After further communication and interviews, Westrup was appointed "as evangelizing, organizing, and soliciting missionary in Mexico" on March 10, 1870. Later that same year Santiago Díaz and José María Uranga were also financially supported by the Mission Society to direct the work in Cadereita and Santa Rosa respectively. Churches were also established in Ebanos, Montemorelos, Durango, and Jerez. The Mission Society was disappointed with the slow progress made during the 70's and with the political strife throughout Mexico. When Westrup resigned in 1874 the Mission Society accepted his resignation with the following comment, "This Board does not consider the success of Mr. Westrup sufficiently encouraging to appoint a successor to labor in that disorganized field."[6] Without outside financial assistance, the Baptist churches struggled. Nevertheless, they were able to report some conversions and baptisms.

The Foreign Mission Board of the Southern Baptist Convention demonstrated interest in sending missionaries to Mexico as early as 1846. In 1851 its Committee on New Fields affirmed the following:

> It is the opinion of your committee that Mexico should constitute a field for our Foreign Mission enterprise. The country has peculiar claims upon us for her proximity, from the bearing her national character will have upon this continent, and from her degradation under the influence of a perverted religion.[7]

At the same time the Home Mission Board reported work taking place along the Mexican border at Brownsville. Their missionary, J. H. Wombell had established a day-school, regular church services, and distribution of Bibles and tracts in both English and Spanish. But the Southern Baptists did not formally enter Mexico at this time. Due to the Civil War and its consequences, Southern Baptists did not begin work in Mexico until the 1870's.

> In 1870 various families from Texas established residence in the northern part of Mexico, where they exploited the rich mineral deposits. They soon organized small congregations into which were received with joy, the Mexican converts. Mr. William Harvey (husband of Isabel Westrup), an intelligent miner who was working the mines near San Juan, near Músquiz, invited his brother-in-law, John O. Westrup, of Monterrey, about 1878, to help him with carpentry work, since Westrup supported himself with a trade as did many of the preachers of his day. Upon moving to Músquiz Westrup

[5]For a more extensive treatment of this schism, see chapter 2.

[6]Quoted in Patterson, Century of Baptist Work, 37.

[7]Ibid., 37.

naturally began to preach and was invited to pastor the church and to cultivate the work near there. Having been reared in Mexico, John Westrup spoke Spanish like a Mexican. His salary was paid by the church, with additional help from certain Christians in Texas.[8]

Santiago Díaz, one of Hickey's converts and pastor of the Baptist church in Cadereita, helped organize a church in Músquiz in 1877. John Westrup became the church's second pastor and started churches in Progreso, Villa de Juárez and San Juan de Sabinas.

Since the American Baptist Home Mission Society no longer supported the work in Mexico, the Southern Baptists felt free to enter. Their Foreign Mission Board together with the Baptist State Convention of Texas officially started supporting John Westrup in September 1880. Two months later, Westrup and his companion Basilio Flores, were murdered near Progreso.[9] William and Victoria Flournoy were appointed in December 1881 to take Westrup's place. Mrs. Flournoy immediately began a day-school with thirty two students that later rose to over a hundred.

Under the leadership of missionary William Powell, located in Saltillo, and nationals such as Alejandro Treviño Osuna, many Baptist churches and schools were begun throughout northern Mexico. Powell was not afraid to enter into the political realm to extend the work of the church. According to Treviño, Powell

> was a friend of governors and public officials. . . . He was a good friend of President Porfirio Díaz, who gave him special attention at any time he had business to present. Through his influence with these officials he was used by the missionaries of all denominations to secure guarantees, when fanatical authorities denied them their rights.[10]

The school that the Powells organized in their home soon outgrew those facilities. Powell obtained the support of Governor Evaristo Madero to establish a school for girls in Saltillo. The governor also offered, on behalf of the state government, properties to build schools in Parras and Patos. Powell took Mayor Fernández of Saltillo and José Cárdenas, Superintendent of Public Education for the state of Coahuila to Richmond, Virginia to meet with the Foreign Mission Board. Due to their convictions regarding the separation of church and state, the Southern Baptists could not accept the properties as gifts from the government. But the

---

[8]Alejandro Treviño, Historia, 31-32. John Westrup and Thomas Westrup, mentioned earlier in this chapter, were brothers.

[9]Ibid., 32.

[10]Treviño, Historia, 187.

Baptists formed an association to purchase and administer the properties.[11] Thus, the Madero Institute was opened in October, 1884 in Saltillo. José Cárdenas resigned as Superintendent of Public Education to become the Principal of the Madero Institute.

By 1884 eight churches in northern Mexico formed the "Primera Asociación Bautista Mexicana."[12] Three national missionaries were appointed and financial support was raised for them. Powell and José Cárdenas started publishing the newspaper El Heraldo Mexicano.

During the 1880's the Southern Baptists sent twenty-six new missionaries to Mexico. Churches were started in Aguascalientes (1887), Guadalajara (1888), Zacatecas (1888), Orizaba (1892), Toluca (1893), Morelia (1894), Chihuahua (1902) and in numerous smaller towns. Dwight L. Moody preached in Toluca in 1895 with quite favorable results.[13] Schools were also started in Zacatecas (1887) and Toluca (a girl's school in 1902 and a boy's school in 1903).

Problems among the foreign missionaries (Powell, Steelman, McCormick, Rudd, Watkins and Wilson) caused serious setbacks among the Baptist work in general from 1896 to 1898. Charges were leveled against various missionaries for doctrinal deviance and administrative disagreements. Patterson describes the consequences as follows:

> It is lamentable that this series of incidents, known as the Exodus, led to the loss of eleven missionaries, closed Madero Institute, divided the Saltillo church, set nationals against nationals, and in general set the mission work back by at least a decade.[14]

One positive side-effect of the "Exodus" was that many Mexicans assumed leadership not only for the local churches, but also for the national work. Among the more notable were Ernesto Barocio, Manuel Treviño Flores, Cerefino Guajardo, Eliseo Recio, Samuel Domínguez, Florencio Treviño, Benjamín Müller, Pablo

---

[11]There is irony in this issue of the separation of church and state. Governor Madero became the President of the Board of Trustees and two other government officials were members of the Board together with six Baptists.

[12]The association's name was soon changed to Coahuila Baptist Association because all of the churches were located in that state.

[13]James Garvin Chastain, Thirty Years in Mexico (El Paso: Baptist Publishing House, 1927), 133-34, described Moody's event as follows, "The last meeting was a veritable pentecost. The Mexicans present who could not understand English were amazed and dazed. The people wept, laughed, shouted and embraced each other, beside themselves with joy. The influence was permanent and far-reaching and marked an epoch in Mexican missions. Through succeeding years thousands were converted to God."

[14]Patterson, Century of Baptist Work, 56-58.

Rodríguez and Porfirio Rodríguez.[15]

The American Baptist Home Mission Society resumed their support of Thomas Westrup in 1881. Their goal was to establish two important centers in Monterrey and Mexico City and then as early as possible, to turn the work over to nationals. Their philosophy differed somewhat from that of the Southern Baptists as they would send out fewer missionaries, but would financially support more Mexican national workers. In general, the relationships between the churches established by the Southern Baptists and the American (Northern) Baptists were quite friendly and cooperative. A large edifice was finished in 1885 for the Monterrey church. The International School (Colegio Internacional) started by the Thomas Westrups a year earlier moved to the church building and soon enrolled many students from Monterrey. The work prospered until 1897 when the church divided and a small group formed the Emmanuel Baptist Church in Monterrey with Francisco Treviño as pastor. Thomas Westrup caused much controversy when he switched denominational affiliations and worked with the Disciples of Christ. He became the leader of the Disciples of Christ work in Monterrey until his death in 1909.

The American Baptist Home Mission Society started work in Mexico City in 1883 with missionary W. T. Green. Pablo Rodríguez, one of the first converts in Múzquiz, who had studied at Louisville Theological Seminary, was employed by the ABHMS to help Green. A church was organized in 1884. That same year missionary W. H. Sloan arrived to pastor the church, replacing Green. He began printing the newspaper "La Luz." In 1886 Ora A. Osborne established a day school in conjunction with the church. One of the biggest accomplishments of Sloan was the erection of an impressive church building near the downtown area.[16] The ABHMS began churches in Aguascalientes (1887),[17] San Luis Potosí (1888), and Puebla (1893).

Six ABHMS churches in the Monterrey area formed the Nuevo León Baptist Association in 1885. They soon carried out various projects such as the ordination of pastors, missionary ventures, and the formation of a Bible Institute. They also maintained fraternal relations with the Coahuila Baptist Association. The Baptist Association of Central and Southern Mexico was organized in 1894 with the churches of Mexico City, Puebla, San Luis Potosí, and Aguascalientes.

---

[15]Ibid., 59.

[16]Patterson, Century of Baptist Work, 73, notes that John D. Rockefeller gave $7,000.00 towards the construction. According to La Luz Bautista, it was the first evangelical church building constructed in the capital. Before that, other Protestant churches had bought Catholic church edifices that had been confiscated by the government.

[17]At different times, missionaries from both the Southern Baptists and the American Baptists worked in Aguascalientes, and consequently, both claimed that they had established the church.

By the turn of the century, Baptist work in Mexico had grown considerably. There were 101 churches and missions spread throughout the country with 1910 members. The time had come to provide greater contact and mutual support. After a few years of promoting the concept of a national Baptist convention, it became a reality in 1903. Alejandro Treviño was chosen to be the first president. Evangelization and education went hand in hand as can be seen in their purpose statement:

> The Convention will have as its purpose the strengthening of fraternal relations between the churches, associations and other Baptist corporations of the land, to the end that they may cooperate in evangelizing Mexico, educating youth, and publishing Christian literature.[18]

The formation of the Convention formed a milestone in the life of Mexican Baptists. National leadership began to have greater participation in decisions that had been previously made by the missionaries. In the first decade of the century the Convention implemented plans regarding missionary work among the Indian groups, a Sunday School Board, and a Board of Publications. The idea of a Baptist college was also recommended, but never came to fruition. Many new churches were planted throughout the western and northwestern parts of Mexico.

In addition to the existing schools in Monterrey (Colegio Internacional), Mexico City, Puebla (Instituto Moderno), and Saltillo (Instituto Madero), many new schools were started by Baptists in the last decade of the Porfiriato. A school for English speaking miners' children was started in Chihuahua in 1903, and renamed Colegio Bautista in 1908 when it opened a department for Spanish speaking children as well. In Toluca, the girl's school (Instituto Anglo-Mexicano) and the boy's school (Instituto Central) began holding classes together in 1903, which was the first time co-education had been tried in southern Mexico. An English-Spanish school was started in Guaymas, and when a boarding school was added in 1910, the name was changed to Colegio Occidental. An industrial school for boys and girls was started in Parral, Chihuahua in 1908 by self-supporting missionary Pierson. Most of the 15 boarding school students accepted were orphans.

Baptist medical ministry in Mexico was begun by Rufus Hooker in León in 1904. He soon began another clinic in Guadalajara. Missionary Conwell began a medical ministry out of the First Baptist Church in Mexico City in 1906. Dr. Hallie G. Neal began her medical practice in León in 1907 and later transferred to Toluca.

Baptists had expanded their ministries through diverse periodicals, beginning with Sloan's La Luz in 1886. The Nuevo León Baptist Association had published El Cristiano Bautista since 1904, and also El Expositor Bíblico, a Sunday School quarterly. When Sloan stopped publishing La Luz in 1907, a new

---

[18]Actas, Convención Nacional Bautista (Mexico City: Convención Nacional Bautista, 1903), 1.

periodical, El Atalaya Bautista, was begun. In 1910 this latter periodical and El Cristiano Bautista were fused into El Bautista.

The Revolution affected all of the Protestant churches in Mexico, including the Baptists. Many Baptists, including pastors Anatolio Bautista and Pablo Rodríguez, entered the revolutionary armies. Some church leaders were killed, and some church buildings were destroyed.[19] Most foreign missionaries tried to maintain neutrality. For example, J. E. Davis in León was forced to print posters for both Pancho Villa and the Federalists.

As the war progressed, it took on an anti-American tone. Most missionaries returned to the United States. Only the Neals in Toluca,[20] and the Browns in Puebla were able to stay in Mexico throughout the entire Revolution. No Baptist church in Mexico was fully self-supporting at the time, and therefore, most of the Mexican pastors were receiving at least part of their salaries from one of the two North American missions. As communications became more difficult and dangerous, some pastors used their manual skills and became self-supporting. Many Baptist families fled to Texas. Surprisingly, a large amount of evangelistic activity took place during the war. One convert was the soldier Eugenio Aviña, who later became governor of the state of Colima. He later distributed many Bibles to the soldiers in his state.[21] A mini-revival took place at the First Baptist Church in Mexico City in 1916. A Dutch evangelist of Jewish extraction, A. B. DeRoos preached to large crowds. More than two hundred Mexicans became converted and were baptized. One of these new believers was the private secretary of President Carranza.[22]

The Convention annual meetings were greatly disrupted by the Revolution. The 1911 meeting was cancelled, and the 1912 meeting in Aguascalientes was attended by delegates from only eleven churches. The Convention could not meet again until 1919. Most of the regional Associations also had to cancel their meetings for the duration of the Revolution.

The Revolution brought about many changes in the schools run by the Baptists. The schools in Saltillo, Toluca, Monterrey, Chihuahua, Guaymas, and Guadalajara, as well as the theological seminary in Monterrey were closed during part of the revolutionary years. The Constitution of 1917 forced many missionaries

---

[19] Chastain, Thirty Years in Mexico, 117, reported how Pastor Eustacio García of the Aztec Indian Church was killed when the Zapatistas overran Ajusco, a small town to the south of Mexico City. The Federalists recaptured the town, and destroyed most of the buildings, including the Baptist edifice.

[20] Treviño, Historia, 257-58, 304-05, affirmed that the good reputation gained by Mrs. Neal as a medical doctor enabled her family to ride out the war. From 1914 on she served in the Constitutionalist Hospital in Toluca.

[21] Chastain, Thirty Years in Mexico, 147.

[22] Patterson, Century of Baptist Work, 112.

to give up their teaching positions, with Mexicans assuming many of the administration and teaching responsibilities.[23]

A surprising advance was made in the area of medical missions at the height of the war. In 1915 the ABHMS bought three large buildings in Puebla to be used for a hospital. It was opened in 1917 with Dr. Conwell as director.

The Plan of Cincinnati did not directly affect the Mexican Baptists. The American Baptists sent delegates to the first meetings in Cincinnati, but later decided not to participate in the plan. If anything, the Baptists in Mexico gained indirectly through the plan. While the participating eight denominations were experiencing relocation, uprooting, internal strife, and interdenominational bickering, the Baptists were able to incorporate dissatisfied evangelicals into their fold.

Baptists made conscientious efforts to reach different Indian groups. Samuel García was named missionary to the Zapotec Indians in 1920 and within a few years had established a church in Tlacochahuaya. Miguel Alfaro was renamed missionary to the Tarascans in 1921. By 1925 he had organized congregations in five villages. On February 8, 1925, Moreno Uripache, governor of the Tarahumaras attended a Baptist church in Chihuahua. He urged the pastor to send missionaries to free his people from the slavery of religious idolatry. A year later, Antonio Rosales Pérez was assigned to minister to the Tarahumaras.

Although Mexican Baptists had experienced much persecution throughout the years, that persecution increased during the 1920's. Especially during the Cristiada, Baptists were caught in the middle between the government officials and the Cristeros. For example, the Baptist church building in Irapuato was destroyed in November, 1926 by a group of Cristeros. A year later, Maximiliano Cisneros from the Baptist church in Atoyac, Jalisco was witnessing to people at a ranch in San Juan. A band of men rode up to the house shouting "Viva Cristo Rey." They dragged Cisneros out of the house and demanded that he kiss their religious banner. When he refused to do so, they killed him by hanging.[24]

The Great Depression of 1929 had a retarding effect upon the resources available for the Baptist work in Mexico.[25] The ABHMS budget for Mexico was $56,522.28 in 1925, but had been reduced to $23,373,30 by 1935. The FMBSBC budget for Mexico was $127,709.50 in 1920. By 1937, the funds available were only $22,405.55. In the short term, this produced hardship and retrenchment. For example, no Southern Baptist funds were available for church buildings for almost

---

[23]For example, Eliseo Villareal became director of the Colegio Internacional in Monterrey, replacing foreign missionary Bertha Hume. The Marrs chose to go to Chile, and left the school in Guaymas in the hands of Pastor Eleno Estrada and his wife.

[24]Patterson, Century of Baptist Work, 127.

[25]Ibid., 127, 132.

twenty years. Over the long haul, this reduction in foreign funds contributed to a more nationalistic and self-reliant attitude among the Mexican churches.

The Baptists were growing at such a fast rate that the government took notice and warned them that they were exceeding their number of clergy. Article 130 stipulated that only native born Mexicans could function as ministers and that the state legislatures could set the number of ministers permitted. To get around the harshness of this law (and in agreement with good Baptist theology), the 1934 Convention approved the following report:

> This Convention declares that, in accord with the practice of Baptist churches, the official functions of ministers are: (1) Have charge of the care of the church, (2) Baptize proper candidates, and (3) administer the Lord's Supper. In accord with these stated customs and practices, preaching is not considered the exclusive prerogative of ministers but any member has the right to publicly declare his ideas and give lectures concerning any matter.[26]

Thus, laity and foreigners were able to continue preaching and exercise much pastoral responsibility, even though they were not counted as clergy for government purposes.

The implementation of the 1917 Constitution's anti-religious legislation by President Calles in 1926 forced certain Baptist schools to close. The 1934 change in Article 3 of the Constitution in which "educación laica" became "educación socialista" forced the closure of additional schools operated by the Baptists. The ABHMS felt that it had to withdraw its support of the Colegio Internacional in Monterrey. Director Eliseo Villarreal continued the school with the tuition that he collected. The Colegio Bautista in Puebla (whose name was changed to Colegio Howard in 1922) terminated its educational services in 1935, due to the change in Article 3. The building was used as a hostel (internado) for students attending public schools. The Colegio Occidental in Guaymas closed in 1926. El Instituto Central in Culiacán was founded in 1926, but due to government pressure was closed in 1932. The Escuela Progreso was opened in Morelia in 1923 but closed at the end of 1926. The following report given at the 1927 Southern Baptist Convention reveals much pessimism regarding the future support of schools in Mexico:

> Our school question in Mexico is a serious question, looked at from two standpoints: the Board does not have money to continue many of our much needed schools, and the government does not want any of our schools.[27]

---

[26]Actas Convención Nacional Bautista, 1934, 14.

[27]Annual of the Southern Baptist Convention, 1927, 254-55. The last phrase surely meant that the Mexican government did not want the Baptist schools to continue functioning as Christian institutions. The government did want to take over the Protestant schools and transform them into public schools.

A combined ABHMS and SBC theological seminary was established in Saltillo in 1917. A preparatory school was also established for men. There was additional government pressure to close the school. This factor, coupled with reduced funds due to the Great Depression, caused the seminary to move to San Antonio, Texas in 1936. By the late 1930's virtually all of the Baptist schools in Mexico were closed. The Baptists had lost their important penetration into the educational sphere of society.[28] Only recently have they begun to enter this sphere.[29]

The Avila Camacho and Miguel Alemán administrations were a time of cautious advance for the Baptists. The Southern Baptist greatly increased the number of missionaries in Mexico. In 1938 the Southern Baptists had no active missionaries actually living in Mexico. Twenty years later, there were forty.

The Colegio Howard property in Puebla had been used as a student hostel since 1935. But given the government's new openness to religion, a new school was established in 1944.

"Colegio Nicolás Bravo," formerly "Colegio Howard," meets in

---

[28]Baptist missionary Orvil W. Reid, The Challenge of Mexico to Missions, 68-69, lamented this loss of the Baptist schools. "As a group it could be said that the Methodists and Presbyterians have more wealth and culture because they have placed more emphasis on schools than other groups have. When the Revolution of 1910-17 came, many of our missionaries left the country. As the new constitution made church directed schools illegal and prohibited the teaching of religion in them, practically all Baptist schools were closed down, and our missionaries returned to the United States. These other denominations kept on with their schools, adapting them to the circumstances. The conviction of our Baptist missionaries was that they could not keep the schools going without breaking the law, and even if they should manage to continue them, they could teach nothing in an evangelistic way. As the emphasis was always placed on evangelism, they felt that they could not justify the spending of mission money and workers just to teach secular subjects. Even though the denominations that kept their schools going could not teach religion and were handicapped in many ways, they did much good by exerting a Christian influence; thus they have attracted a more cultured group on the whole than have the Baptists. Now we could wish that our schools had not been closed." Reid was mistaken in his overly optimistic calculations of how many schools were kept open by other denominations. Methodists and Presbyterians also closed most of their schools. His understanding of the relationship between education and evangelism is clearly seen in his analysis "...yet had we faced the circumstances that our missionaries then faced, we might have done the same thing because of our firm belief that education is not an end within itself, but that it is a means to an end, which is to evangelize (emphasis mine)."

[29]Bethel: Una Obra de Fé. 25. Aniversario (Mexico City: 1988), 30-34, describes how one Baptist church in Mexico City recently penetrated the educational sphere in 1983 by establishing a primary school, the Colegio "David Livingston", with plans for upper levels as well. A self-critique of Baptist absence in the educational realms can be sensed in the following: "The Baptist voice in the educational arena in Mexico was silenced after the Revolution of 1910, when almost all the Baptist schools closed. Until 1983 there was no distinctively Baptist school that was mentioned." Five years later the school had more than 350 students. See also Pedro Larson, "Iglesia Bautista Bethel," in México Hoy y Mañana: Documento No. 2 "Estudio de Casos del Crecimiento de la Iglesia Evangélica en la Gran Ciudad de México" (Mexico City: Visión Evangelizadora Latinoamericana and Programa Latinoamericano de Estudios Socio-Religiosos, 1989), 41-51.

> the beautiful property purchased by the Society many years ago. The Society cooperates in the expenses of the school and supplies Miss Mabel Young, who is English teacher and counselor, and helps in many ways in the Baptist work in Puebla. Miss Rena Button, her co-worker, has developed a far-reaching and effective program as advisor to the churches in Christian education and Young People's work.[30]

Southern Baptists began the Benito Juárez School in Guayameo, Guerrero in 1946 with Moisés Arévalo as director. The school's dormitories were on a farm and offered the students the opportunity to pay for their expenses. The school also enjoyed the praise of the local government authorities.[31]

Baptists opened several student hostels in the 1940's to offset government restrictions on church operated schools. Three factors influenced the Foreign Mission Board's decision to move in this direction:

> (1) Capital losses had been great when unfavorable laws forced the closure of its schools in Mexico. (2) Although the wave of anti-clericalism had largely passed, the laws which discouraged church schools still remained. (3) Generally speaking, except in the larger cities, public schools included only six years of elementary work. By establishing student dormitories under proper supervision, young people had opportunity to continue their education, prepare for full seminary work, take professional courses, or otherwise fit themselves for places of leadership.[32]

These student homes were more like "homes" than "student centers." Although students did receive some help in their academic interests, very little impact was made upon the schools that they attended.[33] Homes were opened in

---

[30] Annual Report WABHMS, 1946, 352.

[31] The Annual of the Southern Baptist Convention, 1949, 119-20, reports that "We celebrated the opening of the Benito Juárez School in February, with two normal trained teachers and your missionaries. This school, which has added another teacher and increased its enrollment to ninety-six, is a real triumph of faith. The federal educational inspector speaks highly of it." In 1955 Arévalo reported an enrollment of 225 students. The federal inspector commended the school and expressed his desire for additional schools; Patterson, Century of Baptist Work, 167. An extensive description of Arévalo's ministry can be found in Omar Bustos Busio, "Una Investigación de las Contribuciones de Moisés Arévalo Arias a la Obra Bautista en el Estado de Guerrero" (Licenciatura thesis, Seminario Teológico Bautista Mexicano, 1985).

[32] Patterson, Century of Baptist Work, 167-68.

[33] Reid, Challenge of Mexico, 92-96, who began the student hostel in Guadalajara lamented the fact that so little work was being done among Baptist students. He estimated that the number of Baptist college students had increased tenfold in ten years. Julian C. Bridges, "A Chance to Study," The Commission (April 1967): 25, describes the typical impact made by these student homes on a student, Saúl García. Little attention is given to academic issues.

Guadalajara (1941), Chihuahua (1947), and Mexico City (1957).

As government restrictions were loosened, the Southern Baptist Seminary was able to return to Torreón in 1946. The American Baptists reopened their theological seminary in 1947 in Mexico City. Women students were admitted for the first time in 1953. In 1957 Director Cosme Montemayor reported that the Seminary had registered with the Secretary of State, implying government awareness and tacit approval of theological education. A third theological institution, the Escuela Bíblica Lacy, was begun in 1936 in Oaxaca. After a stormy childhood in which the school was moved to Puebla, Morelia, and to Guadalajara, it finally returned to Oaxaca in 1959.

Not all Baptists working in Mexico belonged to the National Convention. The Baptist Bible Fellowship, headquartered in Springfield, Missouri, sent their first missionary to Mexico in the early 1940's. Shortly thereafter, they offered Mexican Pastor José Bueno economic support for his work in Ciudad Mante and Limón, Tamaulipas. In 1948, he broke with the ABHMS from whom he had previously received financial support. The Mante church became divided, with the majority agreeing with Bueno. The municipal magistrate had to become involved in the situation to determine which sector would be allowed to keep the property and the name "First Baptist Church." He decided in favor of Bueno's group. The Mante and Limón churches broke from the National Convention that same year. In 1951 they formed the Bible Baptist Fellowship and within five years had eighteen registered churches. Their major complaint against the National Baptist Convention was that theological liberalism had infected much of the denomination.[34]

Other churches including the Buen Pastor Church in Mexico City[35] and the Baptist church in Tapachula also left the National Convention to become affiliated with the Bible Baptist Fellowship. Although many of these churches later returned to the National Convention, the experience produced an important impact upon the Convention leadership. Most reacted by moving to a more defensive, conservative theological position. A conservative social posture usually accompanied theological conservatism. Foreign missionaries sent to Mexico were urged to

---

[34]Another group called "Fundamental Baptist Missions" also became part of this Bible Baptist Fellowship. They represented a fairly typical North American fundamentalist Christianity. They affirmed the verbal inspiration of the Bible. They also emphasized prophecy, especially the premillennial second coming of Christ, with the corollary that the church should not be involved in the social and political activities of this world.

[35]This defection was especially painful because the church's pastor, Feliciano Contreras, had served as President of the National Convention for several terms.

abstain totally from involvement in Mexican politics.[36] Mexican pastors generally adopted the same position.

In 1952 missionary Reid went to great lengths to assure his American readers that Mexican Baptists were just as conservative, evangelistic and committed as the Southern Baptists:

> The Mexican Baptist Convention is as conservative in doctrine as the Southern Baptist Convention in the United States. In spite of the constant pressure of persecution in many places against evangelicals, and especially against those who propagate their faith, the Mexican Baptists are evangelistic. Many of them are faithful personal soul-winners. There has also been a remarkable growth in stewardship in the last ten years. Mexican Baptists now give a higher percentage of their income to the Lord's work than do Southern Baptists. However, their incomes for the most part are extremely low.[37]

Open air evangelistic campaigns became commonplace, in part due to the government's more liberal non-enforcement of the legislation in the Constitution. Important campaigns took place in Piedras Negras (1956) and Torreón (1957). The most publicized was when Billy Graham preached in Mexico City, February 11-16, 1958.

The Baptist run Latin American Hospital in Puebla continued its services. An adjunct school of nursing, begun in 1918, also attracted several dozens of students. It later obtained official affiliation with the University of Puebla. In 1949 Dr. Lamar Cole opened a medical clinic in Guadalajara. In 1958 a large tract of land was purchased and a fifty-bed unit was built. Thus, the Hospital México-Americano came into existence. It later added an intensive care unit.[38]

The Student Movement of 1968

The Baptists in Mexico entered the period under study (1964-1991) with the

---

[36]Reid, Challenge of Mexico, 49, bluntly states "the (gospel) message must be free from politics." Yet he himself dedicates an entire chapter to defend the Mexican government's anti-religious legislation as a necessary means to limit Catholic abuses, ibid., 53-64. He does so because "the influence of the Vatican, and other Catholic forces, has been such that the press of the world has not done justice to the Mexican Revolution in regard to these articles of the reformed Constitution of Mexico." Throughout his book he mentions his warm relations with various government officials in diverse areas. During the anti-alcohol campaign, the governor of Jalisco invited Reid to share information about his work. The governor heartily praised Reid's ministry, 104.

[37]Ibid., 77. Reid was urging a greater emphasis on social ministries, but continually emphasized that "it is not to be an end within itself but rather a means even to a more noble end, the salvation of the souls of men.

[38]Paula Kortkamp, "Nurses Arrive When Needed," The Commission (June 1968): 24.

optimism of the age. They had grown by 80% during the decade of the 1950's. They had called a visionary executive director, Roberto Porras Maynes, who was promoting the extension of Baptist churches throughout the country.

But underneath the surface, certain problems were brewing. Those churches and missionaries associated with the Southern Baptists had adopted a more rigid, conservative theological position, with a fairly conservative social posture that supported the status quo.[39] Some of the churches associated with the American Baptist Convention were more liberal, both in their theology and in their social stance. Dissatisfaction with Executive Secretary Porras began to grow among many Baptist leaders.

These differences surfaced in certain problems regarding the theological seminaries. At the 1965 Convention Porras proposed that the Convention utilize outside funding to support a recruiter for the Baptist seminaries. He hid from the Convention the fact that these funds would come from the World Council of Churches[40] Theological Education Fund. Although there would be no "strings attached," the Convention defeated the proposal.

At the same time, Feland Meadows, rector of the Baptist Seminary of Mexico (Tlalpan), was urging the seminary to join the ecumenical Theological Community that was forming near the Mexican University. Porras was a professor at the Seminary and was caught in the middle. He communicated to the Seminary the Convention's objection to such a move, but at the same time, he defended the seminary's right to make their own decision. At the 1966 Convention, charges of theological modernism were leveled against the seminary and certain like-minded churches.[41] Meadows defended the seminary:

> The seminary has an open door policy. If anyone has anything against the seminary they can go there and clarify matters. In the seminary there is no modernism; only differences of opinion.[42]

Meadows was able to secure the approval of the Central and Northeast Baptist Associations to move the seminary to the Theological Community. He was also able to persuade a majority of the members of the Convention's Relations Committee. When the American Baptists received word of this approval, they

---

[39]This is reflected in R. Henry Wolf, "Notes from a Diary–II," The Commission (November 1967): 20. Commenting on a conversation with a lieutenant in Guayameo, Wolf writes, "I assured him I do not mix in politics, am not pastor of the church, do not carry a gun, and believe in obeying the government."

[40]Baptists in Mexico have been very wary of ecumenical ventures. Any connection with the World Council of Churches has been rejected due to the Council's liberal stance in doctrine and social issues.

[41]Some of the seminary professors were charged with denying the infallibility of Scriptures and the virgin birth of Christ, as well as practicing open communion and a more liberal position on baptism.

[42]Unpublished minutes of the CNB, meeting in Mérida, Yucatán, April 28-May 2 1966.

began plans to build at the Theological Community site in San Angel.[43] The Convention of 1970 voted to terminate relations with the Seminary.[44] The American Baptist Home Mission Society terminated its relationship with the Mexican National Baptist Convention. It eliminated the position of Field Missionary. Their work in Mexico was limited to financial support and minor personnel participation in the seminary. Most Baptist churches in Mexico refused to send their youth to the Baptist Seminary associated with the Theological Community.

The Student Movement of 1968 took place against the backdrop of the controversy regarding the seminaries. Although Liberation Theology took hold in the Baptist Seminary later,[45] certain churches and pastors already held a liberal social conscience which was conducive to greater social and political participation both during 1968 as well as afterwards.

The Baptist Student Ministry had been under the leadership of Julian Bridges since 1961. Bridges was well aware of the political dimensions of student ministry. He asked his North American supporters a rhetorical question whether Mexican Baptist students should participate in political demonstrations.[46] He was especially proud of his associate director, Pablo Castellanos, who had converted to Christ from leftist tendencies:

> When we met him several years ago, Pablo C. had just enrolled in the law school of the 94,000-student National University of Mexico.

---

[43]Anuario Convención Nacional Bautista 1967-68, 42-46; and Anuario Convención Nacional Bautista 1969, 149-53.

[44]Anuario Convención Nacional Bautista 1971, 105. In fact, the Convention voted to break off relations with both seminaries (Tlalpan and Torreón). Doctrinal issues were not the factors involved in breaking ties with the Torreón seminary, which was sponsored by the more conservative Southern Baptists. Many of the Mexican Baptists were not in favor of the proposed geographical move to Mexico City. The minutes from that decisive convention read, "May God bless the Baptist Seminary of Mexico; it in its work and us in ours. May God bless the Mexican Baptist Theological Seminary (Torreón); it in its work and us in ours. We ought not elect representatives to their administrative councils." It later renewed relations with the seminary sponsored by the Southern Baptists, even though it did eventually move from Torreón to Satélite, a suburb just outside Mexico City.

[45]Comunidad Teológica Dean Robert Hoeferkamp, interview by author, 14 June 1991, Mexico City. The heyday of Liberation Theology at the Comunidad Teológica was in the decade of the 1970's. One of the most important events was the Theological Encounter held October 8-10, 1977 that included Jürgen Moltmann, James Cone, Harvey Cox, Raúl Vidales, Luis Rivera Pagán, Sergio Arce Martínez, Augusto Cotto, Orlando Costas, José Porfirio Miranda, and Hugo Assmann among others. The papers presented at this Encounter were later published in Jorge V. Pixley and Jean-Pierre Bastian, Praxis Cristiana y Producción Teológica: Materiales del Encuentro de Teologías Celebrado en la Comunidad Teológica de México (8 al 10 de Octubre 1977) (Salamanca: Ediciones Sígueme, 1979).

[46]Julian C. Bridges, "Where the Action Is," The Commission (November 1968): 16.

A social idealist and an outstanding orator, Pablo soon became a popular speaker at the student forums on social and political issues. Thus, he was approached by the Communist party in the school to see if he would run for office on their ticket. About this time, Pablo was enlisted in the Baptist student work on campus. Christ began to make a difference in his life, and he saw that his revolutionary ideas could be channeled through his Christian faith. Now Pablo debates against Communist students and professors on campus, and strongly sprinkles his arguments with quotations from the Bible, especially the teaching of Jesus.[47]

Prior to the student movement of 1968 Castellanos had used his oratorical skills to disperse a crowd of students who were about to take over the Law School at the UNAM.[48]

The Baptist student ministry was going through a period of transition, precisely during the student movement of 1968. Bridges submitted his resignation at the National Convention in April 1968.[49] There were two student centers operating under Bridges' administration. One was near the Ciudad Universitaria and the other was located by the Normal-Polytechnic Schools on the near north side of the city.

When Bridges resigned, another North American, Robert Frike, was designated director of student ministries.[50] At the National Convention of 1969

---

[47]Ibid. Two years earlier Bridges had expressed deep admiration for certain Communists, such as Cheddi Jagan, ex-premier of Guyana. In an interview with Jagan, the premier labeled Christianity "as nothing but pious preachments, with little concrete action in areas of race relations, economic exploitation, and social oppression. We offered some reply about what the church is doing, but our answers seemed feeble, even to us. Are Christians treating the causes as well as the ills? Are we taking the gospel where the action really is? Is it evident to the world that Christians are seriously trying to apply Christ's teaching to 'love thy neighbor as thyself' in all areas of daily living? Our answers were not too convincing to the dedicated Communist confronting us." Julian C. Bridges, "Interview with a Communist," The Commission (January 1967): 5

[48]Julian C. Bridges, "Pablo Calms Rioters," The Commission (July-August 1966): 18.

[49]Julián C. Bridges, "Informe que Rinde el Director del Departamento de Trabajo Estudiantil de la Convención Nacional Bautista de México. Tampico, Tamps, Abril de 1968," in Anuario Convención Nacional Bautista 1967-68, 143-48. One of his last actions as director of student ministries was to oversee the Congreso Nacional Bautista de Jóvenes from April 11-13, 1968. Almost 500 youth attended and made big plans for extending the gospel among students. Julian C. Bridges, "Congress Affects Young People," The Commission (August 1968): 23.

[50]Frike was very pro-American and also outspoken which sometimes caused additional problems with the students. He would frequently place pro-American news clippings on the student center bulletin board, and one of his Mexican student leaders would remove the articles as soon as possible. Alberto Velasco Sarmiento, interview by author, 9 June 1991, Mexico City.

Frike reported that

> student work in general has been forced to reduce its activities both in number and in kind. This reduction is due to the tremendous, devastating student disturbances, which we all know about. There was a period of some four months when the Student Centers in the Federal District had their doors closed.[51]

With both centers closed during the most crucial months of the movement, the student ministry department gave little orientation to the students, Baptists or otherwise. Months after the massacre in Tlatelolco, students and leaders within the department did a self-evaluation and recognized several weaknesses. Their new goals included the "strengthening of our activities on the campuses of higher education," an emphasis on "programs to influence strongly and thoroughly the non-Christian students," and special attention given to "social ministries."[52] Frike resigned in April 1969 to assume a teaching position at the Baptist Seminary in Torreón.

A related student ministry run by the Baptist Convention was the student home. Approximately 20 students, mostly Baptist, were living in the hostel. On three or four occasions, the director had to go down to different police stations to retrieve some of his "kids" who had been picked up by the police at some of the student demonstrations.[53] The director warned the students that if they participated in the movement, they would be asked to leave the dormitory.

The majority of Baptist pastors offered little or no orientation to the students in their congregations. Most followed the lead of the large First Baptist Church. The topic was never discussed from the pulpit. But some of the students participated quite openly in the student movement. One of the officers of the youth group was Alberto Velasco Sarmiento. He was a student in the School of Biological Sciences of the Instituto Nacional Politécnico. He was a gifted speaker and participated quite actively in the movement.[54] He was working part-time for a print shop and was able to obtain ink for many of the protest flyers that were printed at both the University and at the Politécnico. He frequently invited leaders of the student movement to speak to the youth group at the church. The youth responded with great interest to these talks. The church leadership organized a

---

[51]Roberto Frike, "Informe que Rinde el Director del Departamento de Trabajo Estudiantil de la Convención Nacional Bautista de México ante la Misma en su Reunión Anual Celebrada en la Ciudad de Puebla, Puebla, en Abril de 1969," in Anuario Convención Nacional Bautista 1969, 136-40.

[52]Ibid., 138.

[53]Prisciliano Castell Zavoleta, interview by author, 5 June 1991, Mexico City, affirms that these students were just curious on-lookers and did not really participate in the movement.

[54]. Jaime Paredes, interview by author, 10 March 1991, Mexico City. Alberto Velasco Sarmiento, interview by author, 9 June 1991, Mexico City.

youth retreat precisely when the Tlatelolco massacre took place, and therefore, almost all of their youth were isolated from the tragic event.[55]

Some pastors, such as Estrella de Belén's Alejandro Zamora,[56] cautioned their students to be careful and wary of outside infiltrators who would use the student movement for their own purposes.[57] There was a special concern that the students were being used as "cannon fodder" by communist infiltrators.[58]

The Pastor of Horeb Baptist Church,[59] Rolando Gutiérrez was doing studies at the National University. On the evening of September 18, when the

---

[55]It is still unknown whether the church leadership knew of an imminent use of force by the authorities or whether the retreat held at the Aytec camp was "providential".

[56]Pastor Javier Ulloa, interview by author, 30 May 1991, Mexico City. Pastor Alejandro Zamora, interview by author, 30 May 1991, Mexico City. Zamora is a good example of the alliance between the PRI and Mexican evangelicals. Zamora's father was a close friend of Lázaro Cárdenas and was active in the PRI organization in the state of Michoacán. Pastor Alejandro Zamora had been invited by the PRI to return to his home state to run for the office of representative in the national congress (as "diputado"). He declined the offer in order to continue his pastoral ministry in the capital. Although he did not become an active member of the PRI, his political loyalties affected both his perception of the student movement of 1968 as well as his political preferences in 1988. The PAN was rejected for its alleged ties with the Catholic hierarchy. All the leftist parties were rejected due to a perceived incompatibility between the Biblical faith and classical marxism. According to Zamora, Cuauhtémoc Cárdenas betrayed the heritage of his father, President Lázaro Cárdenas, by aligning himself with the left. That is ironic, because President Cárdenas implemented many reforms (nationalization of the oil industry, agrarian reform, socialistic education, etc.) that are usually considered quite "leftist."

[57]Ibid. Zamora affirmed that the outside infiltrators included both leftists and conservative elements of the Opus Dei Catholic organization. On the night the soldiers invaded the National University, Zamora spoke to a large group of college students at the Baptist Student Center. He urged the students not to have any involvement with communists, due to ideological incompatibilities. He admitted that some of the high school students from his church had been swept up into the protest marches. On the Sunday before the Tlatelolco massacre, his sermon "Una Tierra en la cual Mora la Justicia" emphasized that there would not be perfect justice here on earth before the return of Christ. Therefore, students should not risk their lives for a cause that could not deliver the justice that it promised. Only a "changed heart" due to a spiritual conversion would bring about social justice. After the massacre many parents thanked him for his message. They affirmed that his sermon helped persuade their sons and daughters not to go to Tlatelolco on that fateful evening.

[58]Ibid. Zamora mentioned Sócrates Amado Campos Lemus as a communist student leader who used other students for his own purposes. According to Zamora, Lemus later sold out to the government and became part of the "establishment". Cf. Sócrates Amado Campos Lemus, "Que se Hable de lo que se Tiene que Hablar," in Pensar el 68, coord. Hermann Bellinghausen (Mexico City: Cal y Arena, 1988), 197-99.

[59]A description of this influential church can be found in Herman Hofer, "Iglesia Bautista Horeb," in México Hoy y Mañana: Documento No. 2 "Estudio de Casos del Crecimiento de la Iglesia Evangélica en la Gran Ciudad de México" (Mexico City: Visión Evangelizadora Latinoamericana and Programa Latinoamericano de Estudios Socio-Religiosos, 1989), 53-65.

army took over the university campus, Gutiérrez was attending classes. Realizing what was happening, he made several trips in his car transporting trapped students out of danger.[60]

The largest denominational response to the student movement took place at the Primer Congreso Nacional de Estudiantes Bautistas, held in Puebla April 16-19, 1969. It was organized by Baptist students from Puebla[61] as a deliberate attempt to think Biblically and critically about issues raised by the student movement. In the invitation the organizers sounded a rousing exhortation.

> We trust that you have come to begin to build a Church that is strong in CHRISTIAN SERVICE and that you help us to erase the caricature of a static and formal Church THAT HAS NO SOCIAL INVOLVEMENT. This Congress has been organized with the firm purpose to provide you with orientation and to stimulate you in CHRISTIAN SERVICE. Today you begin to form part of a structure full of responsibility and sacrifice.[62]

Two of the key topics addressed were "An Evangelical Analysis of the Student Movement" by Christian sociologist César Moreno and "The Christian and Social Change" by Pastor Rolando Gutiérrez.[63] The Congress produced strong reactions, both in favor and against. It contributed to a greater polarization within the denomination between the "conservatives" who tended to be socially and politically defenders of the status quo, and the "progressives" who desired to bring about social and political change.[64]

Typical of the conservative position was a letter written by Pastor Adolfo Hernández S. to a student in Mexico City. The letter appeared in the Baptist Convention magazine La Luz Bautista. Essentially the letter urged students to

---

[60]Pastor Rolando Gutiérrez, interview by author, 3 December 1990, Quito, Ecuador.

[61]The Puebla Baptist Church had strong connections with the American Baptist Convention, and therefore, a much greater social conscience. Some of that social awareness can be detected in Eusebio Acosta Chávez, Historia de la Primera Iglesia Bautista de Puebla (Puebla: Primera Iglesia Bautista, 1968).

[62]"1 Congreso Nacional de Estudiantes Bautistas," in Anuario Convención Nacional Bautista 1969, 167-71. José Alcántara M., interview by author, 14 June 1991, Mexico City.

[63]Ibid., 167-171.

[64]Some of the organizers of the Congress later became active in different social ministries. José Alcántara who was in charge of choosing the Congress speakers later became a Lutheran. He has been quite active in social ministries such as AMEXTRA (see chapter 3) and the Lutheran Aid Committee. He has also pushed for a more contextualized theological training as director of the Centro de Estudios Superiores de Integración Cristiana (CESIC) and president of the Asociación de Profesores de Instituciones de Educación Teológica (APIET).

postpone struggles for greater justice until they were older and better equipped to do so. They were exhorted to return to their studies.

> Mario, millions of youth have failed simply because when they could have used their complete intellectual resources, they used them in secondary issues or in things that they could have achieved later. Mario, don't you think that our youth by wanting to modify our laws and to ask for, and even demand, the exclusion of necessary articles (spending energy better used in a more worthy cause), I say, don't you think they are committing a great mistake? . . . Don't you think that they are fighting a battle that is not their own? The youth's battle should be in front of their open books. Their goal should be cherishing their diploma which is the crystallization of their effectiveness in their studies and the crystallization of their parents' efforts. . . . Today the place of the youth is in front of their books; their goal, finishing their degree; while we adults labor forward using all the good suggestions, including those of the youth.[65]

The student movement of 1968 was interpreted within the Baptist Convention as part of a struggle between the conservatives and the liberals within the denomination.[66] By and large, those most sympathetic to the students' cause were those associated with the Tlalpan Seminary, and churches associated with the more liberal American Baptists. Both the First National Congress of Baptist Students (April 16-19, 1969) and the following conference with Harvey Cox (1971) were heavily influenced by the more liberal elements of the denomination. When the Tlalpan Seminary moved into the Theological Community, its ties with the Baptist Convention were severed. It later stressed Liberation Theology and had little impact upon Mexican Baptists. Some of the sympathetic pastors who stayed within the denomination, like Horeb's Rolando Gutiérrez, were viewed with great suspicion by the more conservative pastors.[67]

The Student Congress of 1972 was held in Monterrey. The invited speaker was the Methodist Emilio Castro, a Protestant spokesman for Latin American liberation theology. The leadership of the Baptist Convention refused to provide funding for the congress. The students invited the Nicaraguan Baptist leader

---

[65]Adolfo Hernández S., "Carta a un Estudiante," La Luz Bautista (January 1969): 10. It seems that many of the Marios of that generation did not accept the advice given in this letter. Evangelical churches (and Catholic as well) admit that the generation of 1968 is their "lost" or "unreached" generation.

[66]Pat Carter, interview by author, 13 May 1991, Mexico City.

[67]Ibid. This suspicion, to a large extent, has only recently been overcome. Pastor Rolando Gutiérrez was elected denominational president in 1990 by an overwhelming majority. Carter interprets this as Gutiérrez having moved to the "center". Others would argue that the Convention has shifted to a more socially conscious stance.

Gustavo Parajón to fill in for Castro.[68] The radical social-political dimensions of these congresses took on a more "spiritual" tone at this and later student conventions, partly because of the participation of the "Nuevo Nacimiento" (New Birth) movement.[69]

The Nuevo Nacimiento movement was a Mexican version of the Jesus People movement, made up primarily of "hippie" types, including a large number of ex-drug addicts and prostitutes. The Mexican Baptist Convention was the only evangelical denomination that deliberately aided this movement. Certain Baptist leaders such as Alfonso Víctor Muñoz and Eduardo de la Flor had begun an evangelistic ministry "Nuevo Nacimiento" within the Convention in 1967. As the fruits of this ministry became more permanent, several local churches were formed. These churches, by and large, were incorporated into the Baptist Convention. Some have been influenced by Witness Lee's "Local Church" movement.[70] As a consequence, some of these congregations were split and others left the Baptist Convention. Those that stayed have affected the Convention by making it more aware of youth issues (especially drug addiction and prostitution) and by questioning the traditional Baptist model of a one-man pastoral leadership.[71] As these youth gradually left the drug culture behind, they have adopted more "middle-class" values, including formal university education. Consequently, they have developed a more "sophisticated" analysis of their own ministries, including social action.

The decade of the 1970's saw the Baptist Convention itself gradually become more socially and politically aware. There were many reasons for this increased social conscience. The country in general, and the youth in particular were raising many questions and leveling severe criticisms at several institutions,

---

[68]There was much debate over this issue. It is still not clear whether the students gave in to convention pressure, or if Emilio Castro's plans changed and the students responded accordingly. Rebeca Montemayor de Ulloa, interview by author, 30 May 1991, Mexico City.

[69]Pat Carter, interview by author, 13 May 1991, Mexico City. A description of this unique ministry of Nuevo Nacimiento can be found in David Daniell, Stronger than Mushrooms: The Various Facets of Baptist Student Work in Mexico (Nashville: Convention Press, 1976).

[70]This movement grew out of Watchman Nee's writings. Several prominent authors in the United States accused this group of becoming a "cult" and of using "brain-washing" techniques.

[71]The "official" progression of relations between the Baptists and Nuevo Nacimiento can be seen in the annual reports made to the Convention. The Nuevo Nacimiento groups that developed into churches were strongly attracted to a "team ministry" approach. They were greatly influenced by Victor Javier Espinosa Manrique, "La Constitución de los Ancianos-Obispos en la Iglesia Cristiana: I y II Siglo" (Licenciatura thesis, Seminario Teológico Bautista Mexicano, 1984). Alejandro Sáenz, interview by author, 15 October, 1988.

including the church. Some Baptist leaders tried to respond to these youthful questions. Perhaps the most influential person in this process was Pastor Rolando Gutiérrez of the Horeb church. He broke with the ecumenical Baptist Seminary in the early 1970's.[72] He began teaching at the "convention" seminary which had moved from Torreón to Lomas Verdes, a northern suburb of Mexico City. His academic discipline and pastoral vision inspired many young seminarians. Many followed his example of combining both theological and university studies.[73] As these young men (and some women) took over pastoral leadership in Baptist congregations, much more dialogue took place between the academic world and the church. A Fraternidad Teológica Bautista Mexicana was formed to address a wide array of theological and social issues.[74] University students and graduates in Horeb's church[75] as well as throughout the country, such as sociologist Ruhama Ortiz de Mercado, received encouragement from Gutiérrez and began to make significant contributions in their fields.[76]

The Earthquakes of 1985

The centrally located First Baptist Church was by far the most involved in relief work. Many homes in a "vecindario" in front of the church building collapsed. Within hours of the early morning earthquake on September 19, Mrs. Ortiz, the wife of one of the pastors, had already organized a soup kitchen for those whose homes were damaged. In the early stages, the church provided temporary housing for 500 people. It also offered an around-the-clock kitchen for refugees

---

[72]There has been much controversy about this break with the ecumenical seminary. Moisés Méndez, interview by author, 28 November 1990, Mexico City.

[73]Pastors who have a university degree in addition to their seminary training are very uncommon in Mexico. Gutiérrez not only pastors his church, but has a full time teaching position in the Instituto Politécnico Nacional, is currently president of the National Baptist Convention and president of the Fraternidad Teológica Latinoamericana.

[74]All of the principal leaders of the FTMB including pastors Gonzalo Viniegra, Javier Ulloa, Rafael Pola, and Alfredo Niño, recognize a certain early dependence upon Gutiérrez. Most now wield a good amount of influence in their own right. Their magazine Tensión contains the major papers presented at their annual seminars and workshops.

[75]These have included men and women. One example is Susana Chow who has been a leading figure in the oil industry.

[76]Ruhama Ortiz has contributed a Christian perspective to the field of sociology in Mexico through her writings and presentations at congresses. She is currently co-pastoring a Baptist congregation with her husband, Lázaro Mercado.

and rescue teams, and a medical clinic.[77] From this large church food, medicine and clothing were distributed to 20 shelters and churches.

The Estrella de Belén Church in the southern part of the city also played an important role in the relief work. Pastor Zamora, who was denominational president at the time called the Baptist city pastors to coordinate efforts. Families from his church opened their homes to receive those whose homes had been destroyed. His youth provided food, medicine and spiritual counseling to victims in Tlatelolco and the historic downtown area.[78]

James Philpot, administrator of Southern Baptists in Mexico City, attended daily briefings at the United States embassy, and was thus able to coordinate relief supplies sent from Baptist churches in the United States to the most needy distribution sites in Mexico City.

The Baptist Theological Seminary, located in suburban Lomas Verdes, canceled classes for a week and sent its students to help out in evangelism, counseling, and physical labor.[79] Students from the Baptist hostel helped out in similar ways on an individual basis.[80]

Baptists became heavily involved aiding the homeless at four government shelters. In addition to providing food and clothing, they offered counseling and Bible study groups. At the government's request, Baptists continued working in these shelters long past the original target date of December 1985.

There were other visible forms of cooperation between the Baptists and the government. Medical equipment had been donated to the Baptist owned Mexican-American Hospital in Guadalajara in 1983. But due to red tape in the customs department, this equipment had been sitting at the border for two years. Shortly after the earthquakes, the Baptist Convention signed a contract with the government to lend the equipment to the badly damaged Juárez Hospital. After this period it was to be sent to the hospital in Guadalajara.[81]

The Baptists became involved in job training. They developed a project to train 3,000 jobless quake survivors to operate demolition equipment for the 1,000

---

[77]"Help After the Earthquakes," Christianity Today (8 November 1985): 66; Pastor Juan Germán Ortiz, interview by author, 24 April 1991, Mexico City.

[78]Pastor Alejandro Zamora, interview by author, 30 May 1991, Mexico City.

[79]"Help After the Earthquakes," Christianity Today (8 November 1985): 66, and Pat Carter, interview by author, 13 May 1991, Mexico City.

[80]Director Prisciliano Castell Zavoleta, interview by author, 4 June 1991, Mexico City.

[81]"Post-quake Suffering Continues, but Baptists Assist," The Commission (April 1986): 88.

damaged buildings that needed to be razed.[82] During the three week training program, the Baptists provided food for the trainees. Jackhammers and other demolition equipment were also provided for the workers.

The earthquakes had some long term impact upon the Baptists. In the social area, a permanent program of emergency aid (Comité de Auxilio Bautista) was established at the Convention level to respond more quickly and effectively in future disasters.[83] The grass-roots efforts in rescue and reconstruction projects by many Mexicans has established a precedent for Baptist laity to participate more in different ministries of their churches. According to some leaders there has been a virtual "explosion" of lay led ministries. There has been a dramatic increase in the number of new Baptist churches planted in the years immediately following the earthquakes.[84]

The National Elections of 1988

The Baptists, by and large, participated in the 1988 elections, but without enthusiasm.[85] The overwhelming majority of Baptist pastors gave no orientation regarding the civic responsibilities of Christians. The idea of providing parishioners with criteria by which they could evaluate parties or candidates was totally alien to Mexican Baptist thought.[86] One of the most frequently quoted verses on the subject was "Give to Caesar that which belongs to Caesar and to God that which belongs to God." That passage has usually been interpreted as to imply that there are two distinct spheres, the politico-social and the ecclesiastical, and that there is a clear separation between these two realms.

Most Baptist leaders interviewed believed that the majority of their flock voted for Salinas de Gortari because of the traditional alliance between the PRI

---

[82]Martha Skelton, "Mexico City: Life Rises from Rubble," The Commission (December 1985): 10, 41. The Southern Baptist Foreign Mission Board allocated $406,500.00 to buy food and equipment.

[83]"¡El C.A.B. en Acción!" La Luz Bautista (November 1988): 12-15, mentions how this committee helped flood victims in Chiapas in September 1988 and later on that same month victims of hurricane Gilbert in the states of Nuevo León, Tamaulipas, Yucatán, Campeche and Quintana Roo.

[84]For example, the Estrella de Belén Baptist Church has started four new churches in 6 years. The Horeb Baptist Church has also planted several new churches in the same period. Most of these were started by non-ordained laity.

[85]The surveys realized among the Baptist revealed an abstention rate of only 14%, which was less than the 20.5% registered among Presbyterians.

[86]In scores of interviews and conversations with Baptists, only one pastor was mentioned as having addressed the issues involved in the elections, and he was a pastor in the city of Monterrey.

and the Evangelicals.[87] Many mentioned that it was better to have a "mal conocido que un bueno por conocer (a known evil is better than an unknown good)." The PAN party was rejected due to its supposed clerical influence and Cárdenas was rejected for his leftist leanings. Other leaders believed that the vote was roughly split between the PRI and the Cardenistas.[88] They felt that given the younger voters' and the poor's disenchantment with the PRI, these believers would vote in favor of Cárdenas.

The results of the election survey show that the traditional alliance between evangelicals and the PRI party was weakened among the Baptists. The PRI garnered 41.1% of the Baptist vote. Those Baptists affiliated with somewhat "non-traditional" churches[89] were much more likely to vote against the PRI than their Baptist brothers and sisters who belonged to more traditional churches.

Economic factors played an important role as well. Churches in lower economic neighborhoods also tended more to break the "alliance" and vote for Cárdenas, just like their neighbors. Baptists had fewer qualms about voting for the Partido Acción Nacional. Compared with the Presbyterians (14.5%), Baptists in Mexico City voted for PAN in much larger numbers (24.8%). Especially in upper class churches, Baptists voted for Clouthier in large numbers.[90]

One post-election event did win Salinas some support among evangelicals, and especially among Baptists. He named María de los Angeles Moreno Uriegas to his cabinet, to head up the Secretaría de Pesca. She has been a very active member of the Estrella de Belén Baptist Church. She has used her influence to obtain certain meetings between the President and evangelical leaders.[91]

Analysis

Various historical, social, and religious factors have influenced Baptists' social and political participation in Mexico. They entered the period under study with few natural bridges into Mexican society. They had no educational institutions reaching into the non-Baptist world. Even their contacts with other evangelicals was minimal. Their primary links with Mexican society were their hospitals located

---

[87]Associate Pastor Roberto Guazo of the Dúnamis Baptist Church, conversation with author, 20 April 1991, Mexico City, and Pastor Alejandro Zamora of the Estrella de Belén Baptist Church, interview by author, 30 May 1991, Mexico City.

[88]Pat Carter, interview by author, 13 May 1991, Mexico City.

[89]These include Nuevo Nacimiento groups like Misión Cuajimalpa as well as more middle class congregations such as Moriah and Horeb.

[90]Such as in the Anastasis Baptist Church.

[91]The most notable was held on March 6, 1990 between President Salinas and leaders from among the Baptists, Presbyterians, and Methodists.

in Puebla[92] and Guadalajara. In many ways they would fit into Niebuhr's "Christ Against Culture" paradigm.[93]

Except for a few individuals, Baptist pastors and lay leaders had very little participation in the student movement of 1968. Baptist students, on the contrary, not being as grounded in this "isolation from society" mentality, participated in the movement in ways quite similar to their classmates. In the years following, it was those Baptists associated with the more socially aware American Baptists who became involved in responding to students' questions and to social issues.

Baptists participated greatly in the rescue and relief work after the earthquakes of 1985. Those who participated the most were those closest to the need.[94] The magnitude of the need caused the Baptists to be a channel for help that came from outside the country as well as from other evangelical denominations.[95]

In the 1988 elections, Baptists voted very much like their neighbors did. Social, economic, and gender factors were very influential. Precisely, because most Baptist pastors tried to be apolitical, religious factors did not play a significant role.[96]

Baptist theology has had much to do with this isolationist position. A strict separation of church and state has been a long-standing Baptist doctrine. This has been interpreted to mean that the church should not challenge nor criticize the government. One church doctrine book that has circulated widely among Mexican Baptists puts it this way:

> Just as we do not abandon our home when something or someone has violated this institution, neither do we refuse to fulfill our duties towards the government, even when this has been characterized by

---

[92]Since Baptists in Puebla had a hospital, they were more aware of their civic responsibilities than Baptists in most other parts of the country. It was precisely the Baptist Church in Puebla that organized the student congress in 1969 that attempted to respond to the questions raised by the student movement.

[93]Niebuhr, Christ and Culture, 45-82.

[94]The Primera Iglesia Bautista was surrounded by need, and therefore stayed involved over many months.

[95]This international and interdenominational cooperation was due to either the magnitude of the problem or to a weakening of Landmarkism (see below).

[96]For example, the typical evangelical rejection of the Partido Acción Nacional was not evident among Baptists. 24.8% of Mexico City Baptists voted for the PAN, compared with 22% of the population at large. A possible explanation is that historically, the Baptists have not had key individuals within the upper echelons of the various PRI administrations. Therefore, their loyalties to the PRI are much less than certain other denominations, such as the Presbyterians. Their congregationalism is another contributing factor.

corrupt practices. . . . The church should not get involved in political affairs. . . . God commands us to obey the [government's] laws.[97]

To many Baptist leaders, the secularization laws of the Mexican Constitution fit well with this doctrine of the separation of church and state. Although the state has frequently invaded the "sphere" of the church, few Baptists have publicly protested. Many desire that the legal situation continue the way it is. Influential pastor of the Primera Iglesia Bautista and current vice-president of the National Convention, Librado Ramos Lozano, recently stated his view of the Mexican Constitution succinctly:

> I believe that these [proposed] constitutional changes are not necessary; there is no need to get involved in [changing] Article 3, nor 24, nor 130, because we would be opening the gate and giving arms to those who want power. We sustain the postulate of the separation between Church and State; this was taught by the Lord Jesus Christ. I consider that we pastors should not get involved in political activities. We should dedicate ourselves to our work.[98]

Another of the religious doctrines that has shaped Mexican Baptist life has been the "Landmarkian" movement among Southern Baptists.[99] Some of its principal proponents in Mexico have been missionaries Lacy and Engelmann. In Mexico, there has been a strong emphasis on the importance of the local church, to the exclusion of denominational activities or co-operation with other evangelical groups. Therefore, given this exaggerated congregationalism, few presidents of the Baptist Convention have felt that they could speak out on social or political issues, because they could not be sure they would have the backing of their Baptist constituency.

Landmarkism has also meant that few Baptist students have participated in interdenominational ministries such as Compañerismo Estudiantil. Although a few

---

[97]Pablo R. Jackson, La Doctrina de la Iglesia Local (Deltona, Florida: Editorial Bautista Independiente, 1982), 85-86 (emphasis mine).

[98]"¿Qué Dicen los Líderes Evangélicos?" Gracia 70 (May 1990): 12.

[99]Winthrop S. Hudson, Religion in America: An Historical Account of the Development of American Religious Life, 2nd ed., New York: Charles Scribner's Sons, 1973, 173, identifies the main tenets of "Landmarkists" as "a refusal to recognize other 'societies' as true churches and a rejection of 'alien immersion' and 'pulpit affiliation' with non-Baptists." Sydney E. Ahlstrom, A Religious History of the American People, (New Haven and London: Yale University Press, 1972), 722-725, describes 19th century Landmarkism as being a "resurgence of extreme localism, exclusivism, and opposition to supracongregational agencies." Landmarkism continued to thrive into the twentieth century. "A century after the Landmark testimonies began to be widely propagated, both local practices and collective policies of the Southern Baptist Convention still exhibited signs of their influence; the closing of the Lord's Supper to all but Baptists (often even to those of other Baptist congregations), and a general willingness not only to refuse fellowship with other denominations but to deny them the name of Christian."

participate in the Centros Estudiantiles Bautistas, the majority of Baptist college and high school students do not have many opportunities to integrate their faith with academic topics nor social issues. They were also not exposed to evangelical writers such as Padilla, Arana or Escobar. A combination of this congregationalism and conservative theology meant that liberation theologians were essentially off-limits for most Baptists.

Another distinctive factor of Baptist work in Mexico is the large number of North American missionaries living in Mexico. The overwhelming majority of them are from the Southern Baptist Convention and generally tend to be conservative in their theology, politics and social tendencies. Even if they wanted to speak out on social or political issues, their tenuous legal status in Mexico makes it difficult for them to do so.[100] This, in combination with the legal restrictions on pastors' political participation, has caused the Baptist Convention to be largely "apolitical" defenders of the status quo.

Another related factor was the departure of the American Baptist missionaries from Mexico. This more liberal and ecumenical body has had no missionaries in Mexico for twenty years. The seminary that they sponsor has no formal ties with the Baptist Convention and has had very few Mexican Baptist students in its ranks.

These theological, legal and historical factors have all contributed to Baptists' understanding of their role in society. Political participation has been minimal, while other forms of social involvement have been moderate, as the needs have become manifest.

---

[100]Most missionaries are on tourist visas which must be renewed every six months.

CHAPTER 5

THE CHURCH OF GOD IN THE MEXICAN REPUBLIC[1]

Historical Background

Many of the large pentecostal denominations in Mexico have common roots, and therefore great similarities.[2] The Concilio de la Iglesia Cristiana de las Asambleas de Dios (Assembly of God), the Movimiento de Iglesias Evangélicas Pentecostés Independientes (MIEPI), the Iglesias de Dios Evangelio Completo (Full Gospel Church of God), the Fraternidad de Iglesias de Dios en la República Mexicana, the Iglesia de Dios en la República Mexicana y Centro America, and the Iglesia Cristiana Interdenominacional de la República Mexicana can all trace their histories back to common sources.

The modern Pentecostal movement dates from the beginning of the twentieth century.[3] In 1901 Charles Fox Parham led the students at his Topeka Bible College through a detailed study of the ministry of the Holy Spirit in the book of Acts. He concluded that all instances of the "Baptism in the Holy Spirit" were accompanied by speaking in tongues. He then urged them to seek the fullness of the Spirit's blessing. Some began to speak in unknown tongues. One who received the "gift" was a young black hotel waiter, William J. Seymour. Seymour became a minister for the Evening Light Saints movement and started a mission

---

[1]The full name of this church is the Iglesia de Dios en la República Mexicana y Centro América. This church should not be identified with the Church of God denominations in the United States. The denomination whose headquarters are in Anderson, Indiana is a non-pentecostal group with whom the Iglesia de Dios en la República Mexicana has had no contact. The Church of God headquartered in Cleveland, Tennessee is a pentecostal denomination that had relations with the IDRM in the 1940's. This relation was severed during a church split. The IDRM has remained independent of ties with North American denominations since then. The Iglesia de Dios Evangelio Completo, which grew out of this split, has maintained a fraternal relationship with the Cleveland based denomination. A fairly complete history of the Cleveland, Tennessee group, including their foreign missions, can be found in Charles W. Conn, Como un Ejército Poderoso: Una Historia de la Iglesia de Dios, 1886-1976, trans. Wilfredo Estrada Adorno (Cleveland, Tennessee: Pathway Press, 1983).

[2]One of these similarities is that very little has been written by or about these Mexican Pentecostals. The best self-description of the Church of God can be found in their official magazine El Camino a la Vida.

[3]Brief summaries of the Pentecostal beginnings in the United States can be found in Grant Wacker, "The Pentecostal Movement," in Eerdmans' Handbook to Christianity in America, ed. Mark A. Noll and others (Grand Rapids: Eerdmans, 1983), 336-39; Ahlstrom, A Religious History of the American People, 819-22; and Hudson, Religion in America, 345-46, 428-32. Some of the traditions that contributed to Pentecostalism were of the "Christ Against Culture" paradigm. The Wesleyan Holiness movement, the higher Christian life (second blessing), Landmarkism and dispensationalism had demonstrated varying degrees of a separationist mentality.

on Azusa street in Los Angeles. In 1906 a "revival" came to his mission and many received the pentecostal experience. Pentecostalism spread quickly among Blacks and Hispanics. Many Mexican American braceros were reached in the United States. Frequently they returned to Mexico and eagerly proclaimed their new-found faith. Pentecostalism in Latin America has been much more indigenous, precisely because the founders were largely Hispanics, and not foreign missionaries.[4]

The Iglesia de Dios en la República Mexicana (IDRM),[5] more than most Mexican denominations, was greatly shaped by one individual. David Genaro Ruesga,[6] the church's founder, was born in Morelia, Michoacán on July 6, 1898. After studying in a school for priests in Mexico City, Ruesga joined up with the forces of Pancho Villa during the Mexican Revolution. After the war, he went to the United States to work in the film industry. A serious illness brought him near death. Upon hearing the gospel he was immediately baptized and claimed to be miraculously healed. In 1920 he returned to Mexico City and began proclaiming his new-found faith.[7] By 1923 he had organized a small church in rented facilities in the "Plaza de la Concepción Tepisqueuca." This was probably the first pentecostal congregation in Mexico City.

At this time Ruesga came into contact with the Danish missionary Anna Sanders of the Assembly of God denomination.[8] Given the stricter enforcement of religious legislation in 1925, Ruesga's church was told to construct their own church edifice. Sanders was commissioned to raise funds in the United States. On February 28, 1926 the church bought a large plot of land along the Calzada de Guadalupe, on the north side of the city. The congregation grew rapidly to more than a thousand worshippers in less than five years.[9] Their facilities,

---

[4]For a good overview of the distinctives of Latin American Pentecostalism, see Wagner, Avance del Pentecostalismo en Latinoamericana.

[5]The titles "Iglesia de Dios" and "Church of God" are used interchangeably in this dissertation.

[6]Frequently the founder's last name is spelled Ruezga.

[7]Ruesga's personal account of the beginning of the work in Mexico City can be found in "Historia de Nuestras Iglesias: Así Nació 'La Calzada,'" El Camino a La Vida (July-September 1987): 3-5. This was a reprint of an article originally published in 1946. Much of this information was corroborated by Manuel Bustos, interview by author, 31 May 1991, Mexico City, tape recording.

[8]Anna Sanders' personal version of the beginning of the pentecostal movements in Mexico City is described in "El Principio de la Obra de 'Las Asambleas de Dios' en la Ciudad de México, D.F. en su XX Aniversario," in Roberto Domínguez Pioneros de Pentecostés en el Mundo de Habla Hispana: México y Centroamérica Vol. 2, (Hialeah, Florida: Literatura Evangélica, 1975), 47-59.

[9]Ruesga attributed this rapid growth to the numerous healings and miracles that were occurring. He claimed that this was the first outpouring of the Holy Spirit in Mexico City.

designed for 1250 people, became inadequate. A larger church building was constructed in 1931.

During these early years the church gave birth to many new churches throughout the city as well as in the states of Morelos, México, Puebla, and Guerrero. A theological seminary (SEMID)[10] was begun to train pastors and evangelists. Fraternal relations with the Assembly of God movement were formalized in 1929 when Ruesga and the Church of the "Calzada" officially joined the denomination. But, just a few years later, certain church members raised serious allegations against Ruesga. The church divided into many groups. Some established the Assembly of God Church on Plomeros street.[11] Others formed the large Iglesia Cristiana Interdenominacional in the Portales neighborhood.[12] A Danish man split off and formed the Independent Sarón Church. And yet others formed the Movimiento de Iglesias Evangélicas Pentecostés Independientes.[13] Ruesga was able to regroup and due to his "anointed preaching," quickly formed a large congregation. Seminary graduates began new churches in Tuxtepec, Sumidero, Fortín de las Flores, etc.

In 1940, Ruesga received financial assistance for the publication of Christian literature from the Church of God denomination headquartered in Cleveland, Tennessee. A more formal affiliation was later established. Another church split took place and led to the formation of the Iglesia de Dios Evangelio Completo with the "mother" church in the Clavería neighborhood of Mexico City, which has

---

[10]It is frequently claimed that the seminary was begun in 1922. For example, on the cover of the bulletin Acto de Graduación y Clausura: Generación 1985-1988 (Mexico City: SEMID, 1988) it boldly states "SEMID: Fundado en 1922". This date does not seem to correspond to the facts.

[11]The leader of the Plomeros Assembly of God Church was Rubén J. Arévalo. Information about this founder is located in Domínguez, Pioneros de Pentecostés, 19-22. Linda Arévalo de González, interview by author, 16 January 1991, Ixtapan de la Sal, Mexico. Further information can be found in Pablo Pretiz, "Las Asambleas de Dios," in México Hoy y Mañana: Documento No. 2 "Estudio de Casos del Crecimiento de la Iglesia Evangélica en la Gran Ciudad de México" (Mexico City: Visión Evangelizadora Latinoamericana and Programa Latinoamericano de Estudios Socio-Religiosos, 1989), 117-22, and Alfonso de los Reyes Valdez, Historia de las Asambleas de Dios en México: 1 Los Pioneros (Tampico: Alfolletos, 1990).

[12]A brief history of the Portales church as well as one church it has planted can be found in Guillermo Perrow, "Iglesia Getsemaní," in México Hoy y Mañana: Documento No. 2 "Estudio de Casos del Crecimiento de la Iglesia Evangélica en la Gran Ciudad de México" (Mexico City: Visión Evangelizadora Latinoamericana and Programa Latinoamericano de Estudios Socio-Religiosos, 1989), 85-88.

[13]Each of these pentecostal groups has their own version and interpretation of this split. The perspective of the Iglesia de Dios en la República Mexicana can be found in "La Iglesia: En los Vencedores del Siglo XX," El Camino a la Vida (September-December 1990): 94-100. This author has also had access to a rough draft of a history of the IDRM written by José Luis Montecillos, one of the pastors of the Calzada church. This history is scheduled to be published in 1991.

retained ties with the Cleveland, Tennessee group. The Iglesia de Dios en la República Mexicana has since this last split continued an independent, separatist, and more nationalistic path.[14] David Ruesga died in 1960. After his death, the denomination celebrated memorial services in honor of their founder for many years.[15]

Gregorio Muñoz became the ruling bishop in 1960 and continued for twenty five years until his death on November 21, 1985. Face to face, he was a quiet leader, known for his "simplicity and humility,"[16] although he was fairly authoritative in his writings.

The Church of God is governed by a ruling body of bishops. These men tend to exercise great control over the denomination. As a result of this episcopal structure, the denomination shows much less diversity than the Baptists (congregationalism) or Presbyterians (representation by elders).

The 1968 Student Movement

The Church of God entered the period under study not unaware of the social and political problems that surrounded them. But for most of their leaders, the increase of these problems meant that the Second Coming of the Lord was close at hand.

> The tremendous world events make our hearts throb to think that the Lord of the Harvest, whom we serve, is almost ready to appear in His Second Coming to remove His church which He bought with His blood, and take it to glory.[17]

In general, the Church of God leaders believed that all human efforts to solve the world's problems had failed and were doomed to failure. "Neither of the two great, dominant ideologies, that is, neither Democracy nor Socialism have been able to

---

[14]Many IDRM leaders have told the author with pride that they have no missionary ties with churches in the United States. Given their negative experiences with North American church leaders from both the Assembly of God and the Church of God denominations, the IDRM has been more critical of the United States than most other Mexican Protestant groups. In discussing the Mexican-American War, the editor of the denominational magazine described it as an "unjust war" when Mexico "was invaded by North American soldiers" who "stole more than half of Mexico's national territory"; "Septiembre: El Mes de la Patria," El Camino a la Vida (September-October 1964): 3.

[15]For example, homage was paid to David Ruesga in "Recuerdo Perenne," El Camino a la Vida (July-August 1972): 4-6, more than twelve years after his death. For several years memorial services were held in the "Calzada" Church.

[16]Federico Franco Santos, "Rev. Gregorio Muñoz Espinoza: 'Aunque Esté Muerto, Vivirá,'" El Camino a la Vida (May-June 1986): 3-4.

[17]Gregorio Muñoz Espinoza, "El Obispo Presidente Os Habla," El Camino a la Vida (January-February 1964): 3.

solve the profound moral and spiritual problems that snare the youth of our days."[18]

The 1968 student movement was generally ignored by the leadership of the Church of God.[19] Many pastors within the denomination believed that the student movement was "infiltrated by Communists."[20] Parents shared the same views. Some urged their teen-aged children not to participate, because they "should set their sights on spiritual values, not earthly causes."[21] A somewhat different perspective was held by those who were students at that time. The president of the youth group[22] at the "Calzada" Church, Jaime Paredes, was a student in the School of Biological Sciences of the Instituto Politécnico Nacional.[23] He participated in some of the protest marches as well as took up collections to finance the printing of flyers. Part of his willingness to get involved was due to the fact that his best friend, Alberto Velasco Sarmiento, was also a Protestant and an active participant in the movement. He openly mentioned his own participation with the members of the church, although he did not try to force the youth group to become involved in the student movement.[24] Given the fact that October 2 happened to be a Wednesday, he was directing a regularly scheduled meeting of the youth group at the church, and therefore did not attend the protest rally in Tlatelolco. His younger brother, Jorge, was a student in the Vocational High

---

[18]Amós Bustos T., "Joven: Cristo Pide tu Cooperación," El Camino a la Vida (September-October 1964): 9.

[19]The denominational magazine, El Camino a la Vida, made no explicit mention of the student movement in 1968 or 1969. The only statement remotely pertinent to the movement is found in Gregorio Muñoz Espinoza, "Editorial," El Camino a la Vida (January-February 1969): 3, where the bishop affirms "there is no doubt that we are going through truly dangerous times, because the greater part of the people are neglecting spiritual values".

[20]Pastor Jesús Mejía, interview by author, 6 March 1991, Mexico City. Pastor José Luis Montecillos, interview by author, 7 March 1991, Mexico City.

[21]Pastor Jesús Mejía, interview by author, 6 March 1991, Mexico City.

[22]"Grupos de jóvenes" in Mexican evangelical churches are not equivalent to high school youth groups in churches in the United States. Mexican groups frequently include many members who are in their twenties and some over thirty years old. However, they are usually restricted to those who are unmarried.

[23]Jaime Paredes, interview by author, 10 March 1991, Mexico City. Jaime was president of the youth group from 1968 until 1972.

[24]Ibid. Although the youth group did not officially become involved in the student movement, their sympathies were definitely with the youth and against the government, which they felt was corrupt and abusive of its power. The senior pastor of the church, Bishop Gregorio Muñoz, did not provide any orientation to the youth either in favor of or against participation in the movement.

School #7, located in Tlatelolco. Jorge was also active in the student movement. Later, Jorge succeeded his brother as president of the youth group. Some of his social concern, acquired during his participation in the student movement, was communicated to the youth group.

Manuel Bustos was pastor of the Iglesia de Dios "Bethel" in the Obrera neighborhood. Although in general he and his fellow pastors did not get involved in political issues, he did participate in one event during the student protests.[25] His son was a student at the Instituto Politécnico Nacional and invited his father to accompany him during the March of Silence on September 13. Manuel did so. During the march, his son was grabbed by policemen. Although he escaped from them, the incident left a deep impression upon his father. Since then, Pastor Bustos has not been a loyal supporter of the government nor of the PRI.

As a consequence of the October 2 massacre, the youth of the Calzada Church began a more aggressive evangelistic program aimed at non-church youth. Although there was a greater social and political awareness on the part of the youth, this was due more to changes in the population at large, and not to specific Christian factors.

The long term consequences of the 1968 movement were felt within the denomination, but were not clearly identified. Some of the older Christians observed disturbing characteristics among the younger generations.

> In the younger generations one can observe a strong current of arrogance and indifference acquired in their schools and influenced by the environment in which they exercise their professions and jobs. You can see youth, sons and daughters of brethren converted when they lived in a miserable, poor, and sick situation, and when they met God, their situation totally changed. They were able to give their children good education and preparation, but now the children are ashamed of the Church and they refuse to belong to it.[26]

The denomination responded to these changes not by answering the social questions of the youth, but rather by demanding a more "spiritual" lifestyle. For example, the theme of the XXXII Youth Convention in 1979 was "Youth and Holiness" and for the Convention in 1982, "Time for a Revival." Some of the 1968 generation have since left the Iglesia de Dios denomination and are now either in other protestant churches with a greater social conscience[27] or have abandoned

---

[25]Pastor Manuel Bustos, interview by author, 31 May 1991, Mexico City, tape recording.

[26]"La Decada de los 80s: Un Reto," El Camino a la Vida (March-May 1980): 4.

[27]For example, the Paredes families which included three youth group presidents of the "Calzada" Church are now involved in the Centro Comunitario Calacoaya. This large 3,000 member church is also pentecostal, but has many, active social ministries. A brief description of this church is found in Hector Flores, "Centro Cultural Calacoaya" in México: Hoy y Mañana: Documento No. 2 "Estudio de Casos del

the evangelical faith altogether.

Some of the current middle leadership in the Iglesia de Dios at the denominational level participated in the student movement.[28] Although these younger leaders are not very radical about social and political issues,[29] they are more active than the previous generation. One example is Esteban Santiago Ramírez, a medical doctor who has addressed the population explosion problem by advocating a Christian defense of family planning.[30]

The Earthquakes of 1985

The earthquakes of 1985 struck very close to the headquarters of the Church of God. The principal church of the denomination is located on the near north side of Mexico City on the Calzada de Guadalupe #214. The main seminary of the Iglesia de Dios (SEMID) has its classrooms and dormitories at those facilities. On September 19, the seminary students had just ended their early morning prayer session when the killer quake struck at 6:19 am.[31] The church and seminary facilities suffered little damage, but a large apartment building adjacent to the seminary came crashing down. Although the seminarians tried to help rescue those who were trapped, the police soon arrived and did not permit them to enter the building. Over the next three days the students devoted

---

Crecimiento de la Iglesia Evangélica en la Gran Ciudad de México" (Mexico City: Visión Evangelizadora Latinoamericana and Programa Latinoamericano de Estudios Socio-Religiosos, 1989), 21-31.

[28]For example, Juan Calderón Martínez was a participant in the movement of 1968. Although he was raised in a pentecostal family, he himself was not a practicing Christian at the time. He has spent more than twenty years in the Instituto Politécnico Nacional, first as a student, then as a professor. Some of the social concerns of that educational milieu have been incorporated into his life. Three years ago, he became the academic director of the denominational seminary. Professor Juan Calderón Martínez, interview by author, 15 April 1988, Mexico City.

[29]This reticence to speak out on social issues is partially due to the fact that all of the bishops of the denomination are men over fifty who wield an amazing amount of authority.

[30]Esteban Santiago Ramírez, Planificación Familiar en la Vida Cristiana (Mexico City: Publicaciones El Camino a la Vida, 1990). Although his pro-birth control and anti-abortion stance is common among evangelicals in the United States, it goes against the grain of both the conservative Catholics (who are opposed to family planning) and the liberals in Mexico (who are pro-abortion). In addition, there are a large number of Mexican evangelicals who are opposed to family planning. Even talking about sexual themes is still taboo in many evangelical circles. The fact that it was one of the first books published by the denominational publishing house demonstrates a growing openness to social issues.

[31]Pastor Eusebio Chávez, interview by author, 6 March 1991, Mexico City. Pastor Manuel Flores, interview by author, 6 March 1991, Mexico City. Both pastors were seminary students at the time of the earthquakes.

themselves to helping move objects from the rubble, to praying[32] and to evangelizing. Since the authorities tried to evacuate the area, classes were cancelled for two weeks and the students were sent to their homes in the province areas.

The youth of the Calzada church quickly got involved in the rescue efforts. For two weeks they spent sixteen-hour days in Tlatelolco helping in the rescue efforts, providing clothing and food.[33] Some also aided through counseling and providing spiritual orientation.

Pastor Francisco Castellanos of the church in the Peralvillo neighborhood became involved in an alliance of pastors who coordinated their relief efforts in their own neighborhood as well as in the nearby Tepito and Tlatelolco areas.[34]

Neither the church edifice in the Obrera neighborhood nor the homes of the parishioners suffered much damage during the earthquake, although several buildings in the neighborhood were destroyed. The pastor interpreted this as God's protection of His people.[35] Little was done by this church to aid victims.

The National Elections of 1988

The 1988 election campaign brought little official comment by the leaders of the Iglesia de Dios. The denomination's traditional "apolitical" stance was maintained by most of the pastors and other leaders. Little or no orientation was given from the pulpit, regarding the civic responsibilities of Christian believers or criteria by which the different parties and candidates could be evaluated.

On the one hand, many thought there was a widespread negative vote against the PRI. One well-informed member calculated that 65% of the members of the Calzada Church voted for Cárdenas, 30% for the PAN, and only 5% for the PRI.[36] Another long term member suggested just the opposite, with almost a unanimous vote in favor of the PRI.[37]

---

[32]Some of the prayers consisted of "praising God for demonstrating His power" and "thanking God for sparing the lives of the seminarians." Little was mentioned about intercession for others. When the interviewees were asked why the students were praising God, they replied that God had desired to manifest Himself using the earthquakes. The quakes were a public demonstration of His power. For an interesting study of how people interpret "natural disasters," see Wesley Marx, Acts of God, Acts of Man (New York: Coward, McCann & Geoghegan, Inc., 1977).

[33]Jaime Paredes, interview by author, 10 March 1991, Mexico City.

[34]Francisco Castellanos, interview by author, 10 November 1988, Ixtepec, Oaxaca.

[35]Pastor Manuel Bustos, interview by author, 31 May 1991, Mexico City, tape recording.

[36]Jaime Paredes, interview by author, 10 March 1991, Mexico City.

[37]José García Díaz, interview by author, 12 May 1991, Mexico City.

Soon after the elections, an "official" position was stated by José Luis Montecillos, one of the pastors of the "Calzada" Church and director of the denominational magazine El Camino a la Vida. He gave legitimacy to the PRI "victory" and urged his readers to pray for President Salinas.

> On July 6 of this year voting took place to elect the new president of the Mexican Republic for the next six years. And as we all know, the Party of the Mexican Revolution (P.R.I.) won again. But this time, there was a little bit more opposition to the party that won. And by what can be observed, it is possible that for the next six year period (if the Lord Jesus does not come first), the voting will be even more contested; because there is greater civic participation in the elections. We Christians, in addition to voting, have the great responsibility to pray for Carlos Salinas de Gortari who has become the maximum representative of our nation.[38]

Pastor Montecillos went on to elaborate why Christians should pray for Salinas. The ideology behind the PRI was very acceptable:

> In the case of the PRI we know that their ideology is good, because it is based primarily upon the Mexican Political Constitution, which was founded upon the Reform of Benito Juárez. And thanks to that Reform we have freedom of religion. The Catholic hierarchy, which has always coveted more power, has been restrained by this ideology. And we should pray that this ideology continue....As we already said, the PRI ia a party with a correct ideology.[39]

According to his perspective, the PRI was the only acceptable political party. Although not made explicit, the PAN party was too closely identified with the Catholic hierarchy. Cárdenas was also unacceptable because he was supported by much of the Mexican "left." In spite of the PRI's correct ideology it was urgent that Christians pray for Salinas because having studied Political Economics in the UNAM, he must have studied Marx and Engels. These founders of Communism were enemies of the Christian faith.[40]

> Communism tries to penetrate the entire world, to oust God from human hearts. The United States has been able to stop it a little, but it is necessary that we pray for those that are in government in order that they escape from this negative influence, this ideology that

---

[38]José Luis Montecillos Chipres, "Editorial: Responsabilidad Cristiana en la Política," El Camino a la Vida (October-December 1988): 2 (emphasis mine).

[39]Ibid.

[40]Ibid., 3. Montecillos quotes from Marx "I desire to take revenge upon Him who governs upon high . . ." and "the abolition of religion as an illusory happiness of humanity is a requisite for true happiness" to show the inherent anti-Christian position of Marx.

> is totally against God. For this reason, let us pray for Salinas de Gortari that he might not be influenced by these ideologies that he must have studied.[41]

The author then showed a picture of Evangelist Billy Graham sitting with and "evangelizing" ex-president José López Portillo. Although López Portillo closed his heart to the gospel,[42] perhaps together with the prayers of evangelical Christians, Salinas de Gortari might respond favorably to the Christian message. Pastor Montecillos, quite openly revealing his convictions, concluded:

> Let us pray that our government might have a just ideology which continues to permit us to have the freedom to seek God, since there have already been some persecutions.
>
> Let us pray that in our government there might be men reborn by the Word of God, since given their [current] corruption, the reaction of the Mexican people almost put into office Communist parties and that would have been a terrible misfortune.
>
> Let us pray that God might use men of God to infiltrate the political spheres and that they would be able to share the message of Jesus Christ with power. And even more, that there might be Christian politicians. Truthfully, brother [or sister], let us pray to God for this necessity. This is our responsibility as Christians in the political arena.[43]

The political surveys realized among the Iglesia de Dios revealed a strong preference for the PRI among the church leadership.[44] With some notable exceptions, most pastors share Montecillo's perspectives.

Since the election of 1988, there has been growing political awareness and commentary by church leaders.[45] As relations between the Salinas administration and the Catholic Church have become more cordial, criticism against the government's new alliance has increased. The lead editorial of the denominational magazine El Camino a la Vida for the spring of 1990 asks the question, "Why is

---

[41]Ibid.

[42]Ibid., 4. Montecillos admitted that part of this rejection of the gospel might have been due to the lack of prayer by Christians. Many within his denomination criticized Billy Graham for being "ecumenical" instead of praying for his ministry to López Portillo.

[43]Ibid.

[44]Among Iglesia de Dios pastors surveyed in May 1991, 84.6% showed a preference for the PRI. Of course, they were not allowed to actually vote in the 1988 elections, being forbidden by law.

[45]Most of the editorials of El Camino a la Vida since 1988 have dealt with public issues involving evangelicals.

the Pope coming to Mexico?"[46] The answer supplied by the author was that the Pope was coming to impoverish the Mexican nation spiritually, socially, and materially.[47] Although the Pope and the Catholic Church were the main targets of this editorial, the government was also implicated.

An important factor in this increased social and political awareness has been a change of topics in the Sunday School curriculum. From May 1989 until December 1990 the entire denomination studied the history of the Christian Church sprinkled with a Biblico-theological critique. Although not all would agree with the content of that critique, the historical study of real people has helped the Iglesia de Dios get its feet planted more firmly on the earth.

Analysis

It is obvious that the Iglesia de Dios is more reticent about political and social activities than either their Baptist or Presbyterian companions. Here again, historical, social, doctrinal, and structural factors all help to explain these differences.

The history of the Iglesia de Dios en la República Mexicana differs greatly from that of the Presbyterians or the Baptists. They created no schools nor hospitals, and therefore never had that kind of penetration into the Mexican society. On the other hand, when Mexican legislation forced the closing of evangelical schools, the Iglesia de Dios did not feel the restrictions of that church-state power play. During the War of the Cristeros, the Iglesia de Dios was not established in areas of fighting. Consequently, they were not caught in the middle, as Presbyterians and Baptists were.

They had no highly educated foreign missionaries nor missionary funding to utilize. Thus, they were more indigenous in their methods and could identify better with the common people. They had to promote much sacrificial giving among their people with amazing results.[48]

Although they have a few large urban churches, their strength comes from numerous churches in the rural areas. These congregations have faced much persecution. To help defend these churches, David Ruesga participated in the

---

[46]José Luis Montecillos Chipres, "Editorial: ¿A Qué Viene el Papa a México?" El Camino a la Vida (May-August 1990): 2-3.

[47]Ibid.

[48]The giving habits of Latin American Pentecostals are remarkable. Although they tend to be poorer, they give more to the work than their wealthier non-pentecostal brothers and sisters. Many pentecostals give more than a tithe of their income.

executive committee of the Comité Nacional Evangélico de Defensa.[49] The Iglesia de Dios participated relatively little in other interdenominational ventures. This is perhaps due to the early divisions with the Assembly of God and Church of God movements. Overall, Pentecostal groups in Mexico have had a long tradition of divisions, rivalries, and lack of cooperation.

The Iglesia de Dios has ministered primarily among the poorer classes both in the urban centers as well as in the rural areas. That has on the one hand enabled their church to be very sensitive to the needs of the poor,[50] yet frequently they have proposed simple, spiritual solutions and do not recognize the complex and interrelated structural causes of poverty.

The Iglesia de Dios has certain organizational structures which facilitate stability and conservative, traditional practices. Given the large proportion of rural churches, the Mexican "cacique" model dominates the entire denomination. There is a strong episcopal chain of command, with several older men[51] who make most major decisions. They assign superintendents to direct the work in each district. These in turn, assign pastors to the local churches. Each church must accept the pastor that is designated for them. The pastor has great authority over his congregation, even in matters of dress and food.[52] Pastors and members are severely disciplined if they overstep certain boundaries. Youth are rewarded for Bible memorization, but not for creative application of those same scriptures. Further uniformity is guaranteed as all of the churches must use the same Sunday School materials, hymnal, and version of the Bible. Frequent denominational conferences and ministerial meetings enhance that uniformity.

The Iglesia de Dios is heavily influenced by dispensationalist doctrine.[53] Especially in the area of eschatology, a dispensationalist pre-millennial theology

---

[49]Over the years the Church of God has continued to participate in this organization at different levels. Noé González Rangel, "Magna Concentración Evangélica," El Camino a la Vida (May-June 1986): 5-7, describes the participation of the Iglesia de Dios in the annual march to the Juárez Hemiciclo on March 21, 1986. This march has always been organized by the Comité Nacional Evangélico de Defensa.

[50]Biblical passages that deal with the sharing of material possessions, such as James 2, have been taught and practiced in depth; eg. Gregorio Muñoz, "Hacedores de la Palabra," El Camino a la Vida (July-August 1981): 26-28, had as his purpose the "raising of consciousness and helping believers live as Christians, in order to express their faith by satisfying human needs".

[51]Most of these men are in their sixties or seventies.

[52]One pastor, from the pulpit, rebuked a young woman for wearing earrings to the worship service. She meekly removed them and has not worn earrings to a church service again. Abraham Franco, conversation with author, 15 April 1988, Mexico City.

[53]Most Pentecostal churches in Mexico have dispensational theology, which is quite ironic. Bastions of Anglo American dispensationalism such as Dallas Theological Seminary, Talbot Seminary, and the Scofield Bible are quite adverse to the Pentecostal movement.

dominates.[54] According to this view, the church will be taken out of the world at the time of the rapture, before the world is to be judged. As a logical consequence, dispensationalists tend to withdraw from the world. They tend to see their mission in terms of a "lifeboat" mentality, in which they are to rescue individuals instead of reforming a corrupt, degenerating society. Biblical passages that refer to social justice are interpreted as applying to a different dispensation, usually in the future, millennial kingdom.[55]

A corollary of dispensational theology is the extensive use of typologies. If much of the Bible is for previous or for future dispensations, one way to make these passages relevant for our present age is to interpret certain Old Testament persons as "types" of Jesus Christ. Thus, we can find Jesus "spiritually" prefigured in the Hebrew Scriptures. Pastor José Luis Montecillos, the current director of the denominational magazine, wrote an extensive volume to "discover the Lord Jesus Christ and his work in every book of the Old Testament."[56] The practical consequences of this typology hermeneutic are far-reaching. The social and political implications of the exodus, for example, are spiritualized away and only prefigure the work of Jesus.[57] That kind of interpretation lends itself to an "apolitical" stance in society.

The Iglesia de Dios has a strong belief in divine healing and God's supernatural intervention in human affairs. Most non-pentecostal churches would admit God can heal directly, but that divine healing normally comes "natural" channels (eg. medicines and doctors). There is a strong tendency within the Iglesia de Dios (and many other Pentecostals) to reject the use of medicines and doctors, and rely only on God's supernatural healing. That same kind of reasoning

---

[54]Rafael Vázquez Olmedo, "¿Qué Nos Depara el Futuro?" El Camino a la Vida (November-December 1970): 11-13; Manuel Bustos H., "Las Cosas que han de Suceder Después de Estas," El Camino a la Vida (November-December 1982): 4-5; "La Iglesia: En el Exodo hacia las Estrellas," El Camino a la Vida (September-December 1990): 101-4.

[55]A typical example of this is found in Gregorio Muñoz, "El Reino Mesiánico que Viene," El Camino a la Vida (May-June 1971): 34-36. The strong peace-making message of Isaiah 2 is applied to a future reign after Christ returns. The author wants his "students to understand that the only solution to bring about peace in the world corresponds to the Lord Jesus Christ when he literally reigns upon the earth." Given that dispensationalist interpretation, it is logical for members of the Iglesia de Dios to shun participation in political affairs.

[56]José Luis Montecillos Chiprés, Cristo en el Antiguo Testamento (Mexico City: n.p., 1988), 7. These lessons originally were published for use in all the Sunday Schools of the denomination. They were later grouped together in this extensive volume.

[57]It is ironic that although most dispensationalists are strict literalists in their view of Biblical inspiration, they are at the same time among the least literalistic in their interpretation and application of those same scriptures, due to their extensive use of typology.

is frequently applied to social and political problems as well.[58]

On the theological spectrum, the Iglesia de Dios is placed on the extreme conservative end. Billy Graham, who is usually considered quite conservative by most analysts, is classified as "modernist and liberal" by many Church of God pastors. Of course, Liberation Theology is rejected for many reasons.[59]

One of the most cherished doctrines among the older generation is "separation from the world." There is a strong tendency among leaders of the Church of God to demand a clear separation from "worldly habits." When that line of demarcation was not sufficiently sharp, certain denominational leaders issued a strong warning: "in these last years the line that used to separate the people of the world from the Christian people has almost completely disappeared."[60]

Another strong conviction within the denomination is a belief in a strict separation of church and state. Very little Biblical data is cited to support their view.[61] An historical argument is used. According to this view, the Roman Catholic Church deviated from the truth when it became allied with the Roman Empire under Constantine.[62] Since then, the Catholic Church has always pursued power. In Mexico, this Catholic thirst for political power can be seen in their struggles against Don Benito Juárez and in the War of the Cristeros. By way of contrast, "the Evangelical Church never covets power, because its gaze is fixed upon Christ and upon the salvation of humanity."[63]

Although there is a strong belief in the separation of church and state, nevertheless, the official position of the Church of God is total obedience to the government. Commenting on the classical passage of church-state relations, Romans 13:1-7, the official denominational commentary reads

> . . . because the civil government is an institution of God, every Christian should conscientiously and in good faith respect it and obey it in every one of its laws.[64]

---

[58]"Prayer and patience" are frequently heard exhortations.

[59]"La Iglesia: En los Vencedores del Siglo XX," El Camino a la Vida (September-December 1990): 94-100.

[60]Genaro Ruesga, "La Letra y el Espíritu," El Camino a la Vida (March-May 1980): 33-34.

[61]Baptists, who share the same view of separation of church and state, usually try to defend their position with a Scriptural basis.

[62]A brief presentation of this argument is given by José Luis Montecillos Chipres, "Editorial: La Persecución de la Iglesia Católica a la Evangélica," El Camino a la Vida (January-April 1989): 2-3.

[63]Ibid., 2.

[64]"La Iglesia como Agencia Pacificadora," El Camino a la Vida (August-September 1980): 13.

Any hint of a prophetic stance vis-à-vis the government was rejected because "on many occasions we do not like certain laws nor authorities, nevertheless, it is the divine will that we submit ourselves to them without murmurings."[65] It is probable that the minority status of the Church of God and its weak relations with other Protestant groups, combined with government restrictions on church participation to produce a very passive posture within the Mexican political arena.[66]

The Church of God is very conservative in its traditions. Recently, the presiding bishop, Julio Tejeda Bello, wrote an "epistle" to all the churches of the movement warning them against adopting "modernistic" habits.[67] One of these was the adoption of the 1960 version of the Bible instead of the official Casidoro de Reina version of 1909.[68] Although the examples of translation changes cited by the bishop were not of great transcendence and were based on solid linguistic foundations, there was no reason given to reject the new version except that the Constitution of the Church of God only permitted the 1909 version. A similar argument was used to rebuke those churches and pastors who were not using the official hymnbook.[69]

The bishop used selected Biblical passages to defend the practice of women wearing veils to cover their heads in the worship services as well as to argue against the use of charismatic "dancing in the Spirit."[70] But his main criticism of these practices was that "all of this is modernism."[71]

This legalistic view of the Christian life has permeated the denomination for

---

[65]"El Cristiano y la Democracia," El Camino a la Vida (August-September 1980): 16.

[66]A strong questioning of the government by the church could be based on Revelation 13. But, the dispensationalist interpretation of the Iglesia de Dios places this passage in the future, after the rapture of the church.

[67]Julio Tejeda Bello, "Una Epístola del Siglo XX: El Hno. Obispo Julio Tejeda a la Iglesia de Dios en la Rep. Mexicana," El Camino a la Vida (September-December 1990): 2-3.

[68]Ibid. Bishop Tejeda criticized two changes that appeared in the 1960 version (Luke 2:22 and I Thessalonians 4:4). The first involved a slight change (from "ella" to "ellos") based upon more numerous and more ancient manuscripts, following the accepted canons of textual criticism. The second involved a change in translation of the word "vaso" to "esposa" to make it more understandable in its context.

[69]Ibid., 2. Article XVIII, paragraph 3, stipulated that only the "Himnario de Adoración" be used.

[70]This was a veiled reference to a very recent phenomenon among some rapidly growing charismatic groups in Mexico, such as Amistad Cristiana. The Church of God has lost quite a few of its members to these newer groups. The bishop affirmed that these practices were "modernistic" and came from the United States.

[71]Ibid., 3.

many years. The exhortations against alcoholic beverages, smoking, dancing, movies, and extramarital sex were common in the Church of God and typical of most Mexican Protestants. But in the mid 1970's there was a vitriolic attack against pastors who wore bell bottom pants or short sleeve shirts.[72] Long hair on men was also condemned as was the use of fingernail polish, pants, and earrings by women.[73]

These epistles from the bishop reflect the conservative and traditional nature of the Church of God. Since social and political involvement would be construed as elements of the "modernistic" Social Gospel, it was almost inconceivable that the Church of God officially would have become involved in the 1968 student movement, or any other social protest movement in Mexico.

There are signs that the "apolitical" stance of the Iglesia de Dios is changing. Over the last four years the editor of the denominational magazine has made many political pronouncements. Although he has been decidedly "pro-PRI," he has also criticized certain policies of Salinas. Much of the future social and political involvement of the IDRM depends upon whether this younger generation of leaders is given continued and greater access to positions of authority in the denomination.

---

[72]Isaías Pérez Hernández, "Responsabilidad Ministerial," El Camino a la Vida (March-April 1976): 8 (emphasis mine). The original in Spanish does state "camisas de manga corta." The custom among the pastors of the Church of God is to use coats and ties (and long sleeve shirts!) even in the hot, tropical zones.

[73]Isaías Pérez Hernández, "¿Por Qué No Llega un Avivamiento (Hab. 3:2)?" El Camino a la Vida (March-April 1976): 16. Strangely enough, immediately after criticizing the outward appearance of some Christian youth, the author identifies "criticism" as one of the reasons why revival does not come to the church. "To criticize brothers and sisters [in the faith] is not good, it shows a lack of Christian conscience. But in spite of knowing this, how many Christians go to church just to criticize, either their brothers and sisters or their pastor. These persons lack fraternal spirit, and are nothing more than weeds in the midst of the wheat of the Lord. Criticisms impede that souls be saved, and that the rest grow, because those who have interest in spiritual things feel oppressed by the critical stares of others."

CHAPTER 6

CONCLUSIONS

This dissertation has traced the historical development of three major Evangelical denominations in Mexico City, especially regarding their social and political involvement in Mexican life. Some answers have emerged for the questions raised at the beginning of this study.

(1a) As the PRI shifted from a liberal to a conservative political stance, did Protestants also shift to a more conservative political posture, or did they maintain their liberal persuasion? By and large, the Protestant community in Mexico City has moved towards a more conservative political position over the last seventy years. Protestants were consolidating the gains they had achieved during the Revolution and were also trying to expand their constituency. Placing a high value on numerical growth and religious freedom, Protestants benefited from the relative stability Mexico has enjoyed under the PRI administrations. Therefore, Mexican Protestants have given support (vocal or silent) to the ruling PRI administrations in exchange for the freedom to carry out their religious activities. That tendency towards a more conservative stance has been somewhat modified in the more recent past, especially within the historical denominations. The Student Movement of 1968, the Marxist influence in the universities in the years following, and the political developments of 1988 have produced a more questioning spirit among many Mexican Protestants.

(1b) Has the Protestant alliance with the PRI been weakened in the last quarter of a century, and if so, why? The strength of the PRI-Evangelical alliance is currently at its lowest level since the 1930's. Much of this can be attributed to the growing persecution of Evangelical Christians by Catholics, especially in the rural areas. President Salinas' warm relations with the Catholic Church hierarchy have further annoyed the Protestant community. Many Protestant leaders link these two events. They assert that some rural Catholic priests, trusting in the growing rapport between Salinas and the Catholic hierarchy, have stirred up mobs against the Protestants. The surveys of the 1988 presidential election revealed a substantial rejection of the PRI by Mexico City Protestants.[1] That rejection has probably been somewhat offset by certain achievements of the Salinas administration in non-religious areas (eg. Free Trade Agreement, reduction in

---

[1]The amount of rejection varies from denomination to denomination. The election survey revealed that roughly 60% of Protestants who voted, chose a candidate other than the PRI's Salinas. Church of God members remained more loyal to the PRI than did most other Protestants, as 64.3% of their people voted for Salinas.

inflation, etc.).[2]

(1c) How have the anti-clerical laws of the 1917 Constitution, although originally directed against the Catholic Church, affected Evangelical participation in society? The restrictive laws of the Constitution have greatly contributed to Mexican Protestant "apoliticism." The fact that pastors cannot vote and foreign missionaries must work secretively in Mexico, together with additional restrictions placed upon churches (Article 130), has almost completely silenced the political voice of the Church. The loss of the Evangelical schools (Article 3) and other humanitarian institutions (eg. orphanages) has sharply reduced the Protestant presence in Mexican society, and consequently, their awareness of certain social problems.[3] Mexican Evangelical leaders have grown accustomed to these restrictions, and some have even suggested that the Mexican Constitution possesses a certain amount of "inspiration." By and large, Mexican Protestants have come to believe that it is the government, and not the Church, that has primary responsibility for the educational, medical, and social needs of Mexicans.

There are many indications that conversion to the Protestant faith has produced upward social mobility among adherents in Mexico City.[4] (2a) Has this upward social mobility of Mexican Protestants been a factor in shaping their socio-

---

[2]Saúl Cruz, interview by author, 17 July 1991, Mexico City, believes that the hard working Salinas has recovered much respect from the Mexican people even though the 1988 elections were fraudulent. The mid-term elections of August 18, 1991 tend to confirm his opinion. The PRI received 45% of the vote in Mexico City, up from 27% in 1988. Although opposition parties again denounced the elections as fraudulent, President Salinas has gained the support of more of the populace. It is probable that some of these gains have taken place among Evangelicals.

[3]Other Latin American countries where Evangelical political influence is high, such as Peru and Guatemala, also have strong Evangelical educational institutions and hospitals. The latter has been an important factor in the development of the former.

[4]The difficulty in obtaining hard evidence to susbstantiate this affirmation is recognized. Cf. J. Merle Davis, The Economic Basis of the Evangelical Church in Mexico (London: International Missionary Council, 1940). Much of the evidence is non-quantifiable, such as personal testimonies, and impressions and observations of the author. It is also recognized that this upward social mobility might be due to other factors (eg. migration to Mexico City has been associated with upward mobility for many campesinos, due to greater opportunities for employment, cheaper products and services, etc.). Nevertheless, it is an accepted maxim among Mexican Evangelicals that most conversions lead to a higher economic status. The argument used is simple and persuasive. Money previously spent on alcohol and cigarettes is now spent on education, more nutritious food and "wholesome" recreation. The Protestant "work ethic" is emphasized, and consequently, Evangelicals tend to work more and to get well-paying jobs. The belief in a higher standard of living for Protestants (a prosperity Gospel) is communicated in evangelistic messages and reinforced by personal testimonies. Many second, third, and fourth generation Protestants send their children to expensive private schools. Many drive late-model cars. Church buildings and members' homes tend to be among the better constructions of the neighborhood. Although the purchasing power of Mexicans has declined since 1982, it appears that Evangelicals have maintained a relative economic advantage and mobility over their non-Protestant neighbors.

political action? The historical churches have prospered economically. Presbyterians and Baptists are generally considered middle class denominations.[5] As their members gained more personal affluence, their desire for social change declined. The newer Pentecostal denominations have worked more with the poor and disenfranchised. Yet, even their converts experienced much upward social mobility at an individual and family level. The surveys revealed that the wealthier Protestants voted for Clouthier and Salinas, whereas those who voted for Cárdenas came from the lower economic strata (see Table 1).[6] This was quite similar to the voting of the general populace. If the upward mobility tendency is accurate, then those most desirous of change would be the recent converts, especially from among the poorer classes. Generally, once Protestants have reached a middle class status, they prefer that the government structures retain a large degree of stability, so that they can continue their upward movement.[7]

Table 1
Evangelical Voter Preference According to Income

Income	Cárdenas	Clouthier	Salinas
0-500,000 pesos p/month	55.3%	13.2%	31.5%
500,000-1,500,000	40.9%	18.2%	40.9%

[5]Although both denominations have congregations in poorer neighborhoods, the expectation is that their members will rise up the socio-economic ladder rather quickly. The seminaries and home offices of both denominations are located in rather wealthy neighborhoods. Seminary courses are designed with middle class churches in mind.

[6]These conclusions are based on the totals shown in Table 1. The same conclusions can be drawn from the economic data within each denomination (eg. lower income Baptists voted for Cárdenas in greater proportions than Baptists with higher incomes). An apparent contradiction surfaces when comparisons are made between different denominations. For example, Presbyterians voted for Cárdenas in higher proportions than did members of the Church of God. This occurred in spite of the fact that Presbyterians, in general, have higher incomes than their Pentecostal counterparts. This demonstrates that income is not the only factor involved in voter preference. In this particular case the fact that denominational leaders from the Church of God publicly took a pro-PRI position was surely influential in persuading their membership to vote for Salinas in great numbers. A more detailed analysis of the factors involved in the voter preferences of Church of God members is found in chapter 5.

[7]One additional factor needs to be recognized. Since 1982, with the drop in oil prices, the Mexican economy has experienced a long recession. Purchasing power has declined about 60% since then. Those who had reached the middle class by the early 1980's became increasingly dissatisfied with the government as their economic buying power continued to decline. That explains, in part, the middle class rejection of the PRI in the 1988 elections. With the negotiations of the Free Trade Agreement, the reduction in inflation to 15% annually, a 5% improvement in the purchasing power of workers, and the re-privatization of certain government owned industries, Salinas has recovered some support among the middle class, as shown by the 1991 mid-term elections.

1,500,000-3,000,000	36.2%	23.4%	40.4%
3,000,000-6,000,000	30.0%	15.0%	55.0%
6,000,000-10,000,000	8.3%	58.4%	33.3%
More than 10,000,000	0.0%	71.4%	28.6%

(2b) Has the reduction in social organizations (such as Evangelical schools) caused Mexican Evangelicalism to be more "isolationist"? Evidence suggests an affirmative answer. Whereas Protestants are very involved and quite demanding at a personal and family level (eg. repentance from personal "vices"),[8] they have separated themselves from Mexican society in more visible spheres. Protestant Churches have almost no voice in mass media (whether it be newspapers, magazines, radio, or television). Churches, as institutions, have little influence in education, politics, or the economy. Although Protestants individually have made substantial contributions to Mexican society, Evangelical Churches have not organized themselves for social causes. One decisive factor was the closing of their schools, hospitals, and orphanages in the 1920's and 1930's. It was as if Evangelicals lost their ability to organize themselves for anything other than purely religious purposes. Their main forays into public spheres since then have been for the defense of religious freedom and for university ministry.

The third area of investigation has treated the relationship between theology and socio-political action. (3a) Have Mexican Evangelicals, with their conservative theology, been defenders of the status quo? (3b) If not, have they taken "prophetic" stands on any major issues in the recent past? Over the last three decades Mexican Evangelicals, in general, have been staunch defenders of the "status quo." In fact, they have not challenged the federal government "prophetically" on any major issue.[9] On occasions, Protestants have criticized local government authorities for not providing sufficient protection for their religious freedoms. In these cases they have had to appeal to state governors or federal officials in order to obtain the desired protection.

Mexican Protestants place much value on the authority of the Bible in their lives. (3c) Has their theological understanding of Scripture, therefore, guided their

---

[8]The importance of this personal and family level should not be minimized. Many cultural stereotypes, (eg. the marital infidelity associated with machismo or the supposed inferiority of women) are sharply challenged. Over an extended period of time significant cultural changes have taken place. The suggestion made by Stoll, Is Latin America Turning Protestant?, that changes at this micro level lead to substantial changes at the political level has some merit.

[9]There have been several issues where a prophetic voice would have been appropriate. The Tlatelolco massacre in 1968 was an event that could have provoked much criticism, although few organizations of any kind provided such. Numerous strikes, fraudulent elections and frequent mismanagement of public funds were appropriate occasions for a prophetic voice. Political corruption, pollution, pornography, school textbooks, and abortion are issues that have received much public comment by Protestants in other countries, but not in Mexico.

political and social involvement, or, conversely, has their socio-economic setting greatly conditioned their reading of the Bible? Although Mexican Evangelicals use the Bible extensively for some areas such as family life, social and political issues receive little theological reflection. Few sermons, Sunday School classes, or articles in denominational magazines discuss socio-political themes. Given their lack of social and political activity, it does not appear that all of Scripture has been the Evangelicals' authority for all of "faith and practice." This "blindness" to certain Biblical injunctions cannot be explained only by their growing economic affluence, for the poorer Pentecostals have been just as "apolitical." The limitations placed upon churches in the 1917 Constitution apparently have influenced Protestants' reading of the Bible and consequently, their understanding of the Church's mission, essentially eliminating a prophetic voice in the public arenas.[10]

Finally, (3d) what theologies have Mexican Protestants developed to articulate their understanding of Christian participation in the social and political spheres? The isolationist heritage of fundamentalism has been a critical factor. Biblical passages dealing with social issues are seldom treated. Romans 13:1-7 has been the most frequently cited, with usually a passive, almost blind, obedience interpretation given. Within this fundamentalism, dispensational theology has played a significant role. A typological interpretation of much of the Old Testament, combined with a sharp distinction between Israel and the Church, has led many Mexican Protestants to dismiss the Old Testament as irrelevant for Christian social ethics. Their understanding of the New Testament has caused them to maintain a pessimistic view of society in this dispensation.[11] They have taught that God will bring about a pre-tribulation rapture of the Church from this evil world.[12] Given this perspective, the mission of the Church is similar to that of a lifeboat used to save a few individuals before the ship (=society) sinks. Consequently, Christians should not be overly concerned about the decadent

---

[10]The legal restrictions seem to an important factor. Time and time again, when asked why the Protestant Church had not spoken out on certain issues, the interviewees responded that the Mexican Constitution prohibited them from doing so (and that they must obey the government). Protestants in Peru and Colombia have essentially the same conservative, evangelical theology as their Mexican counterparts. They are also similar in their relative size compared with their national population. Yet the Peruvian and Colombian Protestants have been more active in political spheres, as shown by the recent elections in these countries. The legislation in Peru and Colombia gives greater political freedom to churches than is permitted in Mexico. See Mecham, Church and State, 115-38, 160-78, 340-415, for a comparative study of church-state relationships and legislation in these countries.

[11]I Tim. 4:1; II Tim. 3:1-4; Mat. 24:12.

[12]I Thes. 4:13-18;

nature of society.[13]

Landmarkism has had great influence among Mexican Baptists. Although it is not necessarily "apolitical" in its understanding of the Church's role in society, its extreme localism and congregationalism have contributed to the Baptist apolitical stance at the national level.

Mexican Evangelicals' understanding of the gospel and social action reveals much dichotomization. Church life and politics are apparently unrelated. Certain passages in the Bible receive emphasis at the expense of others. A theological critique is offered at the end of this chapter.

It appears, however, that winds of change are blowing in Mexico. Recent trends suggest that Evangelicals may be becoming more wholistic in their understanding of the gospel. What factors are contributing to those changes?

Recent Trends

In each of the three denominations studied there is a great deal of polarization, which will make it difficult for these churches to participate socially or politically with one united voice. Within the Presbyterian church some of the more debated topics are the ordination of women[14], the use of higher criticism in Biblical Studies, the relation of church and state, and the pentecostalization of Presbyterianism.[15] Baptists are debating "open" versus "closed" communion, the role of women in church, evangelism versus social concern, and the charismatic movement. The Church of God, given its episcopal structure, has less diversity in its ranks. Even so, they are experiencing growing tensions which are expressed as differences between various generations and between their rural and urban churches. The role of higher education, medicine and modern technology in the Christian life is also being debated.

---

[13]Some have even taught that Christians should rejoice as society goes from bad to worse. The increasing decadence of society means that the Second Coming of the Lord is that much nearer.

[14]Bernabé V. Bautista Reyes, La Ordenación de las Mujeres (Mexico City: Ediciones Manantial, 1988) has written against the ordination of women. Several articles in the magazine El Faro of 1987 advocated greater participation by women in the ministry of the church. The editor at that time, Eliseo Pérez, has now been replaced and is no longer in Mexico. It seems doubtful that women will become ordained, except in the more progressive presbyteries such as the Juan Calvino presbytery in Mexico City. Given the fact that women are not currently allowed even to become deaconesses indicates that their ordination as pastors is not likely in the near future.

[15]Jean Pierre Bastian claims that this pentecostalization of Presbyterian churches is common in the southern part of Mexico. An example of a church with Presbyterian roots that has been transformed into a charismatic congregation is described by Daniel Swanson, "Iglesia Renovación Cristiana," México Hoy y Mañana: Documento No. 2 "Estudio de Casos del Crecimiento de la Iglesia Evangélica en la Gran Ciudad de México" (Mexico City: Visión Evangelizadora Latinoamericana and Programa Latinoamericano de Estudios Socio-Religiosos, 1989), 109-13.

In addition, the barriers that exist between Protestant denominations in Mexico have been described as the "highest in all of Latin America." Intense rivalries also exist between interdenominational agencies vying for the same funds and influence. Even among agencies that are ideologically similar, cooperation has been difficult.[16] Although these polarizations do not bode well for a unified social and political participation, there are definite signs that Mexican Protestants will have a greater visible participation in Mexican society in this decade and in the twenty-first century. It is probable that Protestants will establish numerous civil associations to express their growing social and political concerns.[17]

For most of this century, the majority of Protestant leaders in Mexico have advocated an "apolitical" stance. Although they have claimed certain scriptural support for such a position, it may be Mexican legislation, their minority status, and their own theological traditions that have played a larger role in conditioning them to accept such a posture.

A spiritual, "apolitical" position, however, is not really neutral. Especially in a society with strong authoritarian and centralized structures, an apolitical position enables those in power (political, economic, or social) to maintain their dominance. For example, the longevity of the PRI in power has been described by Mario Vargas Llosa as the "perfect dictatorship."[18] The PRI has used the "apolitical silence" of the Christian Church (both Catholic and Protestant) as moral support for its policies and actions. Therefore, the "apolitical" posture of the Protestant Church has, in effect, been a "pro-PRI" position. The impact of that position has not been lost on the PRI leadership. Frequently the PRI administrations have complimented Protestant Churches for minding their own "spiritual" business and leaving "political" and "social" issues in the hands of the experts.

That "apolitical silence," however, is slowly giving way to a more vocal expression of varying political persuasions. Widely accepted Protestant leaders have demonstrated a growing social conscience. Many, while remaining

---

[16]For example, the Comité Nacional Evangélico de Defensa and CONEMEX had a sharp disagreement in 1990 and have decided to go their separate ways. Strong "cacique" personalities have contributed to this lack of cooperation. Their dominant control over their own organization has not prepared them well for working harmoniously with leaders from other Evangelical organizations.

[17]More than one hundred Protestant civil associations are already active in Mexico City, with a growing number dedicated to social ministries. A partial listing and description can be found in México Hoy y Mañana: Documento No. 3 "Manual de Recursos: Estudio de las Agencias de Servicio que Apoyan a las Iglesias Evangélicas en la Gran Ciudad de México" (Mexico City: Visión Evangelizadora Latinoamericana, Programa Latinoamericano de Estudios Socio-Religiosos, and Liga del Sembrador, 1990).

[18]Mario Vargas Llosa, "Mexico: The Perfect Dictatorship," New Perspectives Quarterly (Winter 1991): 23.

theologically conservative or moderate,[19] have become socially active and at times politically out-spoken. Several key factors have contributed to this growing socio-political dimension of conservative Evangelical faith.

Curriculum changes in theological training account for some of this activism. For example, Saúl Tijerina, former moderator of the National Presbyterian Church and former director of the National Presbyterian Seminary (1974-1981) introduced several sociology courses into the seminary curriculum.[20] Similar changes took place in other seminaries as well. New generations of pastors, with more training in the social sciences, are now taking over greater leadership in their respective denominations.

Another factor has been the growing social and political concern on the part of conservative Evangelicals on the international scene. At the time of the 1968 student movement there was little political activity by conservative Evangelicals anywhere in the world. That has changed dramatically. In the United States, the 1973 Roe vs. Wade decision regarding abortion was the crucial event that brought Evangelicals back into the political arena. The election of Jimmy Carter to the presidency in 1976 was another major turning point as conservative Protestants became aware of their political clout.[21] Evangelical mobilization played an even greater role in the Reagan and Bush victories.[22]

In Latin America, Protestants entered the political arena with greater force in the 1980s. The Ríos Montt regime in neighboring Guatemala was both highly visible and deeply controversial. Noteworthy political contributions were also made

---

[19]In contrast with the left-wing "minoría de una minoría" who have been rejected by the mainstream of Mexican evangelicals, their theological conservatism has permitted these Protestant leaders to maintain a large degree of acceptance by their Protestant constituency.

[20]Eg. certain sociology of religion courses and a course entitled "The Church and the University". These curriculum changes were both a consequence and a cause of socio-political activism. The courses introduced by Tijerina were motivated, in part, by his studies at McCormick Theological Seminary in Chicago in the early 1970's. Students who took these courses in the Mexican Presbyterian Seminary later imparted this growing social awareness to the churches they pastored.

[21]Carter's autobiography Why Not the Best? was translated into Spanish and widely disseminated among Mexican Baptist Churches. Jimmy Carter, Por Qué No lo Mejor? (Mexico City: Editorial Mundo Hispano, 1977).

[22]The personal faith of a politician was not necessarily the main attraction for the Evangelical vote. Carter's personal faith was clearly within the Evangelical camp, whereas Reagan rarely attended church services and practiced several "sins" usually condemned by Evangelicals (eg. serving alcoholic beverages in the White House). The abortion issue was emphasized by the Republican party and by many Evangelical leaders as the main issue or litmus test for the Evangelical vote.

by Evangelicals in Peru, Venezuela,[23] and Brazil.[24] Evangelicals have demonstrated a surprising and greater influence in Latin American politics during the 1990's. For example, the election of Protestant representatives and senators has occurred in many countries. The recently elected President and Vice-President of Guatemala are both Protestants. This political clout has been viewed very favorably by most Mexican Evangelicals. Many hear of these "Evangelical victories" through the networking ministries of CONELA, a conservative agency that represents Protestants in Latin America much like the National Association of Evangelicals (NAE) does in the United States.[25]

Theological developments in Latin America have also contributed to this growing awareness of social and political responsibilities. Dieumeme Noelliste has identified Liberation Theology and the Latin American Theological Fraternity as the two major currents in theological activity. He affirms that

> . . . the emergence of Liberation Theology and the Theological Fraternity on the Latin American scene in the early 1970's fundamentally changed the basis of the church's age-old attitude of social indifference.[26]

The more widely publicized Liberation Theology has had a limited effect upon Mexican Protestantism. Due to its "Marxist" political tendencies and its predominantly Roman Catholic expression, few Evangelicals in Mexico have appropriated Liberation Theology on a large scale. Nevertheless, their wholistic model, which makes explicit the connection between theology and socio-political action, has had an indirect influence upon Mexican Protestants.

The Latin American Theological Fraternity has been somewhat more acceptable to the Evangelical community in Mexico. Given the fact that it is Protestant and less politically radical than Liberation Theology, it is more akin to the Evangelical mindset in Mexico. Even so, it has been regarded suspiciously by

---

[23]Godofredo Marín, La Democracia Basada en la Biblia 2d ed. (Caracas: Imprenta Universitaria de la UCV, 1988).

[24]For examples in various Latin American countries, as well as theological articulations of political involvement, from a Theological Fraternity perspective see Pablo Alberto Deiros, ed., Los Evangélicos y el Poder Político en América Latina (Grand Rapids and Buenos Aires: Nueva Creación, 1986).

[25]CONELA's affiliate in Mexico is CONEMEX. Most Protestant denominations in Mexico are members. Strangely, the Baptists and the Presbyterians are not affiliated, although several of their pastors are members on a personal basis.

[26]Dieumeme Noelliste, "The Church and Human Emancipation: A Critical Comparison of Liberation Theology and the Latin American Theological Fraternity" (Ph.D. dissertation, Garrett-Evangelical Theological Seminary and Northwestern University, 1987), xvii.

some.[27]

Another significant factor in this process has been the growing involvement of the Mexican Catholic Church in "political" affairs. After a long "peaceful co-existence" and "understanding" with the PRI (dating back to around 1940), the Catholic Church has made bolder forays into the political arena in the last few years. The Catholic hierarchy has utilized the Pope's visits to push more energetically for important changes in the Constitution. Recently, it has assumed somewhat of a "conscience of society" position regarding the electoral process.[28] The Catholic Church and the government are also working together on various projects, a cooperation seldom seen in the last fifty years.[29] Denis Goulet concludes

> One thing is certain: the Catholic Church in post-Revolutionary Mexico has lost its persecution complex, its timidity and its passivity in the face of temporal problems. It has entered the public arena, and its voice will be heard ever more loudly.[30]

Growing persecution of Protestants,[31] which has occurred simultaneously with this growing socio-political involvement of the Catholic Church, has caused Protestants great concern. Their anxiety has forced them into exploring anew their own social and political stance. Their self-defense has perhaps been the most influential factor in mobilizing Evangelicals in the political arena.[32] Evangelicals with differing ideological persuasions are now presenting a more united front to

---

[27]There are many causes for this "suspicion." The Fraternity is an interdenominational organization which challenges the "closed communion" mentality of some. Another reason is that Fraternity members have read Liberation Theology and incorporated parts of it into their own. And thirdly, FTL members have criticized different aspects of North American Evangelicalism and have questioned some North American "sacred cows." For example, its Declaration of Jarabacoa, published in 1986, called into question the priority of the "right" of private property over other human rights. Some Protestants in Mexico who read the Declaration immediately rejected it, falsely accusing it of being "communist." See Deiros, Poder Político, 343-61, for the complete text of the Declaration of Jarabacoa.

[28]The 1986 mayoral election in Chihuahua was the first major challenge by the Catholic Church of the PRI's "fraudulent" tactics. It threatened to close its churches (reminiscent of 1926) in protest. The Church played an even larger role in the 1988 elections.

[29]Richard Bautch, "The Great Experiment," America (8 April 1989): 316-17, and Denis Goulet, "The Mexican Church: Into the Public Arena," America (8 April 1989): 318-22.

[30]Ibid., 322.

[31]Chris Woehr, "Mexico: Catholic, Protestant Tensions Rise," Christianity Today (19 March 1990): 44.

[32]Much of this persecution has taken place in the southern states of Chiapas and Oaxaca where the Presbyterians are strong. Many of the victims have been Presbyterians.

defend their persecuted Protestant brothers and sisters.[33]

The social ministries of certain Evangelical organizations are making it more acceptable for other Protestants to become involved in social and political action. Visión Mundial de México, Amextra, and the Salvation Army have very strong social emphases, yet have the general acceptance of the Evangelical community. Both the Fraternidad Teológica Latinoamericana (FTL) and the Confraternidad Evangélica de México (CONEMEX) have affirmed the Lausanne Covenant (with its social agenda) as an appropriate expression of wholistic ministry.[34] The Assembly of God movement has provided active leadership in ministry to the multitude of street children[35] and prisoners in Mexico.[36] Protestant lay organizations are starting several private schools. Undoubtedly, this will bring them into conflict with the government, especially in the areas of curriculum (eg. sex education, evolution versus creationism, etc.).

Younger Protestant leaders, who are now entering into positions of greater influence in their denominations and in society are more critical of the government. The "anti-PRI" attitude of this generation was revealed in the election survey realized for this dissertation (see Table 2). The age group that most abandoned

---

[33]A good example is the growing cooperation between the more conservative director of Milamex, Juan Isáis, and the more progressive campus pastor and journalist Carlos Martínez.

[34]The key statement on wholistic ministry in the Lausanne Covenant is found in article 5: ". . .we express penitence both for our neglect and for having sometimes regarded evangelism and social concern as mutually exclusive....we affirm that evangelism and socio-political involvement are both part of our Christian duty....The message of salvation implies also a message of judgment upon every form of alienation, oppression and discrimination, and we should not be afraid to denounce evil and injustice wherever they exist." The complete Lausanne Covenant can be found in C. René Padilla, ed. The New Face of Evangelicalism: An International Symposium on the Lausanne Covenant (Downers Grove, Illinois: InterVarsity Press, 1976). Padilla and other FTL leaders have been influential advocates of the Lausanne Covenant in the English-speaking world as well; cf. Valdir Steuernagel, "The Theology of Mission in its Relation to Social Responsibility within the Lausanne Movement" (Th.D. Lutheran School of Theology, 1988) and Noelliste, "The Church and Human Emancipation."

[35]Many Assembly of God churches have formed civic associations to offer a wide array of social ministries to their local communities. Pastor Benjamín Rivera has spearheaded a ministry to the estimated one million "street children" of Mexico City. See his paper "Caminando al Ritmo de los Niños" presented at the Segunda Consulta de Reflexión Bíblica: Ser Humano, Varón y Mujer, November 1-3 1990, Mexico City.

[36]Pastor David González directs a prison ministry, Confraternidad Carcelaria de México. Since this ministry is affiliated with Chuck Colson's prison ministry in the United States, a certain amount of political activism regarding prison reform can be expected.

the PRI in the last election was the age bracket between 40 and 49.[37] This group is precisely the generation of 1968 which still resents the authoritarianism of the government.[38] As this generation comes into the upper echelons of denominational leadership (in combination with the energetic "rebeldía" of the youth), it is probable that a more vocal, prophetic stance will be taken by most of the Evangelical denominations.

Table 2
Evangelical Voter Preference According to Age[39]

	Cárdenas	Clouthier	Salinas
29 and under	40.0%	20.0%	40.0%
30-39	33.3%	22.2%	44.5%
40-49	48.4%	22.6%	29.0%
50 and over	34.0%	18.8%	47.2%

Even among older leaders, a more vocal attitude can be seen. Juan Isáis, a theological conservative and the Mexican director of Misión Lationamericana, has encouraged several social ministries in many denominations[40] and has adopted a more critical stance vis-à-vis the government.[41]

In the sphere of formal politics, Mexican Protestants seem to be increasing their participation cautiously. The surveys showed that only 3% of Mexico City

---

[37]Only 29% of this group voted for the PRI. The next group was the youngest sector (ages 21 to 29) who voted 38% in favor of the PRI. Those who are 30 to 39 and those 50 or older voted for the PRI at 43% and 44% respectively.

[38]In 1968 those in this age bracket were between 17 and 26 years old.

[39]This refers to the age of those surveyed at the time of the survey, May-June 1991.

[40]Juan Isáis, considered "very conservative" by some of his more progressive Presbyterian brothers and sisters, has become quite involved in social issues. His Misión Latinoamericana participated heavily in earthquake relief over the long haul, helping in the construction of about 50 homes for earthquake victims. He has frequently invited John Perkins, a black, evangelical, social justice advocate to speak at his large youth congresses. Isáis claims that a very large number of Mexican evangelical youth have developed creative "wholistic ministries." Architect Esteban Montejo, interview by author, 28 June 1991, Mexico City; Pastor Juan Isáis, conversation with author at the Fraternidad Teológica Mexicana meeting, 27 June 1991, Mexico City.

[41]Isáis was directing an all-night prayer meeting near the town of Ajusco on the outskirts of Mexico City on February 2, 1990 when his group was attacked by Catholics stirred up by the local priest. Many were injured and had to be taken to hospitals in seven ambulances. This persecution has led Isáis to a more confrontational posture towards the government and the Catholic Church. For both sides of the story, see Carlos Monsiváis, "La Resurección de Canoa," Proceso 694 (19 February 1990): 26-27; cf. "Persecución en el Ajusco," Gracia 69 (March 1990): 9.

Evangelicals participated in the 1988 election campaign. A slightly larger number, 8%, are members of a political party. But 86% of the Evangelicals in Mexico City believe that those elections were not "clean," and 17% of those actively protested against what they perceived as fraud.

This growing political and social activity of the Protestants should not be exaggerated. The legal restrictions, the social indifference of their theological heritage, and their minority status will probably not change overnight. Nor does it mean that Evangelicals in Mexico will necessarily be leaving the PRI in record numbers. A large number of influential Evangelicals, such as Jonás Flores[42] and César Moreno, defend the PRI as the most viable Evangelical option. There are signs, however, that the traditional alliance is breaking down. President Salinas de Gortari's growing warmth towards the Roman Catholic Church, together with an increase in verbal attacks and physical persecution by Catholics against Protestants,[43] has led many Evangelicals to reconsider that alliance with the PRI. The surveys implemented for this dissertation regarding the 1988 presidential elections tend to confirm that observation (see Appendix B).

Since the election, Salinas has committed several acts which have greatly irritated Evangelicals. In his inauguration on December 1, 1988, several Catholic priests were his invited guests. Taking advantage of this new openness, the Conference of Mexican Bishops sent a public letter to President Salinas on June 5, 1989, urging modifications in Articles 3, 5, 24, 27, and 130 of the Constitution.[44] In February 1990, Salinas appointed Agustín Téllez Cruces as his personal ambassador to the Pope. During the Pope's visit to Mexico in May 1990, he received an unusually cordial welcome from President Salinas and many PRI

---

[42]Lawyer Jonás Flores has been the most vocal exponent of the PRI among Evangelicals. He has served as a representative in the Congress under the PRI banner. He frequently speaks to evangelical groups to provide them an "objective" understanding of their civic duties. But he has used these occasions to promote the PRI's cause. This false "neutrality" (in addition to the fact that he belongs to a Unitarian group) has led many Evangelicals to reject his participation; Arturo Torres, interview with author, 1 May 1991, Guadalajara.

[43]Many Protestant periodicals frequently carry reports of persecution; see Oralia Castillo, "Persecución en Oaxaca: 'Estamos Dispuestos a Morir,'" Gracia 69 (March 1990): 8-11. CONEMEX sponsored a "Consulta sobre Persecución en México" in 1990 to establish priorities of self-defense against attacks. President Salinas has not encouraged this persecution. It has primarily occurred in rural areas, urged on by the local priests.

[44]Conferencia del Episcopado Mexicano to Señor Licenciado Carlos Salinas de Gortari, Open letter, 5 June 1989, Servicios Informativos Procesados, A.C., Mexico City. The refusal to submit to these same articles provoked the War of the Cristeros in 1926 (see discussion in chapter 1).

public officials.[45] The Catholic hierarchy in Mexico has returned the favor offering much support for Salinas' policies, including the Free Trade Agreement with Canada and the United States. On July 9, 1991 Salinas visited the Vatican and spoke with Pope John Paul II. There was great expectation that upon his return to Mexico, the President would urge many reforms in the Constitution.[46]

Church-State relationships[47] are one of the hottest topics among Evangelicals. In addition to the events sponsored by the three denominations studied,[48] there is a growing plethora of Protestant comment on the topic. At the fortieth annual Evangelical March in Mexico City on March 21, 1990, fifteen thousand Protestants[49] gathered at the Juárez Hemiciclo monument in the Parque Alameda. They heard the speaker Vicente Montes de Oca Hernández defend the separation of church and state, and the various articles of the Constitution.[50] Arturo Córdova, Executive Secretary of the Comité Nacional

---

[45]Homero Campa, "Funcionarios Federales, Clero, Gobernadores, Alcaldes, Empresarios y PRI, Juntos en la gran Tarea de Recibir al Papa," Proceso (April 1990): 20-25, describes with ample facts and figures the preparations made to receive the Pope. Most newspapers and several magazines in Mexico City carried articles sharply criticizing the government for not enforcing the Constitution during the Pope's visit; see "La Próxima, una Semana en que las Leyes se Harán, Publicamente, a un Lado," Proceso (April, 1990): 20. Ironically, 443 priests wrote an open letter to the Pope on March 19, 1990, warning him that his visit to Mexico was being manipulated by the PRI and government. They advised him that "on July 6, 1988, our people clearly manifested, on the one hand, their rejection of the regime of the party in power, which is the cause of social decay, and on the other hand, their clamor in favor of a true democratization on all levels of social life." The events of the following weeks showed that their warning was not heeded. For the contents of their letter, see "La Visita del Papa Podría Ser Manipulada: Sacerdotes," La Jornada (Mexico City), 16 April 1990, 7-8. Most of the left of center political parties also criticized the visit. See Partido Popular Socialista, Dirección Nacional del Comité Central, "La Visita del Papa es Política, no Pastoral," La Jornada (Mexico City), 4 May 1990, 16.

[46]"Será Alentadora para los Católicos la Visita de CSG al Vaticano," La Jornada (Mexico City), 6 Julio 1991, 5.

[47]Evangelicals are quick to point out that the topic is not "Iglesia-Estado" as if the Catholic Church were the only religious group, but rather "Iglesias-Estado" to include all Protestant churches and non-Christian religious groups as well.

[48]See the discussion in chapters 3, 4, and 5.

[49]Evangelical observers estimated that there were 40,000 participants.

[50]Vicente Montes de Oca Hernández, "La Colección de Nuestro Derecho Constitucional," Discourse pronounced at the XL Marcha Juarista de la Iglesia Cristiana Evangélica in Mexico City on 21 March 1990 (Mexico City: Comité Nacional Evangélico de Defensa, 1990). For a description of the protest march, see "Marcha Juarista de Evangélicos," Gracia 70 (May 1990): 15. Many pro-government banners were raised, affirming "Mr. President, the Evangelical people pray for you" and "we want the separation of church and state to continue." A similar march in Villahermosa, Tabasco attracted 20,000 Evangelical protesters, the

Evangélico de Defensa, urging Evangelicals to become politically active, affirmed, "I hope that there are no changes in the Constitution, but we cannot count on that; now is when we should participate."[51] The magazine Gracia also dedicated its May 1990 issue to Church-State relations, concentrating on possible modifications of the Mexican Constitution. Interviews with Evangelical leaders revealed a wide array of opinions, varying from proposals for no modifications at all to changes in Article 130 and legal recognition of all churches.[52] In an attempt to achieve greater understanding and unity among Evangelicals, the Mexico City chapter of the Fraternidad Teológica Latinoamericana is dedicating several months to study this topic and to offer concrete proposals in the political arena. Alberto Rosales, a theologically conservative pastor and teacher has recently written a history of Mexican Church-State relations with special emphasis on Protestants.[53] Specifically, Rosales examines certain problems in the current relations between the churches and the government and recommends substantial changes in the Constitution.[54]

The government is aware of this political re-awakening among Protestants, and is trying not to alienate its old ally. Baptist Cabinet member María de los Angeles Moreno Uriegas arranged for the much-publicized meeting between President Salinas and Methodist, Presbyterian, and Baptist leaders on March 6, 1990.[55] Salinas promised them that there would be no changes in the Constitution. He also praised them for being serious denominations and not causing any problems for the country.

In June of 1991 CONEMEX, the conservative association of churches, was chosen by the government to be the official voice of Protestantism with whom it would dialogue. CONEMEX is beginning to take the pulse of its constituency in order to express Evangelical concerns to the government.

Doctrinal and religious reasoning will definitely be included in the debate. Biblical passages dealing with the relationship between believers and government

---

largest march in that city in the last fifteen years.

[51] Arturo Córdova, "Entrevista con Arturo Córdova," Gracia 70 (May 1990): 14-17. Córdova blames the foreign missionaries for having taught that Christians should not get involved in politics. He urges Christian laity, not pastors, to get involved in the political battles facing Mexican Protestantism.

[52] "¿Qué Dicen los Líderes Evangélicos?" Gracia 70 (May 1990):12-13.

[53] Alberto Rosales P., Estado e Iglesia en México: Legislación Religiosa (Mexico City: n.p., 1990). Since there are few extensive books on this subject from an Evangelical perspective, Rosales' volume is getting a wide hearing by Mexican Protestants.

[54] Ibid., 339-67. Alberto Rosales Pérez, conversation with author, 5 July 1991, Mexico City.

[55] "Evangélicos ante el Presidente Salinas de Gortari," Gracia 70 (May 1990): 17;

authorities will receive much attention in the upcoming discussions.[56] Although a "blind obedience" interpretation of Romans 13 has dominated most Protestant churches in the last fifty years,[57] a more discriminating "limited obedience" position is gaining momentum, together with a more "prophetic" challenge to the authorities.[58]

Theological Critique

Mexican Protestants affirm a "high"[59] view of scriptural authority for their faith and practice. Nevertheless, this high view of the Bible is not readily seen in their social and political involvement in society. A superficial (and from the author's perspective, a mistaken) interpretation of certain passages has been used to justify an "isolationist" and "apolitical" attitude towards Mexican society. A more detailed study of these sections, together with the majority of pertinent passages in the Bible, actually leads to a greater interaction with the surrounding society.

One of the more frequently quoted "political" sayings by Jesus is "my reign

---

56 [56]Carlos Escorcia, "Las Asambleas de Dios en Nicaragua," Amanecer: Reflexión Cristiana en la Nueva Nicaragua 38-39 (December 1985): 22-25, affirms that there was a significant shift in church-state theologizing in Nicaragua after the Sandinista victory. "In our country [Nicaragua], before the revolutionary triumph emphasis was given to the text of Romans 13, in which Christians are commanded to obey the duly constituted authorities. After July 19, 1979, this passage suddenly disappeared from the evangelical vocabulary and was substituted by others such as the expression of Peter in the Book of Acts, that says: 'It is necessary to obey God rather than men,' or the saying of Christ in the Gospels: 'You cannot serve two masters.'" Although the current situation in Mexico is quite different from the early Sandinista period in Nicaragua, this development in a nearby Latin American country shows that Evangelicals can shift their theological articulation of a given political stance in a relatively short period of time. This happened in Mexico in the later Porfiriato. See Baldwin, Mexican Revolution: Missionaries, Ministers and Social Change, and Jean Pierre Bastian, "Itinerario de un Intelectual Popular Protestante, Liberal y Francmasón en México: José Rumbia Guzmán, 1865-1913," Cristianismo y Sociedad 92 (1987): 91-108. If the PRI no longer serves the interests of Protestants, it is probable that Evangelicals will develop a more confrontational political theology.

[57]An example of this would be the open letter of the Comité Nacional Evangélico de Defensa to C. Lic. Carlos Salinas de Gortari, Novedades (Mexico City), 22 May 1989, 2, in which Romans 13:7 is quoted to defend the position of obedience to the laws. But even in this document, a docile, totally passive position is no longer maintained. An exhortation is given to the government to retain the Constitution as it is, and to defend the Evangelicals from the attacks of their persecutors.

[58]See C. René Padilla, "El Estado Desde una Perspectiva Bíblica," in Los Evangélicos y el Poder Político en América Latina, ed. Pablo Alberto Deiros (Grand Rapids and Buenos Aires: Nueva Creación, 1986), 23-39.

[59]This "high" view implies that the Bible is the primary authority in their lives, much higher than tradition, contemporary mores, reason, etc.

is not of this world."[60] It is usually inferred that Jesus did not have anything to do with the political affairs of this world, and that his followers should not either. Yet, the immediate context has Jesus directing this phrase towards Pilate, an official representative of the Roman Emperor. In the following verse, Jesus affirms that he, in fact, is a king, and for this very reason he was born and came into the world. His reign is not "worldly" in the sense that neither he nor his followers accept the (sub) moral standards of this world (eg. his followers do not use military weapons to defend him). Yet, his reign is "worldly" in the sense that it is located and extended here on earth. This can be seen by the immediately preceding passage of John 17. Jesus was not "of" the world, but he was "in" the world. His followers were likewise not "of" the world, but were sent "into" the world. By parallel, Jesus' reign is not "of" the world, but is located "in" the world. Since the value system of Jesus' reign differs greatly from that of this world, it frequently interacts with society in a confronting, "prophetic" manner.[61] Christians, to the degree that they are faithful to Christ's reign, can contribute to the conscience of society.

Another commonly quoted passage is Romans 13:1-7: "Let every person be in subjection to the governing authorities." The usual interpretation is that followers of Jesus should obey[62] their earthly government in everything.[63] Yet the verb "upotassesthai" does not imply blind obedience. Verses 3 and 4 delineate certain elements (ie. promotion of the general good and punishment of evil) of the government's "job description" as a minister (diakonos) of God. Christians are subsequently directed to use these criteria to evaluate earthly governments. The apostle Paul, for example, had spent much time in Roman prisons and, therefore, knew that frequently it was necessary to disobey human authorities in order to obey higher orders.

C. E. B. Cranfield makes a strong argument for a different translation of "upotassesthai."[64] Because the same word is used in Ephesians 5:21 to refer to

---

[60]John 18:36.

[61]Cf. C. K. Barrett, The Gospel According to St John: An Introduction with Commentary and Notes on the Greek Text, 2d ed. (London: SPCK, 1978), 536-37, and Rudolf Schnackenburg, The Gospel According to St John, vol. 3 (New York: Crossroad, 1982), 248-50. Schnackenburg essentially agrees that Jesus' reign "has an unworldly nature but it is not shut off from the world; rather it manifests itself just there in the world wherever his voice is heard." However, he does minimize the political relevance of Jesus' Kingdom for human society.

[62]"Obedience" is the way Sanday and Headlam translate "upotassesthai" as does C. K. Barrett.

[63]Some exceptions are allowed, citing "we must obey God rather than men (Acts 4:19-20; 5:29)" but in general total obedience is stressed.

[64]C. E. B. Cranfield, A Commentary on Romans 12-13 (Edinburgh: Oliver and Boyd, 1965), 69-72.

a reciprocal obligation among Christians, it cannot mean simply "obey." Cranfield (borrowing from Calvin) sees it as the respect due to others because they are Christ's representatives to us. In the context of Romans 13, the prescribed action "will not be uncritical, not a blind obedience to the authority's every command; for the arbiter of what constitutes "upotassesthai" in a particular situation is not the civil power but Christ."[65] Both interpretations lead to the same conclusion: Christians are to have a "prophetic" ministry towards the government, urging it to truly be God's minister. Especially in twentieth century "democracies," greater (not lesser) ethical responsibility is placed upon the citizenry of a nation, including the Christians. Ethicist Stephen Mott states it clearly:

> Romans 13:1-7 and I Peter 2:13-17 do, in fact, imply a limit to government. The authority of God, under which government functions, provides the basis for judging specific acts of governments. Further, <u>those purposes of government raised in the argument can serve as a yardstick for evaluating laws and the conduct of governments</u>. . . . If the ruler is sent by God, one might acknowledge the ruler's wrong-doing without viewing the injustice as one for the subjects to correct. But these passages go further, authorizing obedience on the grounds of the critical discernment of what is duty and what serves the Lord. From the fact that conscience is to be a motivating force in obeying government <u>a basis may be inferred for disobeying government when its actions are not in conformity with the voice of informed conscience</u>.[66]

Numerous additional passages could be cited to show a strong Biblical basis for a prophetic stance vis-à-vis the government. The "exodus" stands out as a powerful example of God's values being in sharp contrast with the policies of the Pharaoh. Joseph, Rahab, Esther, Nathan, Daniel, John the Baptist, Stephen, Peter, John and Paul all challenged their earthly governments on different occasions. Revelation, the last book in the Christian canon, includes a powerful chapter (13) in which God's reign does battle against the governments of this world.[67]

Dispensationalism, as an hermeneutical methodology, has a wide following among Mexican Pentecostals, and to a lesser degree, non-Pentecostals. In its classical expression, dispensationalism, with a pre-tribulation rapture of the Church

---

[65]Ibid., 71.

[66]Stephen Charles Mott, <u>Biblical Ethics and Social Change</u> (New York: Oxford University Press, 1982), 150 (emphasis mine).

[67]It is recognized that there are many diverse interpretations of Revelation 13:1-10, especially regarding the time of fulfillment. But most do coincide in affirming that God's reign does confront an evil, human government, which is the main application advocated here.

and a pre-millennial second coming of Christ, has usually resulted in an "apolitical" stance. Nevertheless, prominent dispensationalists in the United States have shown that their theology and political activism are not incompatible.[68] Modern defenders of dispensationalism, such as Charles Ryrie,[69] have modified the classical expression of their theology, eliminating some of the more extreme positions.[70] Many hope that as dispensationalists wrestle with the present (as well as the future) dimension of the "Kingdom of God" motif in Scripture, not only will they become more socially and politically active, but that their activity will become more discerning.

It is perhaps the "Kingdom of God" motif, however, that provides the clearest guidelines for Mexican Evangelicals in the realms of social and political action. Although it was Liberation Theology that began to show the importance of "God's Reign" for Latin American society, it is more likely that the thought of the Latin American Theological Fraternity[71] will have a greater influence upon Mexican Protestantism.

C. René Padilla, emphasizing both the present and future dimensions of

---

[68]The most widely-read "fundamentalist futurologist," Hal Lindsey, has used a classical dispensationalism for his interpretation of prophecy. See his The 1980's: Countdown to Armageddon (King of Prussia, Pa.: Westgate Press, 1980) for a combination of dispensationalism and political "right-wing" activism. He urges, p. 175, that "we need to get active electing officials who will not only reflect the Bible's morality in government but will shape domestic and foreign policies to protect our country and our way of life. We need to elect men and women who will have the courage to make the tough decisions needed to insure our nation's survival. They must be willing to clamp down on big government, cut exploitation of the welfare system, keep our strong commitments to our allies and stand up to communist expansion. We need people who see how important a strong military is to keeping peace for us and what remains of the free world."

[69]Charles Ryrie, Dispensationalism Today (Chicago: Moody Press, 1965).

[70]Some dispensational theologians do admit greater continuity between the Old Testament (Hebrew Bible) and the New. Whereas earlier dispensationalists made sharp distinctions between Israel and the Church, modern proponents admit some overlap (I Peter 2:9-10). As that false dichotomy begins to fade, the social and political realities of the Biblical Israelites will shed light on Christian involvement in society today. Another hopeful area of dialogue deals with the relationship between eschatology and social ethics. Modern dispensationalists increasingly admit that most (if not all) eschatological sections of Scripture do have some practical implications for ethics today. As their "pessimistic" view of history gives way to a more balanced understanding of human nature and society, greater participation in society can be expected.

[71]The FTL spans many spectrums. For example, at their twentieth anniversary conference in Quito, Ecuador (December 1990), liberationist José Míguez Bonino and pacifist John Howard Yoder were the keynote speakers. Both have made important contributions to the field of "social Christian ethics." See José Míguez Bonino, Toward a Christian Political Ethics (Philadelphia: Fortress Press, 1983) and John Howard Yoder, The Priestly Kingdom: Social Ethics as Gospel (Notre Dame: University of Notre Dame Press, 1984).

God's reign, affirmed that

> . . . social action motivated by Christian love is simply the normal expression of new life in Christ. As a response to the action of God in Christ Jesus and as a sign of the Kingdom that is already in the midst of people, it is to be expected from Christians.[72]

Pablo Pérez, Mexican Presbyterian pastor and one of the founding members of the Theological Fraternity, expressed the social and political demands upon the Christian in this way:

> The task of the Church of Christ in our continent is clearly outlined; the Lord wants his followers to participate with Him in the proclamation of his liberating message in our lands in order to make disciples liberated by the supreme Liberator. He wants new men and women and with them a new humanity of transformed structures.[73]

Rolando Gutiérrez, current president of both the Mexican Baptist Convention and of the Latin American Theological Fraternity, also affirms this wholistic understanding of the "Gospel of the Kingdom":

> The work of the Church requires consciousness of its position in the Kingdom. To regenerate relations and to reconstitute the society with the dimensions of the teachings of the Sermon on the Mount, continue to be urgencies that cannot be left for "mañana."[74]

As the "Kingdom of God" motif takes hold upon Mexican Evangelical thinking and practice, a corresponding increase in social and political action will also occur. An increased use of the social sciences, more numerous political options, possible changes in the Mexican Constitution, and greater involvement in social ministries, together with theological development along the lines of the Latin American Theological Fraternity will probably result in a more diversified and a more questioning socio-political posture among Mexico City Evangelicals in the years to come.

---

[72] Padilla, El Evangelio Hoy, 92-93.

[73] Pablo Pérez Morales, Misión y Liberación: La Liberación como Móvil en América Latina (Mexico City: El Faro, 1976), 109.

[74] Rolando Gutiérrez Cortés, Creencias Bautistas (Mexico City: Horeb, 1985), 122.

APPENDIX A

EVENTS ATTENDED BY THE AUTHOR

November 8-10 1988	National Ministerial Meetings of the Iglesia de Dios en la República Mexicana, Ixtepec, Oaxaca.
February 14-16 1989	Urban Ministry Conference, sponsored by Visión Mundial de México, Mexico City.
February 21 1989	Pastor's Training Conference, Campo Mazahua, Estado de México.
March 2-4 1989	Retreat of the Asociación Bautista Central, Valsequillo, Puebla.
March 17 1989	VELA Meeting on Protestant Church History, Mexico City.
April 23 1989	Sunday services of the Iglesia Evangélica, San Luis Potosí, SLP.
May 4-6 1989	Primera Consulta de Reflexión Bíblica: La Participación de la Mujer en la Iglesia y en la Sociedad, sponsored by several evangelical organizations, Mexico City.
June 3 1989	Meeting of the Asociación de Profesores de Instituciones de Educación Teológica (APIET), México City.
June 10 1989	Graduation service of the Instituto Evangelístico de México, Mexico City.
July 12-15 1989	Meetings of the Fraternidad Teológica Bautista Mexicana, Mexico City.
August 27 1989	Ordination Exam of Gamaliel Novelo, Bible Society staff and Pastor of the Iglesia Evangélica Libre "El Renuevo", Mexico City.
September 9 1989	Youth Rally of the Convención Bautista del Estado de Morelos, Jojutla de Juárez, Morelos.

October 14 1989	Anniversary Celebration of Compañerismo Estudiantil, Mexico City.
November 2 1989	Youth Rally of the Fraternidad de Iglesias de Dios, Mexico City.
November 4 1989	Ordination Service for Lázaro Mercado, Baptist Pastor, Iglesia Monte Moriáh, Mexico City.
November 10 1989	Chapel service of Visión Mundial de México, Mexico City.
November 26 1989	Meeting of the Esfuerzo Cristiano of the "Berith" Presbbyterian Church, Mexico City.
December 3 1989	Meeting of the Esfuerzo Cristiano of the "Berith" Presbbyterian Church, Mexico City.
March 5 1990	Meeting of COMIMEX, Mexico City.
March 25 1990	Sunday evening service of the "Filadelfia" Presbyterian Church, Cuernavaca, Morelos.
April 2 1990	Meeting of COMIMEX, Mexico City.
April 26 1990	Quadrennial meeting of CONELA, Acapulco, Guerrero.
April 27-May 1 1990	Retreat of the Esfuerzo Cristiano of the "Puerta de Salvación" Presbyterian Church, Kikotén, Morelos.
May 4-5 1990	Presbyterian Consultation on Church-State Relations, Mexico City.
June 8-9 1990	Graduation Exercises of the Instituto Evangelístico de México, Mexico City.
June 25-27 1990	Theological Lectures at the Instituto Bíblico Bautista, Veracruz, VC.
June 30 1990	Graduation service of the Seminario de la Iglesia de Dios en la República Mexicana, Mexico City.

July 11 1990	Youth Rally of the Fraternidad de Iglesias de Dios en la Republica Mexicana, Mexico City.
August 28 1990	Chapel service of Visión Mundial de México, Mexico City.
August 30 1990	Evening service at the La Calzada Church, Mexico City.
September 11 1990	Meeting of the AMPIET, Mexico City.
October 20 1990	Retreat of Pastors of the Iglesia de Dios - Séptimo Día, Chula Vista, Morelos.
November 1-3 1990	Segunda Consulta de Reflexión Bíblica: El Ser Humano: Varón y Mujer, sponsored by several evangelical organizations, Mexico City.
November 3 1990	Presbyterian Conference on Evangelism, Satélite, Mexico.
November 24 1990	Evangelistic Breakfast, Iglesia Evangélica Libre "Bethel", Mexico City.
November 30 1990	Fraternidad Teológica Mexicana, Mexico City.
December 2-12 1990	20th anniversary of the Fraternidad Teológica Latinoamericana, Quito, Ecuador.
January 15-17 1991	Annual meeting of CONEMEX, Ixtapan de la Sal, México.
January 20 1991	Iglesia Pentecostés Independiente "Maranatha", Mexico City.
January 25 1991	Fraternidad Teológica Mexicana, Mexico City.
April 27 1991	Anniversary celebration of the Unión Bíblica, Mexico City.
June 9 1991	10th anniversary of the Esfuerzo Cristiano of the Antioquía Presbyterian Church, Mexico City.

June 23 1991	Graduation service of the Instituto Evangelístico de México, Mexico City.
June 26-27 1991	Workshop "Avance Urbano" '91 sponsored by Visión Mundial de México, Metepec, Puebla.
July 2-5 1991	Primer Simposio Bíblico-Teológico of the National Presbyterian Church with the general theme "La Autoridad de la Biblia Hoy," Mexico City.
July 16-18 1991	Recursos de Evangelismo y Discipulado - Seminar on Pastoral Counseling.

In addition, I had the opportunity to be a guest speaker or professor at the following institutions: Instituto Evangelístico de México, Seminario Teológico Presbiteriano de México, Seminario Metodista, Comunidad Teológica, Centro de Estudios Superiores de Integración Cristiana, Instituto Bíblico de Reflexión Pastoral, Seminario de la Iglesia de Dios en la República Mexicana, Seminario de la Fraternidad de Iglesias de Dios, Seminario de la Iglesia Apostólica, and the Seminario de la Iglesia de Dios-Séptimo Día.

APPENDIX B

ELECTION SURVEY

The presidential election of 1988 was the closest and most disputed of this century. In Mexico City, the "official" results gave Cárdenas 48% of the vote, Salinas 27%, and Clouthier 22%. With the capital city population divided in three substantial blocks, the presidential election was a very appropriate event to be studied.

There have been no published surveys regarding the voter preference of Protestants in the election of 1988. Given the confidential nature of voting in Mexico, it was necessary to survey a large number of Protestant congregations in order to obtain a reliable sampling of voter preference and other data. Students and faculty of the Seminario Teológico Presbiteriano de México, the Instituto Evangelístico de México, the Instituto Bíblico de Reflexión Pastoral (Baptist), the Seminario de la Iglesia de Dios en la República Mexicana, and the Centro de Estudios Superiores de Integración Cristiana aided the author by surveying the churches that they attended. In order to obtain the greatest similarity of conditions possible, adults were surveyed during their Sunday School classes. In general, these adults would be among the most acuve members of the Evangelical Churches (and thus show the greatest Protestant influence, if any). The surveys were realized during the months of May and June 1991. 492 surveys were received representing twenty-three churches. The following survey (translated from Spanish into English) was used.

The information solicited in this survey is for a doctoral dissertation regarding the political participation of Christians in Mexico. Thank you for your valuable help. Do not write your name on the survey in order to preserve the anonymous nature of the information.

Local Church__________ Denomination____________

Age____________________ Sex_____________________

Schooling (highest level acquired)
Primary___ Junior High___ High School___ College___

Monthly Family Income
0-500,000 pesos________ 500,000-1,500,000_________
1,500,000-3,000,000_____ 3,000,000-6,000,000_______
6,000,000-10,000,000_____ More than 10,000,000_______

Who did you vote for in the 1988 elections?
Cárdenas___ Clouthier___ Salinas___ Other___ Abstention___

Are you a member of a political party?___ Which one?___

Did you participate in the election campaign?___ If so, how?______________________________
____

Do you believe that the elections were clean?___ If your answer was negative, did you protest in any way?___ How?______________________________
____

The surveys were tabulated and the results[1] are found in Table 3.

Table 3

Evangelical Voter Preference According to Various Criteria

	Cárdenas	Clouthier	Salinas	Abstention[2]
Denomination				
All Protestants	37.8%	21.4%	40.8%	17.3%
Presbyterian	48.3%	14.5%	37.1%	20.5%
Baptist	34.1%	24.8%	41.1%	14.0%
Church of God	28.6%	7.1%	64.3%	17.6%
Gender				
Males	42.4%	20.7%	36.9%	17.9%
Females	33.7%	22.1%	44.2%	16.8%
Age[3]				
29 or younger	40.0%	20.0%	40.0%	24.5%
30-39	33.3%	22.2%	44.5%	19.1%
40-49	48.4%	22.6%	29.0%	13.9%
50 or older	34.0%	18.8%	47.2%	10.2%
Education				
Primary	41.9%	16.2%	41.9%	17.3%
Junior High	35.5%	19.3%	45.2%	13.9%
High School	40.6%	21.6%	37.8%	17.5%
College	36.1%	22.9%	41.0%	19.4%

---

[1]Certain limitations regarding the survey are readily admitted. For example, since older adults tend to participate in Sunday School classes more than younger adults, the survey is somewhat skewed towards older adults. Another factor is that not all Presbyterian, Baptist, and Church of God congregations in Mexico City were surveyed. An effort was made to cover a fair cross section of churches.

[2]The percentages of abstentions are based upon the total number of respondents. The percentages for the three candidates are based upon the number who voted excluding the abstentions.

[3]The age refers to the respondent's age at the time of the survey (May-June 1991).

Family Income				
0-500,000	55.3%	13.2%	31.5%	17.4%
500,000-1,500,000	40.9%	18.2%	40.9%	15.4%
1,500,000-3,000,000	36.2%	23.4%	40.4%	16.1%
3,000,000-6,000,000	30.0%	15.0%	55.0%	25.9%
6,000,000-10,000000	8.3%	58.4%	33.3%	14.3%
10,000,000 or more	0.0%	71.4%	28.6%	0.0%

Political Party Affiliation	
No Affiliation	90.6%
PRI	7.8%
PRD	1.6%

Participation in the Election Campaign	
Participation	3.3%
No Participation	96.7%

Belief that the Elections were Clean	
Clean	17.1%
Not Clean	82.9%
Protested[4]	14.3%

Many results were expected, although there were also some surprises. The income level was a decisive factor in voter preference. Those with lower incomes voted for Cardenas in greater numbers. Those with the highest incomes favored Clouthier. This was probably due to the campaign promises of Cardenas to favor greater redistribution of wealth, and of Clouthier to favor the development of capitalism.

Denomination affiliation played a key role. Members of the Church of God, in spite of coming from the lower economic classes, showed strong preference for Salinas. Different factors contributed to this preference. First of all, the episcopal government of their own denomination closely parallels that of the PRI. Dissent from the established order or deep questioning of authority has not been encouraged nor rewarded. Secondly, some pastors and denominational leaders made it known, through both oral and written comments, that neither the PAN (due to its Catholic tendencies) nor the Cardenistas (due to their leftist leanings) would

---

[4]Percentage of voters that believed elections were not clean.

be appropriate choices for Pentecostals.[5] The PRI was the lesser of the evils. A third factor was the Church of God's relatively low level of formal education. This, in combination with a strong authoritarian style of leadership, hampered members from using other criteria upon which to base their candidate selection.

The higher levels of income and formal education of Baptists and Presbyterians permitted them to take other criteria into account as they cast their ballots. Although income played a major role, some religious factors also contributed. The Baptist Horeb Church and the Presbyterian Puerta de Salvación Church are of similar economic composition. Yet Horeb members voted for both Cárdenas and Clouthier in greater proportions than did their Presbyterian counterparts. Perhaps Horeb's history and reputation of being a "non-traditional" congregation contributed to this tendency. Horeb's pastor also preached more frequently on social themes that did the minister at Puerta de Salvación.

The age of the voters was another important factor. The 40 to 49 age bracket was the group that gave the least support to the PRI (only 29% of those who voted). Whereas in most countries members of this age bracket desire political stability in order to maintain the economic position they have obtained, in Mexico, just the opposite occurred. One explanation is that this is precisely the generation of 1968 that experienced both police brutality during the Student Movement and a much more politicized education in the following years.

The youngest age group showed a common characteristic of high abstention, together with a higher preference for Cardenas than the two remaining age brackets. The fifty and over bracket gave Salinas the highest percentage (47.2%). It was more difficult for this group to break from their long-standing alliance with the PRI, as well as from their traditional opposition to the PAN. Those sixty years and older showed an even greater loyalty to the PRI.(?% voted for Salinas).

The role of gender was surprising. Evangelical women were much more likely to vote for Salinas than their male counterparts (44.2% to 36.9%). Formal education alone seemed to have little direct effect upon voter preference.[6] A slight correlation existed between education and voter preference for the PAN. The more formal schooling Evangelicals received, the greater was their willingness to vote for the Accion Nacional Party.

The "apolitical" nature of Mexican Protestants was very evident. More than 90% do not belong to any political party. Over 96% did not participate in the election campaign. Nevertheless, this political indifference did not mean they accepted the "official" results released by the government. More than 80%

---

[5]Not all Pentecostals were so strongly in favor of Salinas. Many Assembly of God churches, with a quite similar theology, were decidedly pro-Cárdenas.

[6]Although in combination with other factors (eg. the Church of God's authoritarianism), the degree of formal education was a significant factor.

believed that the elections were not clean,[7] and of these, 14.3% protested in some public way.

[7]It was interesting that half of the Protestants who were members of the PRI felt that the elections were fraudulent. Some of them protested against their own political party.

SOURCES CONSULTED

Bibliography

Acción y Fe. Mexico City: La Unión Nacional de Sociedades Femeniles Cristianas, 1933.

Acosta Chávez, Eusebio. Historia de la Primera Iglesia Bautista de Puebla. Puebla: Primera Iglesia Bautista, 1968.

Acosta González, Emiliano. "La Participación Política de los Cristianos y la Relación Iglesia-Estado." Paper presented at the Foro sobre la Visita del Papa y las Relaciones Iglesia-Estado, Mexico City, 23-27 April 1990.

Actas, Convención Nacional Bautista. Mexico City: Convención Nacional Bautista, 1903.

Actas, Convención Nacional Bautista. Mexico City: Convención Nacional Bautista, 1934.

Actas del Tercer Período de Sesiones de la Conferencia Anual Fronteriza de la Iglesia Metodista de México: Celebrada en la Ciudad de Monterrey (Nuevo León) los días 14 al 18 de Septiembre de 1932. Mexico City: 1932.

Actas Diarias e Informes de la Conferencia Anual de México de la Iglesia Metodista Episcopal. Mexico City: Casa Unida de Publicaciones, 1925.

Acto de Graduación y Clausura: Generación 1985-1988. Mexico City: SEMID, 1988.

Adame Brito, Gamaliel. "Llamado Urgente a los Esforzadores Presbiterianos de México." El Faro (July 1970): 19.

Adame Goddard, Jorge. El Pensamiento Político y Social de los Católicos, 1867-1914. Mexico City: UNAM, 1981.

"Against All Odds." Newsweek (7 October 1985): 38-40.

Aguilar García, Eliú. "La Iglesia Urbana: Algunos Problemas y como Superarlos." Licenciatura thesis, Seminario Teológico Presbiteriano de México, 1978.

Aguilar Ochoa, Daniel. "¡Libertad!" El Faro (September 1970): 4-5.

Aguirre Beltrán, Gonzalo. Antología de Moisés Saenz. Mexico City: Ediciones Oasis, 1970.

Ahlstrom, Sydney E. A Religious History of the American People. New Haven and London: Yale University Press, 1972.

Albavera Rodríguez, Salvador. La Constitución Mexicana como Violadora de los Derechos Humanos Religiosos. Necesidad de Adecuarla a la Declaración Universal de Derechos Humanos. Licenciatura thesis, Universidad Autónoma del Estado de Morelos, 1987.

Alberro, Solange. Inquisición y Sociedad en México, 1571-1700. Mexico City: Fondo de Cultura Económica, 1988.

Alcalá, Alfonso. "El Proyecto de un Concordato con la Santa Sede en Dos Misiones Diplomáticas Mexicanas (1835-1845)." Miscelanea Historiae Pontificiae 50 (1983).

Alvarado Bianchi, Alberto. Estudios acerca del Espíritu Santo. Mexico City: El Faro, 1970.

_____. Tratado de Homilética. Mexico City: El Faro, 1989.

Alvarez, Alejandro. La Crisis Global del Capitalismo en México, 1968-1985. Mexico City: Ediciones Era, 1987.

Alvarez, José Rogelio. Enciclopedia de la Iglesia Católica en México. Mexico City: Enciclopedia de México, 1982.

Alvarez Icaza, José. "Cronología del Desarrollo de las Sectas Religiosas en México, 1987-1988." Iglesias 5:58 (October 1988): 8-10.

_____. "Las Comunidades Cristianas de Base, Marginadas por la Iglesia al Dar su Apoyo al Movimiento Estudiantil." Uno Más Uno (Mexico City), 3 October 1988.

_____. "Los Obispos Mexicanos ante las Elecciones." Iglesias 5:55 (July, 1988): 24-25.

Alvear Acevedo, Carlos. La Iglesia en la Historia de México. Mexico City: Jus, 1975.

Alves, Rubem. Protestantism and Repression: A Brazilian Case Study. Translated by John Drury and revised by Jaime Wright. Maryknoll: Orbis Books, 1985.

Anderson, Lorna and Ofelia Ibáñez, eds. Directorio Evangélico de México: 1969-1970. Mexico City: Mexico Missionary Services, 1970.

Annual of the Southern Baptist Convention. 1927.

Annual of the Southern Baptist Convention. 1949.

Annual Report WABHMS. 1946.

Anuario Convención Nacional Bautista 1967-68. Mexico City: Convención Nacional Bautista, 1968.

Anuario Convención Nacional Bautista 1969. Mexico City: Convención Nacional Bautista, 1969.

Anuario Convención Nacional Bautista 1971. Mexico City: Convención Nacional Bautista, 1971.

Arana Quiroz, Pedro. Providencia y Revolución. Lima: Estandarte de la Verdad, 1970.

_____, comp. Teología en el Camino: Documentos Presentados en los Ultimos Veinte Años por diferentes Comunidades Cristianas de América Latina. Lima: Ediciones Presencia, 1987.

Arias, Mortimer. Venga tu Reino (La Memoria Subversiva de Jesús). México: CUPSA, 1980.

Arjona, Susana. "La Escuela Pública de México." El Faro (January 1969): 18-19.

Arteaga Nava, Eliezer. "Proyección de Nuestra Iglesia en la U.N.A.M." Licenciatura thesis, Seminario Teológico Presbiteriano de México, 1964.

Asamblea General de la Iglesia Presbiteriana en México. Actas de la Segunda Reunión Ordinaria, verificada en el Templo Nacional Presbiteriano "El Sinaí" de la Ciudad y Puerto de Veracruz, Ver., los días 12 al 19 de julio de 1950 Y de la Segunda Reunión Extraordinaria verificada en el Templo Nacional Presbiteriano "El Divino Salvador", de la Ciudad de Mérida, Yuc. los días 7 al 11 de febrero de 1951.

_____. Constitución de la Iglesia Nacional Presbiteriana de México. 2d ed. Mexico City: El Faro, 1987.

_____. Disciplina de la Iglesia Nacional Presbiteriana de México. 3d ed. Mexico City: El Faro, 1984.

Asambleas de Dios. Los Fundamentos de la Educación Cristiana: Tesis. Mexico City: Asambleas de Dios, Departamento de Educación Cristiana, 1987.

Athey, Lois E. "Democracy and Populism: Some Recent Studies." Latin American Research Review 19:3 (1984): 172-83.

Avila Arteaga, Mariano. "Historia Social y Política de la Iglesia Evangélica en México en Perspectiva Bíblica." Philadelphia: Fraternidad Teológica Latinoamericana, 1990. Photocopied.

Báez, Guadalupe. "2 de Octubre: La Iglesia y el 68." Iglesias 5:58 (October, 1988): 7.

Báez Camargo, Gonzalo. Biografía de un Templo. Mexico City: Ediciones Luminar, 1953.

_____. Breve Historia del Cánon Bíblico. Mexico City: Luminar, 1980.

_____. "Church, State and Religious Liberty in Latin America." World Dominion 34 (1956): 29-32.

_____. El Comunismo, el Cristianismo y los Cristianos. Mexico City: Casa Unida de Publicaciones, 1960.

_____. "El Futuro del Protestantismo Latinoamericano." Pensamiento Cristiano 96 (December 1978): 101-09.

_____. El Por Qué del Protestantismo en México. Mexico City: CUPSA, 1930.

_____. El Protestantismo en Iberoamérica. Mexico City: CUPSA, 1945.

_____. Genio y Espíritu del Metodismo Wesleyano. 2d ed. Mexico City: Casa Unida de Publicaciones, 1981.

_____. Hacia la Renovación Religiosa de Hispanoamérica. Mexico City: Casa Unida de Publicaciones, 1929.

_____. Is There Religious Persecution in Mexico? New York: n.p., 1926.

_____. La Nota Evangélica en la Poesía Hispanoamericana. Mexico City: Luminar, 1960.

_____. La Verdad y los Errores del Marxismo. Mexico City: Ed. Alba, Casa Unida de Publicaciones, 1934.

_____. "Los Protestantes en la Revolución Mexicana." Estudios Ecuménicos. (November 1971): 14-16.

_____. "Mexico--Quest for Stability." Christianity Today (19 July 1953).

_____. Protestantes Enjuiciados por la Inquisición en Iberoamerica: Documentos Inéditos o muy Raros para la Historia del Protestantismo en Iberoamerica. Mexico City: CUPSA, 1959.

_____. "Protestantism in Latin America: Mexico." Religion in Life 27.1 (1957): 35-44.

_____. "Punish Mob for Attack on Chapel." The Christian Century 70 (2 September 1953).

_____. "Rectificaciones que Son de Justicia." Estudios Ecuménicos. (November 1971): 82-84.

_____. The Evangelical Situation in Mexico. London: World Dominion Press, 1949.

Báez Camargo, Gonzalo, and Kenneth G. Grubb. Religion in the Republic of Mexico. London: World Dominion Press, 1935.

Báez Camargo, Gonzalo, comp. Apuntes sobre los Comienzos del Protestantismo en México. Mexico City: Centro Evangélico Unido, 1954.

_____, comp. Indice General Anotado de Literatura Evangélica. Mexico City: Comité de Literatura Cristiana del Comité de Cooperación en la América Latina, 1958.

Bailey, David C. ¡Viva Cristo Rey! The Cristero Rebellion and the Church-State Conflict in Mexico. Austin: University of Texas Press, 1974.

Baird, Joseph Armstrong, Jr., and Hugo Rudinger. The Churches of Mexico: 1530-

1810. Berkeley: University of California Press, 1962.

Baker, Stephen. "For Salinas, The Real Campaign is Just Beginning." Business Week (5 December 1988): 48.

Balderrama, Luis C. El Clero y el Gobierno de México: Apuntes para la Historia de la Crisis en 1926. Mexico City: Cuauhtémoc, 1927.

Baldwin, Deborah Jo. "Broken Traditions: Mexican Revolutionaries and Protestant Allegiances." The Americas 40 (1983): 229-258.

_____. "Diplomacia Cultural: Escuelas Misionales Protestantes en México." Historia Mexicana 36.2 (1986): 287-322.

_____. Protestants and the Mexican Revolution: Missionaries, Ministers, and Social Change. Urbana: University of Illinois Press, 1990.

_____. "Variation within the Vanguard, Protestants and the Mexican Revolution." Ph.D. dissertation, University of Chicago, 1979.

Baqueiro, Oscar G. "La Iglesia Metodista en México: Entrevista." Estudios Ecuménicos. (November 1971): 17-23.

_____. Metodismo Mexicano: Periodo 1948-1973. Mexico City: Iglesia Metodista de México-Publicaciones del Centenario, 1974.

Barnett, Das Kelley. The Mission of the Anglican Mission to Mexico and Central America. Austin: Research Center in Christian Theology and Culture, 1961.

Barrett, C. K. The Gospel According to St John: An Introduction with Commentary and Notes on the Greek Text. 2d ed. London: SPCK, 1978.

Bastian, Jean Pierre. Breve Historia del Protestantismo en América Latina. Mexico City: Casa Unida de Publicaciones, 1986.

_____. "Estructura Dinámica del Campo Religioso." Taller de Teología 10 (1982): 67-70.

_____. Historia del Protestantismo en América Latina. Mexico City: Casa Unida de Publicaciones, 1990.

_____. "Itinerario de un Intelectual Popular Protestante, Liberal y Francmasón en México: José Rumbia Guzmán, 1865-1913." Cristianismo y Sociedad 92 (1987): 91-108.

_____. "La Heterodoxia Religiosa en la Historiografía Mexicanista (1968-1988)." Cristianismo y Sociedad 101 (1989): 47-58.

_____. "La Penetración de las Sociedades Religiosas Norteamericanas en México, 1872-1876." Taller de Teología 14 (1984): 5-30.

_____. "Las Sociedades Protestantes en México 1872-1911: Un Liberalismo Radical de Oposición al Porfirismo y de Participación en la Revolución Maderista." Ph.D. dissertation, El Colegio de México, 1987.

_____. "Las Sociedades Protestantes y la Oposición a Porfirio Díaz, 1877-1911." Historia Mexicana 37:3 (January-March 1988), 469-512.

_____. "Los Cristos Históricos Protestantes en México." Taller de Teología 6 (1980): 5-15.

_____. Los Disidentes: Sociedades Protestantes y Revolución en México, 1872-1911. Mexico City: Fondo de Cultura Económica and El Colegio de México, 1989.

_____. "Metodismo y Rebelión Política en Tlaxcala, 1874-1920." In Memorias del Primer Simposio Internacional de Investigaciones Socio-Históricas sobre Tlaxcala, 108-18. Tlaxcala: Gobierno del Estado de Tlaxcala, n.d.

_____. "Modelos de Mujer Protestante: Ideología Religiosa y Educación Femenina, 1880-1910." In Presencia y Transparencia: La Mujer en la Historia de México, 163-80. Mexico City: El Colegio de México, 1987.

_____. "Protestantismo y Colonia en América Latina y el Caribe: 1492-1838." Taller de Teología 9 (1981): 15-34.

_____. "Protestantismos Minoritarios y Protestarios en México." Taller de Teología 10 (1982): 5-12.

_____. Protestantismo y Sociedad en México. Mexico City: Casa Unida de Publicaciones, 1983.

Bauer-Lee, Oscar. Diez Estratégias Bíblicas para Establecer Iglesias y Declaración de Fe de las Iglesias Bautistas. Mexico City: La Luz Bautista, 1982.

Bautch, Richard. "The Great Experiment." America (8 April 1989): 316-17.

Bautista G., Josué. Huella Sangrienta en México: Los Héroes y los Mártires del Misionismo Evangélico del Presente Siglo. Mexico City: Editorial Nueva Era, 1970.

Bautista Reyes, Bernabé V. La Ordenación de las Mujeres: (Desde una Perspectiva Bíblica, Histórica y Teológica). Mexico City: Ediciones Manantial, 1988.

Bazant, Juan. Los Bienes de la Iglesia en México. Guanajuato: El Colegio de México, 1971.

Beeson, Trevor, and Jenny Pearce. A Vision of Hope: The Churches and Change in Latin America. Philadelphia: Fortress Press, 1984.

Bellinghausen, Hermann, coord. Pensar el 68. Mexico City: Cal y Arena, 1988.

Beltrán, Charles S. Religious Aspects of the Conquest of Mexico. Durham: Duke University Press, 1930.

Beltrán, Enrique. La Lucha Revolucionaria del Proletariado contra la Iglesia. Mexico City: Editorial L.A.R., 1931.

Beltrán del Río, Pascal, Manuel Robles, and Rodrigo Vera. "La Iglesia no Quiere Menos que las Reformas a la Constitución; El Gobierno, a la Defensiva." Proceso 694 (19 February 1990): 6-9.

Beltrán del Río, Pascal, and others. "Téllez Cruces: Niño Aplicado, Juez Obsecuente, Gobernador de Paso, Católico Vergonzante." Proceso 694 (19 February 1990): 10-13.

Bennett, Carlos. Pantano Ardiente: La Iglesia Presbiteriana en Tabasco, 1881-1960. Guadalajara: Ediciones Transformación, 1989.

Bennett, Charles. Tinder in Tabasco: A Study of Church Growth in Tropical Mexico. Grand Rapids: Eerdmans, 1968.

Bernaldez, Benjamín. "Siempre Jóvenes." El Faro (March-April 1985): 55-57.

Bernecker, Walther L. "Intolerancia Religiosa e Inmigración en México (Siglo XIX)." Cristianismo y Sociedad 99 (1989): 7-23.

Bethel: Una Obra de Fé. 25 Aniversario. Mexico City: Iglesia Bautista Bethel, 1988.

Bierzychudek, Eduardo, coord. Bibliografía Teológica Comentada. Buenos Aires: ISEDET, Vol. 1, 1973; Vol. 2, 1974; Vol. 3, 1975; Vol. 4, 1976; Vol. 5, 1977; Vol. 6, 1978; Vol. 7, 1979.

Bilski, Andrew. "Breaks in a Monopoly." MacLeans (18 July 1988): 33.

_____. "A Tarnished Victory." MacLeans (25 July 1988): 18.

Blancarte, Roberto. "La Iglesia Católica en México desde 1929; Introducción Crítica a la Producción Historiográfica (1968-1988)." Cristianismo y Sociedad 101 (1989): 27-42.

_____. "Protestantismo Nacional." La Jornada (Mexico City), 12 March 1990.

Bolaños Martínez, Victor Hugo. Historia de la Educación de México en el Siglo XX contada por sus Protagonistas. Vol. I. Mexico City: Editorial "Educación, Ciencia y Cultura", 1982.

Boni, Felix G. and Mitchell A. Seligson. "Applying Quantitative Techniques to Quantitative History: Poverty and Federal Expenditures in Mexico." Latin American Research Review 8:2 (1973): 105-10.

Bonilla González, Enoc. "La Iglesia en la Vida Social." Licenciatura thesis, Seminario Teológico Presbiteriano de México, 1970.

Booth, John A., and Mitchell A. Seligson. "The Political Culture of Authoritarianism in Mexico: A Reexamination." Latin American Research Review 19:1 (1984): 106-24.

Boraiko, Allen A. "Earthquake in Mexico." National Geographic (May 1986): 654-75.

Braden, Charles S. Religious Aspects of the Conquest of Mexico. Durham: Duke University Press, 1930.

Brandenburg, Frank. The Making of Modern Mexico. Englewood Cliffs: 1964.

Bridges, Julian C. "A Chance to Study." The Commission (April 1967): 25.

_____. "Baptists Help Saul Get His Education." The Commission (February 1967): 23.

_____. "Congress Affects Young People." The Commission (August 1968): 23.

_____. Expansión Evangélica en México. Miami: Ed. Mundo Hispano, 1973.

_____. "Interview with a Communist." The Commission (January 1967): 5.

_____. "Pablo Calms Rioters." The Commission (July-August 1966): 18.

_____. "Where the Action Is." The Commission (November 1968): 16.

Brown, Hubert. Latino America. New York: Young People Missionary Movement, 1909.

Brown, Lyle C., and William F. Cooper, eds. Religion in Latin American Life and Literature. Waco: Markham Press Fund, 1980.

Buckingham, Jamie. Fuerza para Vivir. Mexico City: Arthur S. Demoss Foundation, 1989.

Buendía, Manuel, and Sánchez de Armas, Miguel Angel. La Ultraderecha en México. Mexico City: Ediciones Oceano, 1984.

Bustos Busio, Omar. "Una Investigación de las Contribuciones de Moisés Arévalo Arias a la Obra Bautista en el Estado de Guerrero." Licenciatura thesis, Seminario Teológico Bautista Mexicano, 1985.

Bustos H., Manuel. "Las Cosas que han de Suceder Después de Estas." El Camino a la Vida (November-December 1982): 4-5.

Bustos T., Amós. "Joven: Cristo Pide tu Cooperación." El Camino a la Vida (September-October 1964): 9-11.

Butler, Clementina. The Founder of Two Missions. New York: Eaton and Mains, 1902.

Butler, John Wesley. History of the Methodist Episcopal Church in Mexico. New York: Methodist Book Concern, 1918.

_____. Mexico: Coming Into Light. Cincinnati: Jennings and Graham, 1907.

_____. "Protestant Christianity in Mexico." The Missionary Review of the World 24 (May 1911).

_____. Sketches of Mexico. New York: Hunt and Eaton, 1894.

Butler, Mrs. John Wesley. Historic Churches in Mexico with Some of their Legends. New York: Abingdon Press, 1915.

Butler, William. Mexico in Transition. New York: Hunt and Eaton, 1892.

Cabrera, C. M. "Los Dos Pactos: Las Dispensaciones." El Faro (June 1968): 19-21.

_____. "Los Dos Pactos: Transición." El Faro (August 1968): 17-19.

Cadenhead, Jr., Ivie. E., "Jesús González Ortega: Anticlericalist." Journal of Church and State (Winter 1970): 107-20.

Callcott, Wilfred Hardy. Church and State in Mexico, 1822-1857. New York: Duke University Press, 1965.

_____. Liberalism in Mexico: 1857-1929. Stanford University Press, 1931.

Camargo López, Jesús. "La Dependencia Económica de América Latina: Un Enfoque Evangélico." Boletín Teológico 37 (1990): 7-30.

Camarillo, María Teresa, coord. Memoria Periodística del Terremoto (19 de Septiembre-10 de Octubre 1985). Mexico City: UNAM, 1987.

Camp, Roderic A. The Making of a Government: Political Leaders in Modern Mexico. Tucson: University of Arizona Press, 1984.

_____. "The Political Technocrat in Mexico and the Survival of the Political System." Latin American Research Review 20:1 (1985): 97-118.

Campa, Homero. "Funcionarios Federales, Clero, Gobernadores, Alcaldes, Empresarios y PRI, Juntos en la gran Tarea de Recibir al Papa," Proceso (April 1990): 20-25.

Candelaria, Nash. Not by the Sword. Ann Arbor: Bilingual Press, 1982.

Canto Chac, Manuel. "Relaciones Iglesia-Estado en México (Aspecto Político)." Paper presented at the Foro sobre la Visita del Papa y las Relaciones Iglesia-Estado, Mexico City, 23-27 April 1990.

Capistrán Garza, René. La Iglesia Católica y la Revolución Mexicana: Prontuario de Ideas Políticas. Mexico City: Atisbos, 1964.

Cárdenas Pallares, José. El Poder de Jesús el Carpintero. Mexico City: Casa Unida de Publicaciones, 1983.

Cardoso, Joaquín. "La Historia del Protestantismo en México." In El Protestantismo en México, ed. José González B. and others. Mexico City: Buena Prensa, 1946.

_____. Las 20 Principales Sectas Protestantes de México: Sus Contradicciones. Mexico City: Sociedad E.V.C., 1957.

_____. ¿Quiénes son los Testigos de Jehová? Mexico City: Sociedad E.V.C., 1956.

Carrasco Malhue, Pedro. El Catolicismo Popular de los Tarascos. Mexico City: Sep-Setentas, 1976.

_____. Protestantismo y Campo Religioso en un Pueblo del Estado de Oaxaca. B.A. thesis, Instituto Internacional de Estudios Superiores, 1983.

_____. "Sacerdote, Profeta y Brujo, la Conformación del Campo Religioso en un Pueblo del Estado de Oaxaca, México." Taller de Teología 10 (1982): 19-39.

Carrero, Eduardo. La Iglesia Presbiteriana en México: Sus Conquistas, Sus Problemas, Su Actitud. Mexico City: CUPSA, 1927.

Carrillo y Ancona, Crescencio. Orden Circular contra la Progaganda Protestante. Mérida: Imprenta de la Revista de Mérida, nd.

Carter, Jimmy. ¿Por Qué No Lo Mejor? Mexico City: Editorial Mundo Hispano, 1977.

Carter, Pat H. "Missionary, Come Home?" The Commission (April 1968): 6-8.

Case, Alden Buell. Thirty Years with the Mexicans: In Peace and Revolution. New York: Revell, 1917.

Casillas R., Rodolfo. "Pluralidad Religiosa en una Sociedad Tradicional, Chiapas." Cristianismo y Sociedad 101 (1989): 73-87.

Cassaretto, Mary A. El Movimiento Protestante en México. M.A. thesis, UNAM, 1956.

Castañeda, Rubén. "La Situación de la Familia en México: Respuesta Cristiana." Taller de Teología 7 (1980): 21-28.

Castillo, Oralia. "Persecución en Oaxaca: 'Estamos Dispuestos a Morir.'" Gracia 69 (March 1990): 8-11.

_____. "¿Qué Pasa con el Artículo 130?" Gracia 70 (May 1990): 10-13.

Castillo de García, Evangelina, and Débora Castillo de Reyes. Libro Conmemorativo de las Bodas de Plata de la Unión de Sociedades Femeniles del Presbiterio del Distrito Federal: 1954-1979. Mexico City: 1979.

Castleman, William J. On this Foundation: A Historical Literary Biography of the Early Life of Samuel Guy Inman covering the Period 1877-1904. St. Louis: Bethany Press, 1966.

Ceballos, José. "C.E.H.I.L.A. y la Historia de la Iglesia en América Latina." Taller de Teología 7 (1980): 53-54.

Ceballos Ramírez, Manuel. "La Encíclica Rerum Novarum y los Trabajadores Católicos en la Ciudad de México, 1891-1913." Historia Mexicana 38:1 (1983): 3-38.

_____. "La Historiografía Mexicanista y la Iglesia Católica (1968-1988)." Cristianismo y Sociedad 101 (1989): 15-26.

Cervantes Mejía, Patricio. "Guerra Santa vs. las Sectas." Ovaciones August 4, 1987.

Cervantes Salas, Enrique. Presbiterianismo en México. Licenciatura thesis, Seminario Teológico Presbiteriano de México, n.d.

Chao, Jorge. "La Motivación Humana." Conservación Ambiental y Desarrollo Rural. San José, Costa Rica: CMI, Comisión Iglesia y Sociedad, 1988.

Chastain, James Garvin. Thirty Years in Mexico. El Paso: Baptist Publishing House, 1927.

Cidoc Informa. Cuernavaca: CIDOC.

Clavijo Vargas, Augusto F. Radio y Evangelización. Licenciatura thesis, Seminario Teológico Bautista Mexicano, 1982.

Clawson, William Marion. "The Influence of the Catholic Church on the Development of the Mexican Government and its Relationship to Protestant Missions." Ph.D. dissertation, New Orleans Baptist Theological Seminary, 1960.

CLADE II: Documentos Finales. Carta al Pueblo Evangélico de América Latina: Proyecciones Estratégicas. Mexico City: Fraternidad Teológica Latinoamericana, n.d.

Coffin de Ruiz, Maggie. "El Mensaje Mundial del Pbro. Eleazar Z. Pérez." Curriculum Vitae (November 1961): 22.

Coffin Sánchez, José. El General Gutiérrez. 3d ed. Mexico City: El Faro, 1988.

Cole, Jim. "Earthquake Victims Starting Over in Huehuetoca." The Mexico City News, 1 March 1986, 21.

Colburn, Forrest D. "Mexico's Financial Crisis." Latin American Research Review 19:2 (1984): 220-224.

Comisión Episcopal para la Doctrina de la Fe. Iglesias y Grupos Religiosos en México: Cuaderno 1. Mexico City: n.p., n.d.

_____. Iglesias y Grupos Religiosos en México: Cuaderno 2. Mexico City: Editorial La Cruz, n.d.

Comité Nacional Evangélico de Defensa, A.C. to C. Lic. Carlos Salinas de Gortari, et. al. Open letter published in Novedades (Mexico City), 22 May 1989, 2.

Comité Presbiteriano de Emergencia y Rehabilitación. Aid Plan for Victims of the Hurricanes that Devastated the State of Quintana Roo, Mexico, on September 14 and November 20, 1988. Mexico City: COPER, 1988.

_____. Boletín Informativo, Septiembre de 1987. Mexico City: COPER, 1987.

_____. Informe a la Comisión Especial de la R. Asamblea de la Iglesia Nacional Presbiteriana de México. Mexico City: COPER, 1988.

_____. Informe de Actividades ante la R. Asamblea General de la Iglesia Nacional Presbiteriana en su XX Reunión Ordinaria, que Tiene Lugar en la Iglesia "El Divino Redentor" Toluca, Edo. de Mexico, Período en Gestión: Julio 1988-Junio 1990. Mexico City: COPER, 1990.

_____. Informe de la Visita para Llevar Ayuda a los Deudos de los Hermanos Presbiterianos Fallecidos el Día 3 de Diciembre de 1987 en el Río Tulija, Estado de Chiapas, México. Mexico City: COPER, 1987.

_____. Informe que Presenta el Comité Presbiteriano de Emergencia y Rehabilitación (COPER) ante la XIX Reunión Ordinaria de la R. Asamblea General que se Realiza del 13 al 20 de Julio de 1988 en el Seno de la Iglesia "Ebenezer" de Cozumel, Quintana Roo. Mexico City: COPER, 1988.

_____. Report on the Visit to the Amuzgo Brethren in the Sierra of the State of Guerrero, Mexico. Mexico City: COPER, 1986.

_____. Report Presented by the Commission Appointed by this Committee in Joint Meeting with the Officers of the General Assembly of the Presbyterian Church of Mexico, to Take Aid to Victims of the Earthquake in the City of San Salvador, El Salvador, Central America. Mexico City: COPER, 1986.

"Como Cristianos Apoyamos la Candidatura de Cuauhtémoc Cárdenas." Iglesias 5:55 (July 1988): 26-27.

Concha, Miguel, Gari González, and Lino Oscar y Salas. La Participación de los Cristianos en el Proceso Popular de Liberación de México. Mexico City: Siglo XXI-IISUNAM, 1986.

Conferencia del Episcopado Mexicano. "Declaración de los Obispos sobre el Proceso Electoral." Iglesias 5:57 (September 1988): 6-7.

_____. Open letter to Señor Licenciado Carlos Salinas de Gortari, 5 June 1989. Servicios Informativos Procesados, A.C., Mexico City.

Conferencia Nacional de Obreros Evangélicos, Enero 17-19, 1940: Ponencias y Conclusiones. Mexico City: Concilio Nacional Evangélico de México, 1940.

Confesión de Fe de la Iglesia Presbiteriana: Formulada por la Asamblea de Westminster. Mexico City: El Faro, 1973.

Confraternidad Evangélica Latinoamericana. Los Documentos de CONELA. Mexico City: CONELA, nd.

_____. Reglamento Interno de la Confraternidad Evangélica Latinoamericana. Mexico City: CONELA, 1984.

Conn, Charles W. Como un Ejército Poderoso: Una Historia de la Iglesia de Dios, 1886-1976. Translated by Wilfredo Estrada Adorno. Cleveland, Tennessee: Pathway Press, 1983.

Constitución de la Iglesia Cristiana de "Las Asambleas de Dios" en la República Mexicana. Mexico City: Las Asambleas de Dios en la República Mexicana, 1946.

Constitución de la Iglesia Nacional Presbiteriana de México. Mexico City: El Faro, 1983.

Constitución Política de los Estados Unidos Mexicanos: Actualizada. Mexico City: Anaya Editores, 1989.

Consultation sobre la Renovación de la Iglesia que Necesitamos: Celebrada en la Cd. de Monterrey los días 13 al 15 de Octubre, con la Representación Nacional de 14 Denominaciones Evangélicas y 8 Organizaciones Interdenominacionales. N.p.: Federación Evangélica de México, 1969.

Convención Nacional Bautista de México. Programas e Informes para su 59 Reunión Anual del 21 al 27 de abril de 1968. Tampico: 1968.

_____. Programas e Informes, 60 Reunión Anual, abril de 1969. Puebla, 1969.

_____. Libro de Informes: LXXII Reuniones Anuales, julio de 1981. Ciudad Juárez, 1981.

Cook, Guillermo. "The Evangelical Groundswell in Latin America." The Christian Century (12 December 1990): 1172-79.

_____. Profundidad en la Evangelización. San José: INDEF, 1975.

Córdova, Arturo. "Entrevista con Arturo Córdova." Gracia 70 (May 1990): 14-17.

Cosío Villegas, Daniel, coord. Historia General de México. 4 Volumes. Mexico City: El Colegio de México, 1976.

Costas, Orlando E. Compromiso y Misión. San José: Editorial Caribe, 1975.

_____. El Protestantismo en América Latina Hoy: Ensayos del Camino (1972-1974). San José: INDEF, 1975.

_____. "La Misión del Pueblo de Dios en la Ciudad: Comisión de Vida y Misión de la Iglesia." Boletín Teológico 7 (1982): 85-96.

Cotto, Augusto. "Comentario Crítico de la Carta." Taller de Teología 1 (1976): 22-24.

_____. "El Diálogo Necesario entre Cuba y el Resto del Continente." Taller de Teología 2 (1978): 37-44.

_____. "Nuestra Militancia Cristiana." Estudios Ecuménicos (November 1971): 13.

Coxill, H. Wakelin and Sir Kenneth Grubb, eds. World Christian Handbook: 1962 Edition. London: World Dominion Press, 1962.

Craig, Robert M. Our Mexicans. New York: The Board of Home Missions of the Presbyterian Church, 1904.

Cranfield, C. E. B. A Commentary on Romans 12-13. Edinburgh: Oliver and Boyd, 1965.

Creighton, Frank W. A Handbook of the Missions of the Episcopal Church. New York: National Council of Protestant-Episcopal Church, 1936.

_____. The Church in Mexico. Philadelphia: The Church Historical Society, 1929.

Cristo, La Esperanza para América Latina: Ponencias-Informes-Comentarios de la II Conferencia Evangélica Latinoamericana. Buenos Aires: 1962.

"Crusade Council Suggests Calendar." The Commission (February 1967): 31.

Cruz, Saul. God's Healing for Broken Lives in an Oppressed and Neglected Community: Armonía's 1990 Report. Mexico City: Armonía, 1990.

_____. "Middle Class Christians Face Question of Values." Latin America Evangelist 66.4 (October-December 1988): 17.

Cuadernos de Teología. Buenos Aires.

Cuevas, Mariano. Historia de la Iglesia en México. Mexico City: 1946, 5 volumes.

Cumberland, Charles C. Mexican Revolution: The Constitutionalist Years. Austin: University of Texas Press, 1952.

_____. Mexico: The Struggle for Modernity. New York: Oxford University Press, 1968.

Curriculum Vitae. Informative magazine of the Iglesia Nacional Presbiteriana "El Divino Salvador".

Dale, James G. Catarina Neel Dale: Una Doctora entre los Aztecas. Mexico City: CUPSA, 1946.

_____. Katherine Neel Dale: Medical Missionary. Grand Rapids: Eerdmans, 1943.

_____. Mexico and our Missions. Lebanon, Pennsylvania: Sowers, 1910.

Dallal y Castillo, Eduardo. "La Familia como Fenómeno de la Naturaleza." Taller de Teología 7 (1980): 5-10.

Damboriena, Prudencio. Protestantismo en América Latina. Friburgo: Feres, 1962.

Dame, Lawrence. Maya Mission. Garden City, New York: Doubleday and Duran, 1968.

Danel Janet, Fernando. "Carta Abierta a Jürgen Moltmann." Taller de Teología 1 (1976): 24-26.

Daniell, David. Stronger than Mushrooms: The Various Facets of Baptist Student Work in Mexico. Nashville: Convention Press, 1976.

D'Antonio, William V. and Arthur J. Rubel. "Protestantism and Assimilation Among Mexican Americans." Journal for the Scientific Study of Religion. (Fall 1971): 219-232.

Dávalos de Cabello, Ma. del Rosario. "La Labor de la Esposa de un Presidente." El Faro (October 1964): 4-5.

Davis, J. Merle. La Base Económica de la Iglesia Evangélica de México. New York: Concilio Internacional Misionero, 1941.

____. The Economic Basis of the Evangelical Church in Mexico. London: International Missionary Council, 1940.

De la Garza, Yolanda, et al. El Conflicto Lingüístico en la Zona Bilingüe de México. Mexico City: SEP, 1982.

De la Madrid Hurtado, Miguel. Cien Tesis sobre México. Mexico City: Grijalbo, 1982.

De la Rosa, Martín, and Charles A. Reilly, eds. Religión y Política en México. Mexico City: Siglo XXI, 1985.

De las Casas, Bartolomé. Del Unico Modo de Atraer a Todos los Pueblos a la Verdadera Religión. Mexico City: Fondo de Cultura Económica, 1942.

De los Reyes Valdez, Alfonso. Historia de las Asambleas de Dios en México: 1 Los Pioneros. Tampico, Tamaulipas: Alfolletos, 1990.

Deiros, Pablo Alberto. Historia del Cristianismo: Con Enfasis sobre los Evangélicos en América Latina. 2d ed. El Paso: Casa Bautista, 1985.

_____. "Iglesia y Sociedad en el Protestantismo Latinoamericano Reciente." Boletín Teológico 6 (1982): 3-29.

_____, ed. Los Evangélicos y el Poder Político en América Latina. Grand Rapids and Buenos Aires: Nueva Creación, 1986.

Delong, Russell, V., and Wendell Taylor. Fifty Years of Nazarene Missions. Kansas City, Mo.: Beacon Hill Press, 1955.

Dennis, Walter D. Mexican Neighbors. New York: The National Council, 1958.

Díaz de la Serna, María Cristina. El Movimiento de la Renovación Carismática como un Proceso de Socialización Adulta. Mexico City: Universidad Autónoma Metropolitana-Iztapalapa, 1985.

Díaz del Castillo, Bernal. The Discovery and Conquest of Mexico. Translated by A. P. Maudslay. New York: Grove Press, 1956.

"Disaster in Mexico." Newsweek (30 September 1985): 16-21.

Disciplina de la Iglesia Metodista de México. Mexico City: Imprenta Nueva Educación, 1946.

Disciplina de la Iglesia Nacional Presbiteriana de México. Mexico City: El Faro, 1984.

Divas, Luis Armando. La Iglesia Protestante y el Movimiento Estudiantil en México. N.p., 1959.

Dodson, Maurice E. "Ministry Grows under National Pastor." The Commission (June 1968): 25.

Dominación Ideológica y Ciencia Social: El Instituto Lingüístico de Verano en México. México: Nueva Lectura, 1979.

Domínguez, Roberto. Pioneros de Pentecostés en el Mundo de Habla Hispana: México y Centroamérica. Vol. 2. Hialeah, Fl.: Literatura Evangélica, 1975.

Dos Santos, Theotonio, and others. Iglesia y Estado en América Latina. Mexico City: Centro de Reflexión Teológica and Seminario Permanente sobre Latino América, 1979.

Down Mexico Way. Official magazine of the Mexico Mission of the Presbyterian Church, U.S.A.

Drees, Ada M. C., ed. Thirteen Years in Mexico: (From Letters of Charles W. Drees). New York: Abingdon Press, 1915.

Driedger, Leo. "From Mexico to British Honduras." Mennonite Life (October, 1958).

Dussel, Enrique. A History of the Church in Latina America: Colonialism to Liberation (1492-1979. Translated and Revised by Alan Neely. Grand Rapids: Eerdmans, 1981.

_____. De Medellín a Puebla: Una Década de Sangre y Esperanza, 1968/1979. Mexico City: Centro de Estudios Ecuménicos, 1979.

_____, ed. Historia General de la Iglesia en América Latina, México. Volume 5. Mexico City: Cehila-Sígueme-Paulinas, 1984.

"Earthquake Aid." Christianity Today (23 October 1985): 943.

Eaton, James Demarest. Life under Two Flags. New York: Barnes and Co., 1922.

El Abogado Cristiano Ilustrado: Organo de la Iglesia Metodista Episcopal.

"El Aporte Evangélico a la Educación." El Faro (February 1964): 4-6.

"¡El C.A.B. en Acción!" La Luz Bautista (November 1988): 12-15.

El Camino a la Vida. Official magazine of the Iglesia de Dios en la República Mexicana.

El Cristianismo Evangélico en México, Su Tradición Histórica, Su Actuación Práctica, Sus Postulados Sociales. Mexico City: Concilio Nacional de Iglesias, 1934.

"El Cristiano y la Democracia." El Camino a la Vida (August-September 1980): 14-16.

El Evangelista Mexicano. Official magazine of the Iglesia Metodista Episcopal del Sur.

El Exégeta. Official magazine of the Iglesia Apostólica de la Fe en Cristo Jesús.

El Fanal (Lecciones de la Escuela Dominical). Mexico City: El Faro, 1910-1990.

El Faro. Official magazine of the Iglesia Nacional Presbiteriana de México. Mexico City: El Faro, 1885-1991.

El Heraldo. Official magazine of the Iglesia Episcopal Mexicana, 1939-45.

El Mundo Cristiano. Official magazine of the eight denominations that participated in the Plan of Cincinnati, 1919-1929.

Encuentro. Official magazine of the Juan Calvino Presbytery.

Engelmann, L. O. "El Ecumenismo." Defensa (November 1966): 3-79.

_____. "Emanuel, Dios con Nosotros." Defensa (March 1966): 5-76.

Enrique Felix, Jaime. "Tejemanejes de la Nueva Relación Iglesia-Estado." El Pais (Mexico City), 5 April 1990, 9.

Equipo CEDOLASI. "Bibliografía Reciente sobre las Relaciones Iglesia-Estado en México." Cristianismo y Sociedad 101 (1989): 103-110.

Escobar, Samuel. Diálogo entre Cristo y Marx y Otros Ensayos. 2d ed. Lima: Publicaciones AGEUP, 1969.

_____. "El Episcopado Católico en Puebla." Pensamiento Cristiano 95 (September 1978): 24-31.

_____. "Formación del Pueblo de Dios en las Grandes Urbes." Boletín Teológico 7 (1982): 37-83.

_____. "Identidad, Misión y Futuro del Protestantismo Latinoamericano." Taller de Teología 3 (1978): 35-60.

_____. Irrupción Juvenil. Miami: Editorial Caribe, 1977.

_____. La Fe Evangélica y las Teologías de la Liberación. El Paso: Casa Bautista de Publicaciones, 1987.

_____. Precursores Evangélicos: Cartas de Diego Thomson, Memorias de Francisco Penzotti. Lima: Ediciones Presencia, 1984.

_____, ed. Acción en Cristo para un Continente en Crisis: Copilación de la Ponencias, Conferencias, y Estudios Bíblicos del Congreso Latinoamericano de Evangelización, Bogotá, Colombia, Noviembre de 1969. San José, Costa Rica: Editorial Caribe, n.d.

Escorcia, Carlos. "Las Asambleas de Dios en Nicaragua." Amanecer: Reflexión Cristiana en la Nueva Nicaragua 38-39 (December 1985): 22-25.

"Esfuerzo Cristiano en Acción." El Faro (May 1970): 18-20.

Espinosa Manrique, Victor Javier. "La Constitución de los Ancianos-Obispos en la Iglesia Cristiana: I y II Siglo." Licenciatura thesis, Seminario Teológico Bautista Mexicano, 1984.

Esquivel Obregón, Toribio. La Propaganda Protestante en México a la Luz del Derecho Internacional. Mexico City: Publicaciones de la Academia Mexicana de Jurisprudencia y Legislación, 1940.

Estatutos del Movimiento Amigos de Dios Perteneciente a la Iglesia de Dios en la República Mexicana y C.A. Mexico City: Iglesia de Dios en la República Mexicana y C.A., 1989.

Estrada Bojorques, Sergio Antonio. "La Mujer en el Pensamiento de Jesucristo Aplicado a las Iglesias Bautistas en México." Licenciatura thesis, Seminario Teológico Bautista Mexicano, 1982.

"Evangelicals in Mexico." The Christian Century (17 January 1990): 41-42.

"Evangélicos ante el Presidente Salinas de Gortari." Gracia 70 (May 1990): 17.

Evangelismo, Protestantismo y Catolicismo ante la Problemática Social Latinoamericana. Cuernavaca: CIDOC, nd.

Ezcurra, Ana María, and De Lella, Cayetano. La U.P.I. en Puebla: Manipulación Ideológica de la III Conferencia General del Episcopado Latinoamericano. Mexico City: Centro de Estudios Ecuménicos, 1980.

Farris, Norman M. Crown and Clergy in Colonial Mexico, 1759-1821. London: The Athlone Press, 1968.

Fernández Carrero, Eduardo. "Comentando las Noticias." El Faro (July 1968): 9.

_____. "Comentando las Noticias." El Faro (October 1968): 20-21.

_____. "Comentando las Noticias." El Faro (December 1968): 12.

Finkler, Kaja. "Dissident Sectarian Movement, the Catholic Church and Social Classes in Mexico." Comparative Studies in Society and History 25 (1983).

Fish, John H., and John Kretzmann. "Reviving Mexico City: Neighborhood by Neighborhood." The Christian Century (29 November 1989): 1116-18.

Floyd, Olive Beatrice. Doctora en México: The Life of Dr. Katherine Dale. New York: Putnam, 1944.

Fortuny, Patricia. "Difusión e Inserción Protestante en el Campo Yucateco." Taller de Teología 10 (1982): 41-57.

Franco Santos, Federico. "Rev. Gregorio Muñoz Espinoza: 'Aunque Esté Muerto, Vivirá.'" El Camino a la Vida (May-June 1986): 3-4.

Fretz, Joseph Winfield. Mennonite Colonization in Mexico. Akron, Pennsylvania: 1945.

_____. "Mennonites in Mexico." Mennonite Life (April 1947).

G. de Meléndez, Elena. "Escuela 'Fernando R. Rodríguez.'" El Faro (April 1964): 8-10.

Gabriel Muro, Victor. "Religión y Movimientos Sociales en México." Cristianismo y Sociedad 101 (1989): 7-13.

Gandee, Lee R. "The Introduction and Nineteenth Century Development of Protestantism in Mexico." M.A. thesis, Mexico City College, 1949.

Garay, Enrique. "El PAN Llegó al Límite de su Expansión." Iglesias 5:57 (September 1988): 9.

García Ibarra, Daniel. Inicios de la Iglesia Presbiteriana en México. Mexico City: El Faro, 1986.

_____. "La Iglesia." El Faro (October 1969): 12-13.

_____. Los Ancianos Gobernantes: Su Función Hoy Día. Mexico City: Iglesia Nacional Presbiteriana de México, Secretaria de Educación Cristiana, 1970.

Garma Navarro, Carlos. "Las Lágrimas de la Virgen no Caen Aquí: Ritual y Cosmología entre Católicos y Protestantes Totonacos." Cuicuilco 14-15 (July-December 1984).

_____. "Liderazgo, Mensaje Religioso y Contexto Social." Cristianismo y Sociedad 95 (1988): 89-99.

_____. "Liderazgo Protestante en una Lucha Campesina en México." América Indígena 1:44 (1984).

_____. "Los Estudios Antropológicos sobre el Protestantismo en México." Cristianismo y Sociedad 101 (1989): 89-101.

_____. Protestantismo en una Comunidad Totonaca. Mexico City: Instituto Nacional Indigenista, 1987.

Garrison, Winfred E. Los Discípulos de Cristo: Una Breve Historia. Buenos Aires: Editorial La Aurora, 1950.

Garza Marroquín, Juan Leandro. "Colegio Americano." El Faro (May 1964): 16-19.

_____. "El Factor Político en Westminster." El Faro (September-October 1985): 180-90.

_____. La Confesión de Fe de Westminster: Una Versión Popular, Actualizada y Amplificada. Vol. I. Mexico City: El Faro, 1986.

Gatica Sosa, Pedro, and Dr. Roberto García González, "Actividades Realizadas por el Personal Médico y Paramédico de la Delegación Magdalena Contreras, S.S.A., y U.N.A.M., en el Albergue de Casa Popular." Mexico City: Delegación Magdalena Contreras, 1985).

Gaxiola y Gaxiola, Manuel Jesús. La Serpiente y la Paloma: Análisis del Crecimiento de la Iglesia Apostólica de la Fe en Cristo Jesús de México. Pasadena: William Carey Library, 1970.

_____. "Los Pentecostales y el Ecumenismo." Estudios Ecuménicos (November 1971): 1-4.

_____. "Preguntas No-Ecumenistas sobre el Ecumenismo." Estudios Ecuménicos (November 1971): 5-10.

_____, ed. Directorio Evangélico de la Ciudad de México: 1969-1970. Mexico City: Federación Evangélica de México, 1970.

Gilbert, Charles H. "Eighteen Evangelicals in One Cell." The Commission (June 1967): 20.

Giménez, Gilberto. Cultura Popular y Religión en el Anáhuac. Mexico City: Ed. Centro de Estudios Ecuménicos, 1978.

Gladen, Van. "Experts Approve Courses." The Commission (March 1966): 18.

Gómez Ciriza, Roberto. México ante la Diplomacia Vaticana. México: Fondo de Cultura Económica, 1977.

Gómez Pascóe, Nicanor Felipe. "Ahora Sí Soy Su Soldado": Biografía del Mártir Nicanor Gómez. Morelia, Michoacán: n.p., 1935.

Gómez Pascóe, Nicanor Felipe, Fernando Padilla, and Nicanor Gómez R., eds. Libro Histórico de las Bodas de Oro del Sínodo General de la Iglesia Presbiteriana en México: Julio 6, 1901-1951. Mexico City: El Faro, 1956.

González, Justo. Historia de las Misiones en la América Latina. Buenos Aires: La Aurora, 1970.

_____. Historia de un Milagro. Mexico City, Editorial Caribe, 1983.

González B., José, and others, eds. El Protestantismo en México. Mexico City: Buena Prensa, 1946.

González de Alba, Luis. Los Días y los Años. Mexico City: Ediciones Era, 1971.

González Esquivel, Gloria. "Labor Educativa de la Iglesia Presbiteriana de México." Licenciatura thesis, Seminario Teológico Presbiteriano de México, 1987.

González Luna, Efraín. Los Católicos y la Política en México: Condición Política de los Católicos Mexicanos. Mexico City: Editorial Jus, 1988.

González Martínez, Luis Lauro. "Una Investigación del Ministerio de las Iglesias Bautistas Mexicanas hacia los Profesionistas." Licenciatura thesis, Seminario Teológico Bautista Mexicano, 1982.

González Navarro, Moisés. "Separación de la Iglesia y el Estado y Desamortización de Bienes de Manos Muertas." In La Formación del Estado Mexicano, 169-90. México: Porrúa, 1984.

González Rangel, Noé. "Magna Concentración Evangélica." El Camino a la Vida (May-June 1986): 5-7.

Goodman, Felicitas D. "Apostolics of Yucatan: A Case History of a Religious Movement." In Religion, Altered States of Consciousness and Social Change, ed. Erika Bourguignone, 178-218. Columbus: Ohio State University Press, 1973.

_____. Speaking in Tongues: A Cross Cultural Study of Glossolalia. Chicago: University of Chicago Press, 1972.

Goslin, Tomás S. Los Evangélicos en la América Latina: Siglo XIX, Los Comienzos. Buenos Aires: Editorial La Aurora, 1956.

Goulet, Denis. "The Mexican Church: Into the Public Arena." America (8 April 1989): 318-22.

Gouvéa Mendonca, António. O Celeste Porvir: A Insercáo do Protestantismo no Brasil. Sao Paolo: Edicóes Paulinas, 1984.

Granados Roldán, Otto. La Iglesia Católica Méxicana como Grupo de Presión. Mexico City: UNAM, 1981.

Gray, Jr., William H. "Sermon at the Ranch." The Commission (August 1968): 23.

Green, James H. "Willing Sacrifice." The Commission (January 1967): 15.

Greenlan, Fay Sharon. Religious Reform in Mexico. Gainesville: University of Florida Press, 1958.

Greenleaf, Richard E. La Inquisición en Nueva España en el Siglo XVI. Mexico City: Fondo de Cultura Económica, 1981.

_____. "North American Protestants and the Mexican Inquisition, 1765-1820." Journal of Church and State (Spring 1966): 186-99.

_____. The Mexican Inquisition of the Sixteenth Century. Albuquerque: University of New Mexico Press, 1969.

_____. Zumarraga and the Mexican Inquisition. Washington: Academy of American Franciscan History, 1961.

Greenway, Roger S. An Urban Strategy for Latin America. Grand Rapids: Baker Book House, 1973.

_____. Apóstoles a la Ciudad: Estratégias Bíblicas para Misiones Urbanas. Grand Rapids: Iglesia Cristiana Reformada, 1981.

Greenway, Roger S., and others. Con Cristo en la Ciudad. El Paso: Casa Bautista de Publicaciones, 1976.

Gremillion, Joseph B., and others. The Christian Challenge in Latin America. New York: Maryknoll, 1964.

Griffin, Ricardo. 25 Años de Evangelismo en México. Mexico City: Editorial Cuajimalpa, 1986.

Gringoire, Pedro. [Gonzalo Báez Camargo]. El Doctor Mora: Impulsor Nacional de la Causa Bíblica en México. Mexico City: Sociedad Bíblica, 1965.

_____. Las Manos de Cristo. 2d ed. Mexico City: CUPSA, 1985.

_____. Marxismo ¿Ciencia Pura o Ciencia Ficción?. Mexico City: Editorial Jus, 1979.

_____. "Para que el Mundo Crea" (Reflexiones sobre la Unidad Cristiana). Mexico City: B. Costa-Amic Editor, 1971.

_____. Una Exhibición de Ignorancia y Mala Fe. Mexico City: Arte y Periodismo, 1971.

_____. Voces Perdurables de Nuestro Tiempo. Mexico City: CUPSA y Nueva Imagen, 1971.

Groves, Juan L. "¿Es la Cristología una Ideología?" Taller de Teología 6 (1980): 17-19.

Grubb, Kenneth G. An Advancing Church in Latin America. London: World Dominion Press, 1956.

Gruening, Ernest H. Mexico and its Heritage. New York: Appleton Century, 1940.

Guerra, Eleazar, G. Báez Camargo, and Alfredo H. La Misión de la Iglesia Evangélica de México en la Hora Presente: Ponencias y Resoluciones del Primer Congreso Nacional Evangélico, Octubre 10-18, 1939. Mexico City: CUPSA, 1940.

Guerrero, Francisco Javier. "Moisés Sáenz, el Precursor Olvidado." Nueva Antropología 1 (1975): 31-55.

Gutiérrez Casillas, José. Camino Hacia la Unidad: La Realidad Mexicana desde 1917, Iluminada por Textos del Magisterio Eclesiástico. Guadalajara: Suárez-Muñoz Ediciones, 1986.

_____. Historia de la Iglesia en México. Mexico City: Porrúa, 1984.

Gutiérrez-Cortés, Rolando. "Análisis Argumental - La Familia en Crisis." Boletín Teológico 18 (1986): 122-27.

_____. "Capacitación de Discípulos." Boletín Teológico 6 (1982): 37-44.

_____. Creencias Bautistas. Mexico City: Horeb, 1985.

_____. "Cristología y Acción Pastoral en América Latina." Boletín Teológico 8 (1982): 21-38.

_____. "Criterio Pastoral en la Labor de Hermenéutica e Historia." Boletín Teológico 4 (1981): 75-85.

_____. Cuando una Familia enfrenta Problemas. El Paso: Casa Bautista de Publicaciones, 1984.

_____. Educación Teológica y Acción Pastoral en América Latina, Hoy. Mexico City: Horeb, 1984.

_____. El Espíritu y la Palabra en la Comunidad Evangelizadora. Mexico City: Horeb, 1979.

_____. El Mensaje de los Salmos en Nuestro Contexto. Vol. I. El Paso: Casa Bautista, 1978.

_____. El Mensaje de los Salmos en Nuestro Contexto. Vol. II. El Paso, Casa Bautista, 1978.

_____. El Mensaje de los Salmos en Nuestro Contexto. Vol. III. El Paso, Casa Bautista, 1982.

_____. "El Sacerdocio Universal de los Creyentes." Boletín Teológico 30 (1988): 117-25.

_____. "Hacia una Hermenéutica Teológica." Boletín Teológico 5 (1982): 104-21.

_____. ¿Holocausto o Adoración? Una Visión de la Vida, del Hombre, del Mundo, y de la Historia. Mexico City: Horeb, nd.

_____. "La Biblia, el Uso de Presupuesto y Claves Hermenéuticas." Boletín Teológico 10-11 (1983): 1-26.

_____. "La Educación Teológica frente al Reto del Mundo Contemporáneo." Tensión: Revista de Análisis Teológico (1988): 58-62.

_____. "La Familia en Crisis." Boletín Teológico 17 (1985): 46-64.

_____. "La Naturaleza de la Iglesia: Misión y Acción Pastoral." Boletín Teológico 9 (1983): 5-25.

_____. "La Pastoral de la Familia." Boletín Teológico 3 (1981): 63-68.

_____. "Metodología Teológica." Boletín Teológico 20 (1986): 1-3.

_____. "Un Programa Urbano de Evangelización." Boletín Teológico 7 (1982): 1-13.

Hale, Charles A. Mexican Liberalism in the Age of Mora. New Haven: Yale University Press, 1968.

Hart, John M. "Historiographical Dynamics of the Mexican Revolution." Latin American Research Review 19:3 (1984): 223-31.

Hastey, Ervin E. "Gospel Shared on Telecast." The Commission (December 1968): 19.

_____. "Meeting Offers Evangelistic Openings." The Commission (October 1966): 20.

_____. "Pioneer Pastor Sees Work Grow." The Commission (March 1968): 25.

Haven, Gilbert. Our Next Door Neighbor. New York: Harper, 1875.

_____. Iglesia Metodista de México. 1875.

Hefley, James C. Peril by Choice. Grand Rapids: Zondervan, 1968.

_____. "Spiritual Revolution: Second Stage." The Commission (January 1966): 10-11.

Heironimus, Dorothy. Friends in Mexico. Richmond, Indiana: American Friends Board of Missions, 1941.

Helms, James Ervin. Origins and Growth of Protestantism in Mexico to 1920. Ph.D. dissertation, University of Texas, 1955.

"Help After the Earthquakes." Christianity Today (8 November 1985): 66.

Hernández, Ciro. Some Aspects of the Mexican Catholic Social Congresses, 1903-1909. M.A. thesis, Mexico City College.

Hernández Bautista, Ulises. "Trabajo Pastoral de la Familia." Taller de Teología 7 (1980): 15-20.

Hernández Gómez de García, Elisa, and others. "Bosquejo Biográfico del Presbítero Moisés García Chávez." El Faro (March-April 1985): 79.

Hernández Jiménez, José. "La Vida Cívica del Creyente." El Faro (September 1964): 4-5.

_____. "Un Hombre y una Dama ante la Historia." El Faro (October 1964): 2-3.

Hernández S., Adolfo. "Carta a un Estudiante." La Luz Bautista (January 1969): 10.

Herzog, Jesús Silva. Breve Historia de la Revolución Mexicana: Los Antecedentes y la Etapa Maderista. Mexico City: Fondo de Cultura Económica, 1962.

Hinojosa, Oscar. "Damaged Goods: Did Salinas Really Win?" World Press Review (September 1988): 17-18.

Hoeferkamp, Roberto T. "Desde el Cristo Presente hasta el Jesús Histórico." Taller de Teología 6 (1980): 33-37.

_____. "Dogmatismo y Reideologización: Reflexiones Críticas sobre el Encuentro de Teologías." Taller de Teología 3 (1978): 15-23.

_____. "El Discipulado Cristiano según D. Bonhoeffer." Taller de Teología 4 (1979): 24-28.

_____. "Reino de Dios y Actividad Humana." Taller de Teología 1 (1976): 19-21.

Holding, Nannie E. A Decade of Mission Life in Mexico Mission Homes. Nashville: Publishing House of Methodist Church South, 1895.

Howard, Jorge P. La Otra Conquista de América. Buenos Aires: Editorial La Aurora, nd.

Hudson, Winthrop S. Religion in America: An Historical Account of the Development of American Religious Life. 2d ed. New York: Charles Scribner's Sons, 1973.

Huebner, Roberto G. "Cristología de Efesios." Taller de Teología 6 (1980): 27-31.

_____. "La Gran Ausente del Encuentro de Teologías." Taller de Teología 3 (1978): 25-28.

Huegel, Federico J., and others. Los Protestantes y el Segundo Concilio Vaticano. Mexico City: CUPSA, 1964.

Huegel, Juan E., ed. Discípulos y Ministros: Los Ministerios de los Cristianos Hoy Día. Documentos de la Consulta Nacional sobre la Renovación del Ministerio. México D.F. 1 al 5 de febrero, 1980. 2d ed. Guadalajara: Iglesias en Transformación, 1984.

_____. "La Iglesia como Comunidad del Reino." Taller de Teología 6 (1980): 39-41.

_____. "Responde." Pensamiento Cristiano 98 (June 1979): 200-01.

_____. "Un Nuevo Modelo de Ministerio." Pensamiento Cristiano 93 (March 1978): 167-169.

Hugh, Steven. Miracles in Mexico. Chicago: Moody Press, 1972.

Hurtado G., Arnulfo. El Cisma Mexicano. Mexico City: Buena Prensa, 1956.

Ibarra Bellón, Araceli, and Alisa Lanczyner Reisel. "La Hermosa Provincia: Nacimiento y Vida de una Secta Cristiana en Guadalajara." M.A. thesis, La Universidad de Guadalajara, 1972.

Iglesia Metodista de México. Bodas de Diamante del Metodismo en México. Mexico City: Imprenta Nueva Educación, 1948.

_____. La Iglesia Metodista de México. Mexico City: CUPSA, 1930.

_____. La Iglesia Metodista de México y su Herencia Wesleyana. 1953.

_____. Metodismo: Autónomo, Unido, 1930-1980. Mexico City: Iglesia Metodista de México-Dirección de Literatura y Comunicaciones, 1980.

_____. Síntesis Histórica del Metodismo en México. Mexico City: 1987.

_____. Un Pueblo Llamado Metodista. Mexico City: Iglesia Metodista de México-Dirección de Literatura y Comunicaciones, nd.

Iglesia Nacional Presbiteriana de México. Orden de Culto y Liturgia. Mexico City: El Faro, n.d.

_____. Primer Centenario de la Obra Femenil Presbiteriana en México, 1887-1987. Mexico City: 1987.

_____. 1872-1972 Centenario: Iglesia Nacional Presbiteriana de México. Monterrey: Iglesia Nacional Presbiteriana, 1973.

"Iglesia y Política." Revista Mexicana de Sociología 43 (1981).

Iglesias. Official organ of the Centro Nacional de Comunicación Social.

Iglesias, Margaret G. Messenger to the Golden People. Nashville: Broadman, 1968.

Información Punto Inicial. An interdenominational magazine serving Mexico and Hispanics in the United States of America.

Informador. A monthly magazine of the activities of the Jehova's Witnesses in Mexico.

Inman, Samuel Guy. Christian Cooperation in Latin America. New York: Committee on Cooperation, 1917.

_____. New Aspects of Christian Work in Mexico: Report on Recent Developments and a Series of Conferences on Evangelical Work held in Mexico City, March 15-21, 1934. N.p., 1934.

_____. Problems in Pan-Americanism. New York: Doran and Co., 1921.

Instituto de Asesoría Antropológica para la Región Maya. "Protestantismo en Chiapas: Indígenas Urbanos (El Nuevo Cinturón de Miseria de San Cristobal de las Casas)." Taller de Teología 10 (1982): 59-65.

Instituto Lingüístico de Verano: Conformado e Impulsado en México. Mexico City: Instituto Lingüístico de Verano, 1984.

Irelan, Elma C. Fifty Years with Our Mexican Neighbors. St. Louis: Bethany Press, 1949.

Isáis, Elisabeth F. "Mexico: Land of Contrasts, Church-State Tensions." Latin America Evangelist (April-June 1990): 18.

Isáis, Juan M. Cómo No Fracasar en la Vida Cristiana: Consejos para Nuevos Creyentes. Mexico City: Misión Latinoamericana de México, n.d.

_____. Cómo Tener Exito en Evangelismo a Fondo: Manual Práctico. Mexico City: Misión Latinoamericana de México, n.d.

_____. The Other Evangelism: One Man's View of Evangelism in Depth's Revolutionary Results. Winona Lake, Indiana: Brethren Evangelistic Ministries, 1988.

_____. The Other Side of the Coin. Grand Rapids: Eerdmans, 1966.

Jackson, Pablo R. La Doctrina de la Iglesia Local. Deltona, Fl.: Editorial Bautista Independiente, 1982.

Jaramillo Cárdenas, Luciano. "Biblia y Quehacer Teológico en un Mundo de Cambios y Relatividades." Boletín Teológico 10-11 (1983): 73-104.

Jaramillo, Rubén. Autobiografía y Asesinato. 3d ed. Mexico City: Ed. Nuestro Tiempo, 1978.

Joekel, Samuel L. Compaginado Todo: El Argumento de la Biblia. Mexico City: El Faro, 1952.

Johnson, John J., ed. Continuity and Change in Latin America. Stanford: Stanford University Press, 1964.

Johnson, Johnni. "Mission of a Mission." The Commission (August 1968): 18-19.

_____. "People with Mission." The Commission (July 1968): 12-13.

Johnson, Kenneth F. Mexican Democracy: A Critical View. Boston: Allyn and Bacon, 1971.

Jones, Rex Ralph. "Church Planting among Middle Class Families in Mexico City." Ph.D. dissertation, Fuller Theological Seminary, 1984.

Juárez, José Roberto. "The Use of Counter-Oaths in the Archdiocese of Guadalajara, Mexico, 1876-1911." Journal of Church and State (Winter 1970): 79-88.

"Jubileo de Oro de la Maestra Celia García de Alarcón." El Faro (May 1964): 6-7.

Kelley, Francis C. Blood Drenched Altars. 2d ed. rev. Milwaukee: The Bruce Publishing Company, 1935.

Kelly, Maria Ann. "A Chapter in Mexican Church-State Relations." Ph.D. dissertation, Georgetown University, 1975.

Kessler, Juan B. A. "La Historia de la Iglesia en América Latina." Boletín Teológico, 1st Ser., 1-2 (1979): 2-25.

Knight, Walker L. The Land Between. Atlanta: Southern Baptist Home Mission Board, 1966.

Knowlton, Robert J. Church Property and the Mexican Reform, 1856-1910. DeKalb: Northern Illinois University Press, 1976.

Kortkamp, Paula. "Nurses Arrive when Needed." The Commission (June 1968): 24.

"La Década de los 80s: Un Reto." El Camino a la Vida (March-May 1980): 4-5.

"La Educación y las Iglesias Reformadas en México." El Faro: 12-15.

"La Iglesia como Agencia Pacificadora." El Camino a la Vida (August-September 1980): 11-13.

"La Iglesia: En el Exodo hacia las Estrellas." El Camino a la Vida (September-December 1990): 101-4.

"La Iglesia: En los Vencedores del Siglo XX." El Camino a la Vida (September-December 1990): 94-100.

La Iglesia en Respuesta a las Necesidades Humanas: Wheaton '83. Mexico City: Visión Mundial de México, nd.

La Luz Bautista. Official magazine of the Convención Nacional Bautista.

"La Próxima, una Semana en que las Leyes se Harán, Publicamente, a un Lado." Proceso (April 1990): 20.

"La Visita del Papa Podría Ser Manipulada: Sacerdotes." La Jornada (Mexico City), 16 April 1990, 7-8.

Lajara, Cecilio N, ed. Un Pueblo con Mentalidad Teológica. Mexico City: El Faro, 1976.

Lalive, Christian. El Refugio de las Masas. Santiago, Chile: Editorial del Pacífico, 1970.

Lango, Ezequiel. Catecismo Menor Explicado. 4th ed. Mexico City: El Faro, 1973.

Lara-Braud, Jorge, trans. Social Justice and the Latin Churches. Richmond: John Knox Press, 1969.

Larson, Pedro. El Uso Evangélico del X Censo General de Población y Vivienda, 1980. Mexico City: Horeb, 1985.

"Las Olimpiadas." El Faro (July 1968): 4-5.

"Las Relaciones Iglesia-Estado en el México Contemporáneo." Iglesias 5:55 (July 1988): 4-5.

Lea, Henry Charles. The Inquisition in the Spanish Dependencies. New York: The Macmillan Company, 1908.

Lechuga, Graciela, ed. Ideología Educativa de la Revolución Mexicana. Mexico City: Universidad Autónoma Metropolitana-Xochimilco, 1984.

Lee, Allan W. The Burro and the Bibles and Other Vignettes of a Summer in Mexico. Jericho, New York: Exposition Press, 1968.

Lee de Gutiérrez, Edna. "Buenas Nuevas a los Pobres." Boletín Teológico 35 (1989): 249-53.

Lee, James H. "Church and State in Mexican Higher Education, 1821-1861." Journal of Church and State (Winter 1978): 57-72.

León, Luis L. and Manuel Herrera Lasso. El Movimiento Revolucionario y el Clericalismo Mexicano. Mexico City: Imprenta de la Dirección de Estudios Geográficos y Climatológicos, 1926.

León-Portilla, Miguel. Los Diálogos de 1524 según el Texto de Fray Bernardino de Sahagún y sus Colaboradores Indígenas. Mexico City: UNAM, 1986.

Lernoux, Penny. "The Latin American Church." Latin American Research Review 15:2 (1980): 201-211.

Lewis, Oscar. Pedro Martínez: A Mexican Peasant and His Family. New York: Random House, 1964.

Liebman, Arthur, Kenneth N. Walker, and Myron Glazer. Latin American University Students: A Six-Nation Study. Cambridge: Harvard University Press, 1972.

Lipset, Seymour Martin, and Aldo Solari, eds. Elites in Latin America. London: Oxford University Press, 1967.

Lloreda, Raquel. "Campamento Juvenil." El Faro (August 1969): 12-13.

Loaeza, Soledad. "Iglesia-Estado: ¿La Guerra Terminó?" Nexos 113 (May 1987): 5-6.

_____. "La Iglesia Católica y el Reformismo Autoritario." Foro Internacional 25:2 (October-December 1984): 138-65.

López Loredo, Martha Esther. "Trabajo de Investigación sobre la Función del Hombre y la Mujer en el Matrimonio Contemporáneo Presbiteriano Confrontado Biblicamente." Licenciatura thesis, Seminario Teológico Presbiteriano de México, 1984.

Lyon, Roy Lenere. El Evangelio Según la Gran Comisión. El Paso: Casa Bautista de Publicaciones, 1958.

Mabry, Donald J. "Mexican Anticlerics, Bishops, Cristeros, and the Devout during the 1920's: A Scholarly Debate." Journal of Church and State (Winter 1978): 81-92.

MacFarland, Charles S. Chaos in Mexico: The Conflict of Church and State. New York: Harper, 1935.

Macín Andrade, Raul. "El Compromiso de un Pastor Evangélico Mexicano: Entrevista con el Pbro. Raúl Macín." Estudios Ecuménicos 9 (December 1970):57-60.

_____. "La Reforma Radical, un Tema Siempre Nuevo." Taller de Teología 13 (1983): 33-38.

_____. Lutero: Presencia Religiosa y Política en México. Mexico City: Nuevomar, 1983.

_____. Un Profeta Olvidado. Montevideo: Tierra Nueva, 1970.

Mackay, John A. Las Iglesias Latinoamericanas y el Movimiento Ecuménico. 2d ed. Mexico City: Casa Unida de Publicaciones, 1989.

_____. The Other Spanish Christ. London: Student Christian Movement Press, 1932.

Magaña Aguilar, Hugo. "Una Reflexión Pastoral sobre el Ecumenismo: El Movimiento Estudiantil Cristiano en América Latina y el Caribe, 1951-1986." Licenciatura thesis, Instituto Internacional de Estudios Superiores, 1987.

Maldonado de Castellanos, Elia Ruth. "Eminente Posición Espiritual de la Iglesia Nacional Presbiteriana." Curriculum Vitae (November 1961): 15-16.

Manual de Estrategias Bautistas: Area Metropolitana D.F.-Edomex. Mexico City: Comité de Estrategia Bautista, 1988.

"Marcha Juarista de Evangélicos." Gracia 70 (May 1990): 15.

Margarant, Guillermo F. La Iglesia Mexicana y el Derecho. Mexico City: Porrúa, 1984.

Marín, Godofredo. La Democracia Basada en la Biblia. 2d ed. Caracas: Imprenta Universitaria de la UCV, 1988.

Márquez Campos, Alfredo. México, 1968. Mexico City: Editorial Estela, 1969.

Márquez Jiménez, Arturo. "La Lucha por Establecer el Señorío de Cristo en la Iglesia Bautista Galilea." Licenciatura thesis, Seminario Teológico Bautista Mexicano, 1983.

Marroquín, Hazael T. "Circulación e Influencia de la Biblia en México: Biblias Obsequiadas a Presidentes de la República." El Faro (August 1964): 17.

_____. "Circulacıón e Influencia de la Biblia en México: Dos Eventos Trascendentes," El Faro (June 1964): 15.

_____. "Circulación e Influencia de la Biblia en México: 'La Fe es por el Oir.'" El Faro (April 1964): 12-13.

_____. La Agencia Bíblica en México y su Obra. Mexico City: Sociedad Bíblica, 1941.

_____. La Biblia en México. Mexico City: Agencia Bíblica Americana, 1953.

_____. Versiones Castellanas de la Biblia. Mexico City: El Faro, 1959.

Marsden, George. Fundamentalism and American Culture: The Shaping of Twentieth Century Evangelicalism, 1870-1925. New York: Oxford University Press, 1980.

Martin, David. Tongues of Fire: The Explosion of Protestantism in Latin America. Oxford: Blackwell, 1990.

Martín, Manolo. "Y . . . Llega Otro Año." El Faro (January 1969): 4.

Martínez, J. L. Nezahualcóyotl. Mexico City: Fondo de Cultura Económica, 1972.

Martínez García, Carlos. "¿Existe Persecución Religiosa en México?" Uno Más Uno (Mexico City), 11 October 1990.

_____. "Secta: Un Concepto Inadecuado para Explicar el Protestantismo Mexicano." Boletín Teológico 41 (1991): 55-72.

Martínez López, Joel. Orígenes del Presbiterianismo en México. Matamoros: n.p., 1972.

Martínez Sierra, Virgilio Marcial. "La Influencia del Pentecostalismo entre los Ministros Bautistas de México." Licenciatura thesis, Seminario Teológico Bautista Mexicano, 1984.

Marx, Wesley. Acts of God, Acts of Man. New York: Coward, McCann, & Geoghegan, Inc., 1977.

Mather, Cotton. Diary of Cotton Mather. Boston: Massachusetts Historical Society, 1912.

Maust, John. Cities of Change: Urban Growth and God's People in Ten Latin American Cities. Coral Gables, Fl.: Latin America Mission, 1984.

_____. "Gonzalo Báez-Camargo: God's Man in Mexico." Christianity Today (5 March 1982): 28-31.

McAlier T., Miguel. "El Reino de Dios y lo Pastoral." Tensión: Revista de Análisis Teológico (1988): 6-14.

McClelland, Alicia J. Estudios del Evangelio de San Juan. Mexico City: El Faro, 1986.

_____. Mission to Mexico. Nashville: Board of World Missions, Presbyterian Church in the United States, 1960.

McGavran, Donald, John Huegel, and Jack Taylor. Church Growth in Mexico. Grand Rapids: Eerdmans, 1963.

McGuire, Stryker. "A Compromised Election: Despite Cries of Fraud, Mexico's Ruling Party Claims a Close Victory." Newsweek (18 July 1988): 36.

McKechnie, Marianne E. "The Mexican Revolution and the National Presbyterian Church of Mexico, 1910-1940." Ph.D. dissertation, The American University, 1970.

McLean, J. H. The Living Christ for Latin America. New York: The Board of Foreign Missions and the Woman's Board of Foreign Missions of the Presbyterian Church, USA, 1916.

Mecham, J. Lloyd. Church and State in Latin America: A History of Politico-Ecclesiastical Relations. Rev. ed. Chapel Hill: University of North Carolina Press, 1966.

Medina, J. T. Historia del Tribunal del Santo Oficio de la Inquisición en México, 2d ed. Mexico City: Ediciones Fuente Cultural, 1952.

_____. La Primitiva Inquisición Americana. Santiago, Chile: Imprenta Elzeviriana, 1914.

Medina Ascencio, Luis. México y el Vaticano. México: Jus, 1984.

Meléndez, Elena G. "Escuela 'Fernando R. Rodríguez,'" El Faro (April 1964): 8-10.

Memorias del III Encuentro Nacional del Movimiento de Cristianos Comprometidos en las Luchas Populares. Mexico City: Movimiento de Cristianos Comprometidos en las Luchas Populares, 1990.

Méndez, Moisés. "Cristología de Efesios." Taller de Teología 6 (1980): 21-26.

_____. "Las Mujeres en el Nuevo Testamento." Taller de Teología 8 (1981): 45-57.

Mendoza Meza, Lazara. Evangélicos Otomíes de Ixmiquilpan, Hgo. Mexico City: Secretaría de Educación Pública Instituto Nacional Indigenista, 1982.

"Mexican Hayride." National Review (5 August 1988): 19.

Mexican Neighbors. New York: The National Council of Churches, 1958.

"Mexico: The Baptists. Evangelical and Mexican." The Commission (February-March 1986): 28-29.

"Mexico: The Baptists. The Second Century." The Commission (February-March 1986): 26-27.

Mexico: A People Prepared. Mexico City: Lausanne Mexico Committee, 1989.

México Hoy y Mañana: Documento No. 1 "Directorio Evangélico de la Gran Ciudad de México". Mexico City: Visión Evangelizadora Latinoamericana and Instituto Misionológico de las Américas, 1987.

México Hoy y Mañana: Documento No. 2 "Estudio de Casos del Crecimiento de la Iglesia Evangélica en la Gran Ciudad de México". Mexico City: Visión Evangelizadora Latinoamericana and Programa Latinoamericano de Estudios Socio-Religiosos, 1989.

México Hoy y Mañana: Documento No. 3 "Manual de Recursos: Estudio de las Agencias de Servicio que Apoyan a las Iglesias Evangélicas en la Gran Ciudad de México". Mexico City: Visión Evangelizadora Latinoamericana, Programa Latinoamericano de Estudios Socio-Religiosos, and Liga del Sembrador, 1990.

"Mexico: Killer Quake." Time (30 September 1985): 34-43.

"Mexico: Mexico City. Anastasis: God at Work." The Commission (February-March 1986): 32-35.

"Mexico: Mexico City. Bethel: City Vision." The Commission (February-March 1986): 36-39.

"Mexico: Mexico City. Bethesda: Living Hope." The Commission (February-March 1986): 30-31.

"Mexico: Mexico City. Eliacim: Moving Ahead." The Commission (February-March 1986): 40-41.

"Mexico: Night of Sadness." Newsweek (14 October 1968): 45-48.

"Mexico: Olympic Struggle." Newsweek (7 October 1968): 50-55.

Meyer, Jean. "Cincuenta Años de Radicalismo: La Iglesia Católica, La Derecha y la Izquierda en América Latina." Vuelta 82 (September 1983).

_____. "El Catolicismo Social en México hasta 1913." Christus 528 (November 1979): 33-40.

_____. El Sinarquismo: ¿Un Fascismo Mexicano? Mexico City: Joaquín Mortiz, 1979.

_____. Historia de los Cristianos en América Latina. Mexico City: Editorial Vuelta, 1989.

_____. La Cristiada. 3 volumes. Mexico City: Siglo XXI, 1973.

Meyer, Michael C. and William L. Sherman. The Course of Mexican History. 3d ed. New York: Oxford University Press, 1987.

Michaels, Albert L. "Fascism and Sinarquismo: Popular Nationalisms against the Mexican Revolution." Journal of Church and State (Spring 1966): 234-50.

Míguez Bonino, José. Doing Theology in a Revolutionary Situation. Philadelphia: Fortress Press, 1975.

_____. Toward a Christian Political Ethics. Philadelphia: Fortress Press, 1983.

Millet, Richard. "John Wesley Butler and the Mexican Revolution, 1910-1911." Studies in the Social Sciences 17 (1978): 73-87.

_____. "The Protestant Role in Twentieth Century Latin American Church-State Relations." Journal of Church and State 15:3 (1973): 367-80.

Mills, Elizabeth H. "The Mormon Colonies in Chihuahua after the 1912 Exodus." M.A. thesis, University of Arizona, 1950.

Minard, Lawrence. "The New Missionaries." Forbes (14 May 1990): 41-42.

"Miracles Amid the Ruins." Time (7 October 1985): 36-38.

Miranda, Francisco. "Problemática de una Historia Eclesiástica." Historia Mexicana 21:2 (October-December 1971).

Misión. San José, Costa Rica.

Mitchell, James E. The Emergence of a Mexican Church. Pasadena: William Carey Library, 1970.

"Mob Attack Shocks Mexican Evangelicals." Latin America Evangelist (April-June 1990): 3.

Moberg, David O. The Great Reversal: Evangelism versus Social Concern. Philadelphia: Lippincott, 1972.

Moctezuma, Aquiles P. El Conflicto Religioso de 1926. Mexico City: Editorial Ayac, 1929.

Monciváiz, Daniel D. "La Iglesia del Evangelio 'Cuadrangular': Entrevista con el Rdo. Daniel D. Moncivaiz." Estudios Evangélicos 9 (December 1970): 68-76.

Mondragón González, Carlos. El Hombre en el Discurso Skinneriano y la Concepción Social del Sujeto. Licenciatura thesis, Escuela Nacional de Estudios Profesionales, Iztacala, 1983.

_____. "Pastoral en Tiempo de Crisis." Tensión: Revista de Análisis Teológico (1988): 15-19.

Mondragón González, Carlos, and Carlos Martínez García. Presencia Protestante en América Latina: Precisiones Históricas y Conceptuales. Guadalajara: V Encuentro Nacional: Iglesia, Estado y Grupos Laicos, 1989.

Mondragón González, Carlos, and Carlos Martínez García. Religión y Política en el Perú: Los Protestantes en el Gobierno de Alberto Fujimori. Austin: Eleventh Annual Student Conference on Latin America: Institute of Latin American Studies, 1991.

Monsiváis, Carlos. Entrada Libre: Crónicas de la Sociedad que se Organiza. Mexico City: Ediciones Era, 1987.

_____. "La Resurrección de Canoa." Proceso 694 (19 February 1990): 26-27.

_____. "Las Demás Iglesias: Los Mexicanos de Tercera Clase." Nexos (October 1989).

_____. "Muerte y Resurreción del Nacionalismo Mexicano." Nexos (1987).

Montecillos Chipres, José Luis. Cristo en el Antiguo Testamento. Mexico City: n.p., 1988.

_____. "Editorial: ¿A Qué Viene el Papa a México?" El Camino a la Vida (May-August 1990): 2-3.

_____. "Editorial: La Persecución de la Iglesia Católica a la Evangélica." El Camino a la Vida (January-April 1989): 2-3.

_____. "Editorial: Miedo por un Libro." El Camino a la Vida (January-April 1990): 2-3.

_____. "Editorial: Responsabilidad Cristiana en la Política." El Camino a la Vida (October-December 1988): 2-4.

Montemayor, Cosme G. El Protestantismo en México. Mexico City: Casa Presbiteriana de Publicaciones, 1945.

_____. Hickey: El Fundador. Mexico City: 1962.

Montemayor de Ulloa, Rebeca. "Ministerio Social Cristiano: Conceptualización y Praxis." Licenciatura thesis, Seminario Teológico Bautista Mexicano, 1981.

Montes de Oca Hernández, Vicente. "La Colección de Nuestro Derecho Constitucional." Discourse pronounced at the XL Marcha Juarista de la Iglesia Cristiana Evangélica, Mexico City, 21 March 1990.

Montgomery, Tommie Sue, ed. Mexico Today. Philadelphia: Institute for the Study of Human Issues, 1982.

Moody, John. "The Man Behind the Mask." Time (19 November 1990): 20-21.

Moore, Roberto Cecil. La Evangelización de Marcha . . . en América Latina. El Paso: Casa Bautista, 1959.

Mora, José María Luis. Obras Sueltas. 2d ed. Mexico City: Porrúa, 1963.

Morales, Francisco. Clero y Política en México, 1767-1834. Mexico City: SepSetentas, 1975.

Morales de Pérez, Luz. Aplicación de la Enseñanza entre los Alumnos, y Pláticas con los Maestros de la Escuela Dominical. Mexico City: 1943.

Moreno Pérez, César. "México: La Ciudad Más Grande de América Latina (Una Perspectiva Sociológica)." Boletín Teológico 7 (1982): 15-35.

Morrow, Medora A. Enseñándoles. Mexico City: El Faro, 1951.

Morrow, Rufus C. El Almirante Misionero. Mexico City: El Faro, 1962.

_____. El Rey-Mesías: Estudios en el Evangelio según San Mateo. Mexico City: El Faro, 1950.

Moses, Jasper T. "A Survey of Christian Education in Mexico." M.A. thesis, Butler College, 1903.

_____. Today in the Land of Tomorrow: A Study in the Development of Mexico. Indianapolis: Christian Women's Board of Missions, 1907.

Mott, Stephen Charles. Bibical Ethics and Social Change. New York: Oxford University Press, 1982.

Muñoz Espinoza, Gregorio. "Editorial." El Camino a la Vida (January-February 1969): 3-4.

_____. "El Obispo Presidente os Habla." El Camino a la Vida (January-February 1964): 3.

_____. "El Reino Mesiánico que Viene." El Camino a la Vida (May-June 1971): 34-36.

_____. "Hacedores de la Palabra." El Camino a la Vida (July-August 1981): 26-28.

Murray, Alice M. "Díaz and the Church: The Conciliation Policy, 1876-1900." M.A. thesis, Mexico City College, 1959.

Murray, Paul V. The Catholic Church in Mexico: Historical Essays for the General Reader. Mexico City: Editorial E.P.M., 1965.

Narváez Cruz, Alfredo. "Historia de la Iglesia Nacional Presbiteriana de México." Licenciatura thesis, Seminario Teológico Presbiteriano de México, 1983.

"Nationals are the Key." Here's Life World Report 2:3 (June-July 1984): 3-5.

Navarro Pedraza, Enrique. "Problemas y Alternativas de la Evangelización en México." Licenciatura thesis, Seminario Teológico Bautista Mexicano, 1984.

Negrete Salas, Martaelena. Relaciones entre la Iglesia y el Estado en México, 1930-1940. Mexico City: El Colegio de México and the Universidad Iberoamericana, 1988.

Nelson, Wilton M., ed. Diccionario de Historia de la Iglesia. Miami: Editorial Caribe, 1989.

_____. Protestantism in Central America. Grand Rapids: Eerdmans, 1984.

"Ni Modo?: Mexico City Trapped by its own Growth." Partners International 45:4 (October-December 1987): 8-9.

Nida, Eugene A. "Communication of the Gospel to Latin Americans." Practical Anthropology 8.4 (July-August 1961): 145-56.

_____. "The Indigenous Churches of Latin America." Practical Anthropology (May-June 1961).

_____. Understanding Latin Americans: With Special Reference to Religious Values and Movements. South Pasadena: William Carey Library, 1974.

Niebuhr, H. Richard. Christ and Culture. New York: Harper & Row, 1951.

Nieto Anduaga, José. "La Familia Sagrada -¿Es Sagrada la Familia?" Taller de Teología 7 (1980): 29-32.

Nieymeyer Jr., E. V. "Anticlericalism in the Mexican Constitutional Convention, 1916-1917." The Americas 11 (July 1954).

Niño, Nohemí de. "La Pastoral desde la Niñez." Tensión: Revista de Análisis Teológico (1988): 33-40.

Noelliste, Dieumeme. "The Church and Human Emancipation: A Critical Comparison of Liberation Theology and the Latin American Theological Fraternity." Ph.D. dissertation, Garrett-Evangelical Theological Seminary and Northwestern University, 1987.

Noll, Mark A., and others, eds. Eerdmans' Handbook to Christianity in America. Grand Rapids: Eerdmans, 1983.

Nuñez, Emilio Antonio. "La Influencia del Protestantismo en el Desarrollo Histórico de Guatemala." Boletín Teológico, 1st Ser., 2 (1978): 1-15.

Nuñez, Emilio Antonio, and William D. Taylor. Crisis in Latin America: An Evangelical Perspective. Chicago: Moody Press, 1990.

Nyenhuis, Gerald. Etica Cristiana: Un Enfoque Bíblico Teológico. Miami: Logoi, 1981.

_____. "La Gran Necesidad de Buena Predicación." Pensamiento Cristiano 87 (September 1976): 39-41.

Olimón Nolasco, Manuel. "Algunas Claves de Lectura sobre la Relación Iglesia-Estado en la Historia de México." in Sociedad Civil y Sociedad Religiosa. México: Parroquial, 1985.

"Olimpiada en México." El Faro (May 1968): 31.

Olivera Sedano, Alicia. Aspectos del Conflicto Religioso de 1926 a 1929. Mexico City: Instituto Nacional de Antropología e Historia, 1966.

_____. "La Iglesia en México, 1926-1970." In Contemporary Mexico, ed. James W. Wilkie. Los Angeles: UCLA, 1976.

Onderdonk, Frank S. A Glimpse of Mexico. Nashville: Board of Missions, Methodist Episcopal Church, 1930.

Operación Movilización. Carta de Oración, 1957-1990.

Ortega, Miguel. "Don Aristómeno." El Faro (March-April 1985): 62-63.

Ortiz de Mercado, Ruhama. "Pastoral Indígena." Tensión: Revista de Análisis Teológico (1988): 41-57.

Ortiz de Mercado, Ruhama, and Luis Scott, eds. Mujer: Primera Consulta de Reflexión Bíblica. La Participación de la Mujer en la Iglesia y en la Sociedad. Mexico City: Editorial Kyrios, 1990.

Ortiz, Marcelino. Perfiles para el Hombre de Hoy. Mexico City: El Faro, 1973.

O'Shaughnessy, Edith. A Diplomat's Wife in Mexico. New York: Harper and Brothers, 1916.

Osuna, Andrés. Por la Escuela y por la Patria. Mexico City: Casa Unida de Publicaciones, 1943.

_____. Psicología Pedagógica. 5th ed. Mexico City: Sociedad de Edición y Librería Franco-Americano, 1928.

Padilla, Washington. "El Protestantismo en el Ecuador: Breve Reseña Histórica." Boletín Histórico 27 (1987): 135-194.

_____. La Iglesia y los Dioses Modernos: Historia del Protestantismo en el Ecuador. Quito: Corporación Editora Nacional, 1989.

Padilla, C. René. El Evangelio Hoy. Buenos Aires: Ediciones Certeza, 1975.

_____. Misión Integral: Ensayos sobre el Reino y la Iglesia. Grand Rapids: Nueva Creación, 1986.

_____, ed. Nuevas Alternativas de Educación Teológica. Grand Rapids and Buenos Aires: Nueva Creación, 1986.

_____, ed. The New Face of Evangelicalism: An International Symposium on the Lausanne Covenant. Downers Grove, Illinois: InterVarsity Press, 1976.

_____, comp. Fe Cristiana y Latinoamérica Hoy. Buenos Aires: Ediciones Certeza, 1974.

Palmer, Dennis R. "The American Protestant Conspiracy Theory of Mexican History: A Case Study in the Literature of Mexican Militant Catholicism." Ph.D. dissertation, Graduate Theological Union, 1978.

Palmer, Donald C. Explosion of People Evangelism: An Analysis of Pentecostal Church Growth in Colombia. Chicago: Moody Press, 1974.

Palomino López, Salatiel. El Movimiento Carismático: Una Confrontación Crítica. Mexico City: El Faro, 1985.

_____. "Una Boca y un Corazón." El Faro (January-February 1985): 6-10.

_____. Yo Seré tu Dios: Estudios sobre la Doctrina Bíblica del Pacto. Mexico City: El Faro, 1988.

Paredes Muñoz, Nancy and Pedro Carrasco Malhue. "La Biblia Anotada de Scofield, Instituto de Fundamentalismo." Taller de Teología 8 (1981): 27-44.

Partido Acción Nacional. "Resistencia Civil." Palabra. 1 (1988).

Partido Popular Socialista, Dirección Nacional del Comité Central. "La Visita del Papa es Política, no Pastoral." La Jornada (Mexico City), 4 May 1990, 16.

Pascoe, Santiago. Salid de Ella: ¿Puede Uno Salvarse en la Iglesia Romana?. Mexico City: La Antorcha de México, nd.

Pastoralia. San José: Publicaciones CELEP.

Pattee, Richard. The Catholic Revival in Mexico. Washington: Catholic Association for International Peace, 1944.

Patterson, Frank W. A Century of Baptist Work in Mexico. El Paso: Baptist Spanish Publishing House, 1979.

_____. Manual de Finanzas para Iglesias. 3d ed. El Paso: Casa Bautista de Publicaciones, 1971.

Penton, Marvin J. "Mexico's Reformation: A History of Mexican Protestantism." Ph.D. dissertation, University of Iowa, 1965.

Pérez, Lugo J. La Cuestión Religiosa en México. Mexico City: Publicaciones de Centro Cultural Cuauhtémoc, 1926.

Pérez Alvarez, Eliseo. "Centro Social Presbiteriano El Faro." El Faro (September-October 1985): 192.

_____. "Uso del Antiguo Testamento en la Iglesia Presbiteriana de México." Licenciatura thesis, Seminario Teológico Presbiteriano de México, 1978.

Pérez de Camargo, Carmen, and Luis Scott, eds. El Ser Humano: Varón y Mujer. Mexico City: Editorial Kyrios, CUPSA, and Transformación, 1991.

Pérez Hernández, Isaías. "¿Por Qué No Llega un Avivamiento (Hab. 3:2)?" El Camino a la Vida (March-April 1976): 15-16.

_____. "Responsabilidad Ministerial," El Camino a la Vida (March-April 1976): 6-8.

Pérez Morales, Pablo E. "Dimensiones Misionológicas en el Documento Final del Congreso Internacional Ecuménico de Teología." Boletín Teológico 4 (1981): 59-64.

_____. Misión y Liberación: La Liberación como Móvil en América Latina. Mexico City: El Faro, 1976.

"Persecución en el Ajusco." Gracia 69 (March 1990): 9.

Petersen, John H. "Recent Research on Latin American University Students." Latin American Research Review 5:1 (1970): 37-58.

Piedra Solano, Arturo. "La Misión Latinoamericana y los Estados Unidos." Taller de Teología 14 (1984): 57-78.

Pierard, Richard V. "Por qué los Evangélicos Norteamericanos no han Cumplido su Papel en el Campo de la Justicia Social?" Boletín Teológico, 1st Ser. 2 (1978): 16-21.

Pixley, Jorge V. "Contribución a la Lectura del Relato del Becerro de Oro (Ex. 32)." Taller de Teología 8 (1981): 5-15.

_____. "El Diálogo de Moltmann con Míguez." Taller de Teología 1 (1976): 15-18.

_____. "El Discipulado Cristiano: Reflexiones Inspiradas en una Obra de Jon Sobrino." Taller de Teología 4 (1979): 11-16.

_____. "En el Encuentro de Teologías, ¿Hubo Encuentro?" Taller de Teología 3 (1978): 7-13.

_____. "La Familia, ¿Fenómeno de la Naturaleza, Producto de la Ingeniería Social o Epifenómeno del Desarrolio Capitalista?" Taller de Teología 7 (1980): 11-13.

_____. "La Toma de la Tierra de Canaán, ¿Liberación o Despojo?" Taller de Teología 12 (1983): 5-14.

Pixley, Jorge V., and Jean Pierre Bastian. Praxis Cristiana y Producción Teológica: Materiales del Encuentro de Teologías Celebrado en la Comunidad Teológica de México (8 al 10 de Octubre 1977). Salamanca: Ediciones Sígueme, 1979.

Planchet, Regis. La Cuestión Religiosa en México; o sea, Vida de Benito Juárez. Roma: Desclée, 1906.

_____. La Intervención Protestante en México y Sud América. El Paso: Revista Católica, 1928.

Pola Baca, Rafael, ed. "Biblia, Teología y Acción Pastoral." Tensión: Revista de Análisis Teológico (1988).

Poniatowski, Elena. La Noche de Tlatelolco: Testimonios de Historia Oral. (Mexico City: Ediciones Era, 1971).

"¿Por Qué el Trabajo Estudiantil?" El Faro (May 1970): 28-29.

¿Por Qué?. An independent (anti-government) Mexican magazine.

"Post-quake Suffering Continues, but Baptists Assist." The Commission (April 1986): 88.

Porch, Robert S. "The Influence of the Aztecs upon Contemporary Religious Thought in Mexico." M.A. thesis, Columbia Bible College, 1957.

Porter, Eugene O. "The History of Methodism in Mexico." Ph.D. dissertation, Ohio State University, 1936.

Portes Gil, Emilio. La Lucha entre el Poder Civil y el Clero. Mexico City: 1934; reprint, Mexico City: El Día, 1983.

Poythress, Vern S. Understanding Dispensationalists. Grand Rapids: Zondervan, 1987.

Prescott, Lyle. Luz en la América Latina. Translated by Ismael E. Amaya and Sergio Franco. Kansas City, Mo.: Casa Nazarena de Publicaciones, 1967.

Presidencia de la República: Unidad de la Crónica Presidencial. Terremotos de Septiembre: Sobretiro de las Razones y las Obras: Crónica del Sexenio 1982-1988, Tercer Año. Mexico City: Fondo de Cultura Económica, 1986.

Priestley, Herbert I. The Mexican Nation. New York: The Macmillan Company, 1926.

Primer Congreso de Iglesias Evangélicas: Ponencias y Resoluciones. Guadalajara: Comisión Editorial, 1956.

"Primer Congreso Estudiantil Presbiteriano." El Faro (July 1970): 18-21.

Primer Congreso Estudiantil Presbiteriano. Mexico City: Iglesia Nacional Presbiteriana, Departamento de Labor Juvenil-Estudiantil de la Secretaría de Educación Cristiana, 1970.

Primera Consulta sobre Relaciones Iglesia-Estado: Problemática Actual de la Iglesia en México. Mexico City: Iglesia Nacional Presbiteriana, 1990.

"Professions Exceed 1,000 in Regional Campaign." The Commission (1968): 29.

Prospecto de Estudios: Comunidad Teológica de México. Mexico City: Comunidad Teológica de México, 1975.

Prospecto de Estudios: Comunidad Teológica de México. Mexico City: Comunidad Teológica de México, circa 1984.

Puig Casauranc, José Manuel. *La Cuestión Religiosa en Relación con la Educación Pública en México*. Mexico City: Talleres Gráficos de la Nación, 1928.

Purdie Knowles, James. *Samuel A. Purdie: His Life and Letters, His Work as a Missionary and Spanish Writer and Publisher in Mexico and Central America*. Plainfield, Indiana: Publishing Association of Friends, 1908.

Purdie, Samuel A. *Memories of Angela Aguilar de Mascorro: And Sketches of the Friends' Mexican Mission*. Chicago: Publishing Association of Friends, 1885.

"Qué Dicen los Líderes Evangélicos?" *Gracia* 70 (May 1990): 12-13.

Quigley, Robert. E. *American Catholic Opinions of Mexican Anticlericalism, 1910-1936*. Cuernavaca: CIDOC, 1969.

Quirarte, Martín. *El Problema Religioso en México*. Mexico City: Instituto Nacional de Antropología e Historia, 1967.

Quirk, Robert. *An Affair of Honor: Woodrow Wilson and the Occupation of Vera Cruz*. Lexington: University of Kentucky Press, 1962.

_____. *The Mexican Revolution and the Catholic Church*. Bloomington: Indiana University Press, 1973.

R. de Garza Leal, Flora. "XXV Aniversario de la Fundación de los Departamentos de Primaria y Jardín de Niños del Instituto Juárez." *El Faro* (August 1970): 16-17.

Raat, W. Dirk. "Synthesizing the Mexican Experience." *Latin American Research Review* 15:3 (1980): 266-272.

Raat, W. Dirk, and William H. Beezley, eds. *Twentieth-Century Mexico*. Lincoln: University of Nebraska Press, 1986.

Ramos, Marcos Antonio. *Panorama del Protestantismo en Cuba*. San José: Editorial Caribe, 1986.

Ramos Pereira, Jovelino. "The Response of Protestants to the Mexican Revolution, 1910-1940." M.A. thesis, Columbia University, 1973.

Ramos, Samuel. Profile of Man and Culture in Mexico. 3d ed. New York: McGraw, 1969.

Rankin, Melinda. Twenty Years among the Mexicans. Cincinnati: Central Book Concern, 1881.

Ravelo, Renato. Los Jaramillistas. Mexico City: Ed. Nuestro Tiempo, 1978.

Read, William R., Victor M. Monterroso, and Harmon A. Johnson. Latin American Church Growth. Grand Rapids: Eerdmans, 1969.

"Recuerdo Perenne." El Camino a la Vida (July-August 1972): 4-6.

Reid, Orvil W. The Challenge of Mexico to Missions. Guadalajara: Baptist Student Home Print Shop, 1952.

"Relaciones Iglesia-Estado." Christus 587 (August 1985).

Rembao, Alberto. Discurso a la Nación Evangélica. Buenos Aires: La Aurora, 1949.

_____. "La Realidad Protestante en América Latina." Cuadernos Teológicos 22 (1957): 3-13.

_____. Lupita: A Story of Mexico in Revolution. New York: Friendship Press, 1935.

_____. Outlook in Mexico. New York: Friendship Press, 1942.

_____. Pneuma. Mexico City: CUPSA, 19??.

Rengifo Vela, Rolando. "Hacia una Pastoral de la Familia para la Familia Pastoral." Tensión: Revista de Análisis Teológico (1988): 20-33.

Revista Bíblica. Buenos Aires.

Revueltas, José. México 68: Juventud y Revolución. Mexico City: Ediciones Era, 1978.

Reynoso Macías, Angel, and others. Calvino Vivo: Libro Conmemorativo del 450 Aniversario de la Reforma en Ginebra. Mexico City: El Faro, 1987.

Reynoso Macías, Angel, and others. *El Culto es Fiesta*. Mexico City: El Faro, 1988.

Ricard, Robert. *The Spiritual Conquest of Mexico*. Translated by Leslie B. Simpson. Berkeley: University of California Press, 1966.

Richard, Pablo, ed. *Materiales para una Historia de la Teología en América Latina*. San Jose, Costa Rica: Departamento Ecuménico de Investigaciones, 1981.

Richard, Pablo, and Meléndez, Guillermo, eds. *La Iglesia de los Pobres en América Central: Un Análisis Socio-Político y Teológico de la Iglesia Centroamericana (1960-1982)*. San José: Departamento Ecuménico de Investigaciones, 1982.

Rivera, Benjamín. "Caminando al Ritmo de los Niños." Paper presented at the Segunda Consulta de Reflexión Bíblica: Ser Humano, Varón y Mujer, Mexico City, 1-3 November 1990.

Rivera R., Pedro. *Instituciones Protestantes en México*. Mexico City: Editorial Jus, 1962.

_____. *Protestantismo Mexicano: Su Desarrollo y Estado Actual*. 3d ed. Mexico City, 1961.

Roberts, W. Dayton. *Los Auténticos Revolucionarios: La Historia de Evangelismo a Fondo*. San José: Editorial Caribe, 1969.

Rocafuerte, Vicente. *Ensayo sobre Tolerancia Religiosa*. Mexico City, 1831.

Rodríguez Díaz, Daniel. "El Evangelio Social como Ideología hacia el Interior del Capitalismo Norteamericano." *Taller de Teología* 9 (1981): 35-50.

_____. "Lutero, Reformador o Revolucionario." *Taller de Teología* 13 (1983): 23-31.

Rodríguez Morgado, Oscar. "Historia de la Iglesia Presbiteriana en México." Licenciatura thesis, Seminario Teológico Presbiteriano de México, 1982.

Rodríguez, Erwin. *Un Evangelio según la Clase Dominante*. Mexico City: UNAM, 1982.

Roman, Richard. "Church-State Relations and the Mexican Constitutional Congress, 1916-1917." Journal of Church and State (Winter 1978): 73-80.

Romero López, Agustín. Síntesis Histórica del Instituto Militarizado Benjamín N. Velasco de Querétaro: 1890-1971. Mexico City, 1987.

Romney, Thomas C. The Mormon Colonies in Mexico. Salt Lake City: The Deseret Book Company, 1938.

Rosales Pérez, Alberto. "Categorías Religiosas de los Constituyentes: 1856-1857." Licenciatura thesis, Seminario Teológico Presbiteriano de México, 1976.

_____. "El Faro, Organo de Comunicación (durante 100 Años)." El Faro (March-April 1985): 44-51.

_____. "El Faro, Organo de Servicio Social." El Faro (September-October 1985): 166-70.

_____. Estado e Iglesia en México: Legislación Religiosa. Mexico City: n.p., 1990.

_____. "La Génesis de 'El Faro' (En su Primer Centenario)." El Faro (January-February 1985): 13-26.

Rosales, Ray. The Evangelism in Depth Program of the Latin American Mission. Th.M. thesis, Luther Theological Seminary, 1966.

Ross, William G. Sunrise in Aztec Land. Richmond: Presbyterian Committee on Publicactions, 1922.

Ross Torres, Guillermo A. Estudios en las Sagradas Escrituras: Evangelio de Juan. Mexico City: El Faro, 1969.

_____. Estudios en las Sagradas Escrituras: Evangelio de Lucas. 2d ed. Mexico City: El Faro, 1982.

_____. Estudios en las Sagradas Escrituras: Evangelio de Marcos. Mexico City: El Faro, 1967.

_____. Estudios en las Sagradas Escrituras: Evangelio de Mateo. Mexico City: El Faro, 1967.

Rosser, Edwin H. "Beyond Revolution: The Social Concern of Moisés Sáenz, Mexican Educator." Ph.D. dissertation, The American University, 1970.

Ruesga, David G. "Historia de Nuestras Iglesias: Así Nació 'La Calzada.'" El Camino a La Vida (July-September 1987): 3-5.

_____. "Nació en un Pesebre." El Camino a la Vida (January-February 1969): 7-9.

Ruesga, Genaro. "La Letra y el Espíritu." El Camino a la Vida (March-May 1980): 33-34.

Ruiz Castro, Jerjes. Teología Bíblica Latinoamericana: Pautas Hermenéuticas. Licenciatura thesis, Seminario Bíblico Latinoamericano, 1977.

Ruiz Guerra, Rubén. Consideraciones acerca de la Bibliografía del Metodismo en México. Mexico City: n.p., n.d.

Rycroft, W. Stanley. On This Foundation: The Evangelical Witness in Latin America. New York: Friendship Press, 1942.

_____. Religion and Faith in Latin America. Philadelphia: Westminster Press, 1958.

_____. "The Protestant Churches and Religious Freedom in Latin America." Journal of Church and State (Spring 1966): 264-73.

Sáenz, Moisés. "La Educación Pública en México." La Nueva Democracia (May 1924): 10.

_____. México Integro. 2d ed. Mexico City: Fondo de Cultura Económica, SEP/80, 1982.

_____. "¿Para Qué Educamos a Nuestros Hijos?" La Nueva Democracia (September 1924): 8.

Salem, Luis D. Francisco G. Penzotti: Apóstol de la Libertad y la Verdad. Mexico City: Sociedades Bíblicas, 1963.

_____. La Biblia en el Pensamiento Hispanoamericano. Mexico City: Casa Unida de Publicaciones, 1971.

Samuelson, Robert J. "The Mexican Connection." Newsweek (12 December 1988): 53

Sánchez, Sergio. "Working Together Towards a Holistic Transformation: The Case of the Mexican Association for Rural and Urban Transformation (AMEXTRA, A.C.)." Cuernavaca: AMEXTRA, 1990.

Sánchez Cetina, Edesio. "Babilonia." Boletín Teológico 35 (1989): 213-224.

_____. "Ensayo Exegético del Antiguo Testamento." Boletín Teológico 19 (1986): 32-61.

_____. Fe Bíblica: Antiguo Testamento y América Latina (Ensayos Exegéticos). Mexico City: El Faro, 1986.

_____. "La Biblia y su Contexto Histórico." Boletín Teológico 10-11 (1983): 175-221.

_____. "La Familia: Iglesia Doméstica." Boletín Teológico 13-14 (1984): 22-41.

_____. "Lectura de Joel 2:18-32 desde América Latina." Boletín Teológico 21-22 (1986): 25-48.

_____. Question-answer period following paper presented at the Primer Simposio Bíblico-Teológico of the Iglesia Nacional Presbiteriana, 5 July 1991, Mexico City.

Sandeen, Ernest R. The Roots of Fundamentalism: British and American Millenarianism, 1800-1930. Chicago: University of Chicago Press, 1970.

Sansores Caamal, Miguel. "La Iglesia ante las Necesidades de la Comunidad Actual." Licenciatura thesis, Seminario Teológico Presbiteriano de México, 1977.

Santiago Ramírez, Esteban. Planificación Familiar en la Vida Cristiana. Mexico City: Publicaciones El Camino a la Vida, 1990.

Savage, Pedro, and others. El Debate Contemporáneo sobre la Biblia. Barcelona: Ediciones Evangélicas Europeas, 1972.

_____. "El Fruto del Espíritu." Pensamiento Cristiano 97 (March 1979): 172-77.

_____. "La Iglesia como Comunidad Discipuladora del Reino." Boletín Teológico 6 (1982): 61-101.

_____. La Iglesia: Comunidad Discipuladora. Guadalajara: Ediciones Transformación, 1989.

Sawatzky, Harry Leonard. "Mennonite Colonization in Mexico." Ph.D. dissertation, University of California, 1967.

Schmitt, Karl M. "American Protestant Missionaries and the Díaz Regime in Mexico, 1876-1911." Journal of Church and State (1983): 253-277.

_____. Evolution of Mexican Thought on Church-State Relations, 1876-1911. Ann Arbor: University of Michigan Press, 1954.

_____. "The Mexican Positivists and the Church-State Question, 1876-1911." Journal of Church and State (Spring 1966): 200-13.

Schnackenburg, Rudolf. The Gospel According to St John. Vol 3. New York: Crossroad, 1982.

"Scientist's Lectures Aid Student Work." The Commission (November 1966): 29.

Scopes, Wilfred, ed. The Christian Ministry in Latin America and the Caribbean. New York: Commission on World Mission and Evangelism, World Council of Churches, 1962.

Scott, Lindy. "Los Evangélicos Mexicanos en el Siglo XX." Austin: Institute of Latin American Studies, 1991.

_____. "La Acción Pastoral en el Nuevo Testamento." Tensión: Revista de Análisis Teológico (1988): 1-5.

Searfoss L., Esteban. Directorio Evangélico de la República Mexicana - 1982-83. Mexico City: 1982.

"Septiembre: El Mes de la Patria." El Camino a la Vida (September-October 1964): 3.

"Será Alentadora para los Católicos la Visita de CSG al Vaticano." La Jornada (Mexico City), 6 July 1991.

Shapira, Yoram. Mexican Foreign Policy under Echeverría. Beverly Hills: Sage Publications, 1978.

Shaull, M. Richard. Encounter with Revolution. New York: Association Press, 1955.

Shelby Erdman, Margaret. Contentedly Yours, Alice J. McClelland. Cuernavaca: n.p., 1969.

_____. Un Jazmín Floreció en Guerrero: Breve Biografía de la Srita. Alicia Jazmín McClelland. N.p., 1966.

Sigmund, Paul E., ed. Models of Political Change in Latin America. New York: Frederick A. Praeger, 1970.

Siller A., Clodomiro L. "Indigenismo y Protestantismo (Visión Católica)." Taller de Teología 10 (1982): 13-17.

Silva Herzog, Jesús. Breve Historia de la Revolución Mexicana: La Etapa Constitucionalista y la Lucha de Facciones. 2d ed. rev. Mexico City: Fondo de Cultura Económica, 1985.

Simms, Donaldo, Agustín Acosta, Manuel Martínez, Pedro Larson, and Arturo Alarcón. Instituto de Misiones. PRUEBA: Manual de Misiones. Mexico City: 1980.

Simon, Julian L. Basic Research Methods in Social Science: The Art of Empirical Investigation. New York: Randam House, 1969.

Simpson, Leslie Byrd. Many Mexicos. Berkeley: University of California Press, 1969.

Sinclair, John H., ed. Protestantism in Latin America: A Bibliographical Guide. Austin: Hispanic-American Institute, 1967.

_____. Protestantism in Latin America: A Bibliographical Guide. Pasadena: William Carey Library, 1976.

Skelton, Martha. "Mexico City: Life Rises from Rubble." The Commission (December 1985): 10, 41.

Skidmore, Thomas E., and Peter H. Smith. "Notes on Quantitative History: Federal Expenditure and Social Change in Mexico since 1910." Latin American Research Review 5:1 (1970): 71-85.

Smith, Anthony Christopher. "The Essentials of Missiology from the Evangelical Perspective of the 'Fraternidad Teológica Latinoamericana'." Ph.D. dissertation, Southern Baptist Theological Seminary, 1983.

Smolowe, Jill. "Going at Full Tilt." Time (19 November 1990): 16-19.

Sociedad de Estudios Históricos del Metodismo en México. 1986 Anuario. Mexico City: SEHMM, 1986.

Solís Gil, José. "Iglesia y Crisis Energética: Hacia una Ubicación del Pueblo de Dios en la Crisis Energética." Licenciatura thesis, Seminario Teológico Bautista Mexicano, 1981.

Sosa, A. F., L. E. Odell, and José Quiñones, eds. El Cristianismo Evangélico en la América Latina: Informe y Resoluciones de la Primera Conferencia Evangélica Latinoamericana: 18 al 30 de julio de 1949. Buenos Aires: La Aurora, 1949.

Sotelo González, Moisés. "La Influencia del Protestantismo en México." Licenciatura thesis, Seminario Teológico Presbiteriano de México, 1962.

Sotelo González, Isaías. "Historia del Presbiterio del Sur." Licenciatura thesis, Seminario Teológico Presbiteriano de México, 1965.

Souvenir Book of the Golden Anniversary or Jubilee of the Methodist Episcopal Church in Mexico: 1873 - 1923. Mexico City: CUPSA, 1924

"Spell of the Olympics." Newsweek (21 October 1968): 64-65.

Spicer, Edward H. Cycles of Conquest: The Impact of Spain, Mexico, and the United States on the Indians of the Southwest, 1533-1960. 2d ed. Tucson: University of Arizona Press, 1976.

Staples, Anne. La Iglesia en la Primera República Federal Mexicana (1824-1835). México: SepSetentas, 1976.

Steuernagel, Valdir Raúl. "The Theology of Mission in its Relation to Social Responsibility within the Lausanne Movement." Th.D. dissertation, Lutheran School of Theology, 1988.

Stewart, Doug, Mexico City, letter to Dick Dye, 30 March 1986. Photocopy.

Stockwell, B. Foster. The Christian Ministry in Latin America and the Caribbean. New York: World Council of Churches, 1962.

Stoll, David. Fishers of Men or Founders of Empire?. London: Zed Press, 1982.

_____. Is Latin America Turning Protestant? The Politics of Evangelical Growth. Berkeley: University of California Press, 1990.

Strachan, R. Kenneth. Evangelism in Depth: Experimenting with a New Type of Evangelism. Chicago: Moody Press, 1961.

Straughan, Alton C. "A Banana and a Tract." The Commission 29:11:3.

Taylor, Clyde, and Wade Coggins, eds. Protestant Missions in Latin America: A Statistical Survey. Washington: Evangelical Foreign Mission Association, 1961.

Taylor, Jack E. God's Messengers to Mexico's Masses: A Study of the Religious Significance of the Braceros. Eugene, Oregon: Institute of Church Growth, 1962.

Tec Ruiz, Raul B. "La Necesidad de Cumplir en su Totalidad la Misión de la Iglesia." Licenciatura thesis, Seminario Teológico Presbiteriano de México, 1975.

Tejeda Bello, Julio. "Una Epístola del Siglo XX: El Hno. Obispo Julio Tejeda a la Iglesia de Dios en la Rep. Mexicana." El Camino a la Vida (September-December 1990): 2-3.

Temple, Helen. Un Arbol Junto a un Arroyo: La Historia del Dr. C. E. Morales, Predicador Pionero, y Primer Educador y Músico Nazareno en México. Kansas City, Mo.: Casa Nazarena de Publicaciones, 1973.

Tensión. Official magazine of the Fraternidad Teológica Bautista Mexicana.

"Terminó la Era del PRI." Visión (8 August 1988): 6-7.

The Commission. Official missionary magazine of the Southern Baptist Convention.

The Reformation in Mexico. Hartford: Junior Auxiliary Publishing Co., n.d.

The Voice of Mexico: Addresses given at the National Training Conference in Mexico City, January 5-10, 1963 for National and Area Staff Personnel of the American Baptist Convention in Preparation for "Mission to the World". Valley Forge, PA.: American Baptist Convention, 1963.

Thomas, Dani B. and Richard B. Craig. "Student Dissent in Latin America: Toward a Comparative Analysis." Latin American Research Review 8:1 (1973): 71-96.

Thomas, Ethel. The Industrial School: La Escuela Sara Alarcón. Abiline, Kansas: Shodinger and Wilson, n.d.

Thomson, Wallace. Trading with Mexico. New York: Dodd, Mead and Co., 1921.

Tijerina González, Saúl. "Dispensario de Higiene Mental: Una Obra Social en Monterrey para Enfermos de Escasos Recursos." Licenciatura thesis, Seminario Teológico Presbiteriano de México, 1968.

_____. Huellas Imborrables: Historia de la Iglesia Nacional Presbiteriana "El Buen Pastor," de Monterrey N.L.. Mexico City: El Faro, 1984.

_____. "La Influencia Social de 'El Faro' durante un Siglo de Existencia." El Faro Sep-Oct (1985): 162-66.

_____. "Mexican Presbyterians' Adventure of Faith: A Case of Moratorium--Two Interviews." Interviews by J. Gary Campbell. International Review of Mission (April 1975): 200-09.

Timmer, David E. "Meanwhile, South of the Border." The Reformed Journal (October 1988): 5-7.

Toro, Alfonso. La Iglesia y el Estado en México. 2d ed. Mexico City: Ediciones El Caballito, 1975.

Torres Vargas, José de Jesús. "Manual para un Ministerio Hospitalario." Licenciatura thesis, Seminario Teológico Bautista Mexicano, 1983.

Townsend, William Cameron. Lazaro Cardenas: Mexican Democrat. Ann Arbor: George Wahr, 1952.

Trejo Estrada, Evelia María del Socorro, "La Introducción del Protestantismo en México: Aspectos Diplomáticos." Licenciatura thesis, UNAM, 1983.

Treviño, Alejandro. Cincuenta Años en el Ministerio. El Paso: Casa Bautista de Publicaciones, 1937.

_____. Historia de los Trabajos Bautistas en México. El Paso: Casa Bautista de Publicaciones, 1939.

Trujillo, Samuel. "El Ecumenismo en México." Iglesias VI-68 (1989): 4-6.

_____. "El Faro, un Medio de Comunicación." El Faro (March-April 1985): 52-53.

_____. "Renovemos Nuestro Espíritu." El Faro (July 1969): 3.

_____. Santificados para el Compromiso. Mexico City: CELADEC-CENCOS, n.d.

_____. "Solicito una Revolución." El Faro (October 1969): 3.

Un Caballero de Cristo (anonymous). La Salvación Simplificada. Mexico City: Editorial Ingram, 1964.

"Un Programa de Hospitalidad y Orientación en A.C.E. para los Visitantes Mundiales a las Olimpiadas." El Faro (October 1968): 16.

Urbano Barajas, Sergio. "Principios Paulinos para la Observancia de la Cena del Señor, Aplicados a las Iglesias Bautistas en México." Licenciatura thesis, Seminario Teológico Bautista Mexicano, 1985.

Ureña, José. "Mesura, Pide la Permanente a la Jerarquía Católica." La Jornada (Mexico City), 29 March 1990): 7.

Valeriano Esquivel, Marcelino. "Razones del Crecimiento de la Iglesia Evangélica en México." Licenciatura thesis, Seminario Teológico Presbiteriano de México, 1963.

Van Slyke, Lorenzo P. Melodías de Sión. Mexico City: El Faro, 1986.

Varetto de Canclini, Agustina. Juan C. Varetto: Embajador de Cristo. Buenos Aires: Editorial Evangélica Bautista, 1955.

Varetto, Juan C. Diego Thomson. Buenos Aires: Imprenta Bautista, 1918.

Vargas, Felipe. "México: Avance Democrático." Visión (25 July 1988).

Vargas Llosa, Mario. "Mexico: The Perfect Dictatorship." New Perspectives Quarterly (Winter 1991): 23.

Vasconcelo Rezende, María Valeria. "El Feminismo del Movimiento Misionero Protestante en América Latina." Taller de Teología 7 (1980): 33-51.

Vásquez, Felipe. "La Religión Urbana Evangélica en Xalapa." La Palabra y el Hombre 63 (July-September 1987).

Vázquez, Apolonio. Los que Sembraron con Lágrimas. Mexico City: El Faro, 1985.

Vázquez Olmedo, Rafaél. "¿Qué Nos Depara el Futuro?" El Camino a la Vida (November-December 1970): 11-13.

Velasco, Gustavo A. Metodismo Mexicano: Períodos Iniciales. Mexico City: Sociedad de Estudios del Metodismo en México, 1974.

Vidales, Raul. "El Sujeto Histórico de la Teología de la Liberación." Taller de Teología 2 (1978): 9-18.

Videla, Gabriela. Sergio Méndez Arceo: Un Señor Obispo. Cuernavaca: Correo del Sur, 1982.

Villagrán Arjona, Samuel. "Encarnación de la Iglesia en la Sociedad: Coyuntura Actual." Licenciatura thesis, Seminario Teológico Presbiteriano de México, 1985.

Villaseñor, Guillermo. Estado e Iglesia: El Caso de la Educación. Mexico City: Editorial Edicol, 1978.

Villegas, Jorge. Cosas Nuestras. Monterrey: Plus Ediciones, 1988.

Visión de los Vencidos: Relaciones Indígenas de la Conquista. Mexico City: UNAM, 1987.

Voelkel, Jack. Student Evangelism in a World of Revolution. Grand Rapids: Zondervan, 1974.

Wagner, Pedro. Avance del Pentecostalismo en Latinoamérica. Translated by Benjamín Mercado. 2d ed. Revised by Agustín S. Contin. Miami: Vida, 1987.

Walsh, Billy J. "Rich Dividends Realized." The Commission (January 1968): 20.

Weber, Timothy P. Living in the Shadow of the Second Coming: American Premillennialism, 1875-1982. Grand Rapids: Zondervan, 1983.

West, Cornel, Caridad C. Guidote, and Margaret Coakley, eds. Theology in the Americas: Detroit II Conference Papers. Maryknoll: Orbis, 1982.

Westrup P., Horacio. Paladines del Evangelio en México. Mexico City: Casa Unida de Publicaciones, 1953.

Westrup, Enrique Tomás, ed. Principios: Relato de la Introducción del Evangelio en México. Escritos del Protagonista Principalen Dicha Obra: Tomás Martín Westrup. Monterrey: n.p., 1948.

Wheeler, W. Reginald, Dwight H. Day, and James B. Rodgers. Modern Missions in Mexico. Philadelphia: The Westminster Press, 1925.

Wiarda, Howard J. "Corporate Theory and Ideology: A Latin American Development Paradigm." Journal of Church and State (Winter 1978): 29-56.

Wiebe, David V. They Seek a Country. Hillsboro, Kansas: Mennonite Publishing House, 1959.

Wilkie, James W. "Statistical Indicators of the Impact of National Revolution on the Catholic Church in Mexico, 1910-1967." Journal of Church and State (Winter 1970): 89-106.

_____. "The Meaning of the Cristero Religious War Against the Mexican Revolution." Journal of Church and State (Spring 1966): 214-33.

William, John B. La Iglesia y el Estado en Veracruz. México: SepSetentas, 1976.

Willis, Avery T. El Plan Maestro para el Discipulado Cristiano. Mexico City: Casa Bautista, 1986.

Wilson, Boyce. "Church Growth by Church Division: A Mexican Model for Urban Church Growth." D.Miss. Major Project, Trinity Evangelical Divinity School, 1985.

Winton, George B. Mexico Past and Present. Nashville: Cokesbury Press, 1938.

_____. Mexico Today: Social, Political, and Religious Conditions. New York: Missionary Education Movement of the United States and Canada, 1913.

_____. A New Era in Old Mexico. Nashville: Methodist Episcopal Church South Publishing House, 1905.

"Witnessing in Mexico." The Commission (19): 32.

Woehr, Chris. "Mexico: Catholic, Protestant Tensions Rise." Christianity Today (19 March 1990), 44.

Wolf, R. Henry. "It's Like This." The Commission (March 1967): 7-9.

_____. "Notes from a Diary--II." The Commission (November 1967): 21.

Womack, John. "Unfreedom in Mexico: Government Crackdown on the Universities." The New Republic (12 October 1968): 27-31.

Wonderly, William L., and Jorge Lara-Braud. ¿Los Evangélicos Somos Así?. Mexico City: Casa Unida de Publicaciones, 1964.

Woods, Kenneth F. "Samuel Guy Inman and Intervention in Mexico." Southern California Quarterly 46.4 (1964): 351-70.

Yancey, Philip. "Cam Townsend's Mission: Let God Do the Talking." Christianity Today (18 June 1982): 14-18.

Yoder, John Howard. The Priestly Kingdom: Social Ethics as Gospel. Notre Dame: University of Notre Dame Press, 1984.

Zamarripa, Roberto. "La Visita del Papa, Diseñada con Fines Políticos: Cárdenas." La Jornada (Mexico City), 29 March 1990, 6.

Zambrano, Ariel. "Problemas Contemporáneos en los Paises Latinoamericanos." El Faro (February 1970): 18-19.

Zamora V., Abel, and María Guel de Zamora. Jesucristo: Un Estudio Analítico y Crítico de esta Importante Doctrina. Guadalajara: 1989.

Zapata Arceyuz, Virgilio. Historia de la Iglesia Evangélica en Guatemala. Guatemala City: Comisión de Relaciones Públicas y Comisión de Historia y Estadística pro-Centenario, 1982.

Zavala, Iván. "Encuestas: La Brújula Loca." La Jornada (Mexico City), 5 March 1991.

Zermeño, Sergio. México: Una Democracia Utópica, El Movimiento Estudiantil del 68. Mexico City: Siglo Veintiuno Editores, 1978.

Persons Interviewed

Abascal, Salvador, Diputado of the PAN party. Interview by author, 31 October 1989, Mexico City.

Alcántara Mejía, José, professor of the Universidad Iberoamericana and director of CESIC. Interview by author, 14 June 1991, Mexico City.

Alvarado Reyes, Jorge, Presbyterian pastor and seminary professor. Interview by author, 26 October 1989, Mexico City.

Araiza, Eugenio, director of urban ministries for AMEXTRA. Interview by author, 20 October 1989, Mexico City.

Araiza, Verónica, social worker for AMEXTRA. Interview by author, 20 October 1989, Mexico City.

Arévalo, Linda, Assembly of God pastor. Interview by author, 16 January 1991, Ixtapan de la Sal, Mexico.

Arias, Ariel, Baptist sociologist. Interview by author, 17 February 1989, Mexico City.

Bustos, Manuel, Church of God pastor. Interview by author, 31 May 1991, Mexico City.

Calderón Martínez, Juan, Church of God seminary academic dean and professor of the Instituto Politécnico Nacional. Interview by author, 15 April 1988, Mexico City.

Carrillo, Pablo, textile engineer and founder of Magreb. Interview by author, 28 June 1991, Mexico City.

Carter, Pat, psychologist and ex-director of the Baptist seminary. Interview by author, 13 May 1991, Mexico City.

Castañeda, Ignacio, Presbyterian pastor and ex-moderator of the general assembly. Interview by author, 27 November 1989, Mexico City.

Castell Zavoleta, Prisciliano, director of Baptist student hostel. Interview by author, 5 June 1991, Mexico City.

Castellanos, Francisco, Church of God pastor and seminary director. Interview by author, 10 November 1988, Ixtepec, Oaxaca.

Castillo, Enrique, Pentecostal pastor. Interview by author, 8 November 1991, Mexico City.

Celis, Germán, Presbyterian medical doctor. Interview by author, 24 May 1991, Mexico City.

Chávez, Eusebio, Church of God pastor. Interview by author, 6 March 1991, Mexico City.

Clemente, Abel, Presbyterian pastor, ex-moderator of the general assembly and ex-director of COPER. Interview by author, 22 May 1991, Mexico City.

Cortés, Norberto, Baptist missionary to the Mazahuas. Interview by author, 20 March 1989, Mexico City.

Cruz, Saúl, Baptist psychologist and founder of Armonía. Interview by author, 17 July 1991, Mexico City.

De Koster, Pedro, Methodist turned Pentecostal businessman. Interview by author, 13 April 1991, Mexico City.

Delgado, Francisco, Reformed Presbyterian pastor and seminary professor. Interview by author, 11 November 1989, Mexico City.

Deras, Sergio, Presbyterian sociologist. Interview by author, 26 June 1991, Metepec, Puebla.

Díaz Ordaz, Hector, Presbyterian pastor and ex-rector of the Presbyterian seminary. Interview by author, 17 November 1989, Mexico City.

Dixon, Sara, Presbyterian missionary to Mexico. Interview by author, 19 September 1990, Mexico City.

Duchamps, Oscar, Baptist packaging manager of Coca Cola de México. Interview by author, 23 November 1989, Mexico City.

Dueñas, Eduardo, Presbyterian businessman and ex-committee member of the Cruzada Estudiantil. Interview by author, 11 October 1990, Mexico City.

Echegollen, Artemisa, Mexican director of the Instituto Lingüístico de Verano, 8 April 1989, Mexico City.

Flores, Manuel, Church of God pastor. Interview by author, 6 March 1991, Mexico City.

Franco, Abraham, Church of God pastor. Interview by author, 15 April 1988, Mexico City.

García Díaz, José, Church of God layman. Interview by author, 12 May 1991, Mexico City.

García Ibarra, Daniel, Presbyterian pastor and academic dean of Presbyterian Seminary. Interview by author, 26 October 1989, Mexico City.

González, David, Assembly of God pastor and director of Confraternidad Carcelaria de México. Interview by author, 16 January 1991, Ixtapan de la Sal, Mexico.

González, Lázaro, Baptist seminary professor. Interview by author, 5 November 1989, Mexico City.

Guazo, Roberto, Baptist pastor. Interview by author, 20 April 1991, Mexico City.

Gutiérrez, Rolando, Baptist pastor, president of the convention, professor at the Instituto Politécnico Nacional, and president of the FTL. Interview by author, 3 December 1990, Quito.

Hoeferkamp, Roberto, Lutheran seminary professor and academic dean of the Comunidad Teológica. Interview by author, 14 June 1991, Mexico City.

Isáis, Elizabeth, journalist. Interview by author, 13 March 1990, Mexico City.

Isáis, Juan, Presbyterian pastor and director of the Misión Latinoamericana-México. Interview by author, 27 June 1991, Mexico City.

Juárez, Alejandro, Baptist pastor. Interview by author, 15 February 1988, Chicago.

Juárez, Carmen, Presbyterian pastor and seminary professor. Interview by author, 29 November 1989, Mexico City.

Larson, Pedro, Baptist seminary professor. Interview by author, 31 May 1990, Mexico City.

Legters, David, Presbyterian seminary professor. Interview by author, 20 May 1991, Mexico City.

López, Abner, Presbyterian pastor and rector of seminary. Interview by author, 2 November 1990, Mexico City.

Mann, Lloyd, Baptist Campus minister. Interview by author, 18 June 1991, Mexico City.

Martínez, Carlos, Mennonite journalist. Interview by author, 28 February 1991, Mexico City.

Martínez, Juan José, Methodist pastor. Interview by author, 28 June 1990, Mexico City.

Medina, Rubén, Presbyterian layman and director of Visión Mundial de México. Interview by author, 9 May 1991, Mexico City.

Mejía, Jesús, Church of God pastor. Interview by author, 6 March 1991, Mexico City.

Méndez, Moisés, Baptist seminary professor. Interview by author, 28 November 1990, Mexico City.

Mercado Hurtado, Elías, Presbyterian medical doctor. Interview by author, 15 April 1991, Mexico City.

Mondragón, Carlos, psychologist and professor of the ENEP-Iztacala. Interview by author, 28 February 1991, Mexico City.

Montecillos, José Luis, Church of God pastor and magazine editor. Interview by author, 7 March 1991, Mexico City.

Montejo, Esteban, Lutheran arquitect. Interview by author, 28 June 1991, Mexico City.

Montemayor de Ulloa, Rebeca, Baptist professor. Interview by author, 30 May 1991, Mexico City.

Ortiz, Juan Germán, Baptist pastor. Interview by author, 24 April 1991, Mexico City.

Paredes, Jaime, Church of God layman. Interview by author, 10 March 1991, Mexico City.

Pech, Abram, Presbyterian pastor. Interview by author, 1 December 1989, Mexico City.

Pentecost, Edward, ex-IFES missionary to Mexico. Interview by author, 1 July 1988, Washington, D.C.

Pérez de Camargo, Carmen, ex-staff worker of Compañerismo Estudiantil and co-founder of Enlace. Interview by author, 5 October 1990, Mexico City.

Pérez, Eliseo, Presbyterian seminary professor and ex-director of El Faro. Interview by author, 14 May 1990, Mexico City.

Pérez, Pablo, Presbyterian pastor and professor at various theological institutions. Interview by author, 23 May 1990, Mexico City.

Perkins, John, Afro-American community development expert. Interview by author, 30 June 1991, Mexico City.

Porras, Aristómeno, journalist. Interview by author, 19 March 1989, Mexico City.

Rébora Greene, Ernesto, Presbyterian politician and businessman. Interview by author, 31 October 1989, Mexico City.

Rengifo, Rolando, Baptist pastor and founder-director of Visión Ahora. Interview by author, 15 September 1989, Mexico City.

Robles, Ascención, director of the Instituto Evangelístico de México. Interview by author, 19 July 1990, Mexico City.

Robles, Connie, academic dean of the Instituto Evangelístico de México. Interview by author, 19 July 1990, Mexico City.

Rosser, Edwin, ex-Presbyterian missionary in Mexico. Interview by author, 2 March 1991, Austin, Texas.

Sáenz, Alejandro, Baptist bi-vocational pastor. Interview by author, 15 October 1988, Mexico City.

Saldaña Zamarrón, Angel, Catholic journalist for CENCOS. Interview by author, 1 June 1990, Mexico City.

Sánchez, Sergio, ex-staff member of Compañerismo Estudiantil and founder of AMEXTRA. Interview by author, 15 April 1991, Mexico City.

Stewart, Doug, IFES missionary in Mexico. Interviews by author, 29 June 1990 and 9 May 1991, Mexico City.

Stewart, Marilyn, IFES missionary in Mexico. Interview by author, 19 June 1990, Mexico City.

Tijerina, Saúl, Presbyterian pastor, ex-moderator of general assembly and ex-academic dean of seminary. Interview by author, 5 July 1991, Mexico City.

Tinley, Fred, Presbyterian missionary to Mexico. Interview by author, 17 September 1990, Guadalajara.

Trujillo, Samuel, Presbyterian pastor. Interview by author, 9 June 1991, Mexico City.

Ulloa, Javier, Baptist pastor and seminary professor. Interview by author, 30 May 1991, Mexico City.

Ulloa, Sergio, Baptist pastor and seminary professor. Interview by author, 30 May 1991, Mexico City.

Velasco Sarmiento, Alberto, Baptist layman. Interview by author, 9 June 1991, Mexico City.

Velazco, José Luis, director of Casa Unida de Publicaciones. Interview by author, 6 December 1989, Mexico City.

Villaseñor, Raúl, Baptist businessman. Interview by author, 19 October 1989, Mexico City.

Viniegra, Gonzalo. Baptist pastor. Interview by author, 26 June 1990, Veracruz.

Zamora, Alejandro, Baptist pastor and ex-president of the convention. Interview by author, 30 May 1991, Mexico City.

Videocassettes

UNICEF, 19 de Septiembre. 27 min. 1986. Videocassette.

Visión Mundial de México. Emergencia. Terremoto: Ciudad de México, 1985. 30 min. 1986. Videocassette.

_____. Terremoto de la Ciudad de México. 26 min. 1986. Videocassette.

PUBLICATIONS OF EDITORIAL KYRIOS

A TI LA GLORIA
(Latin American songbook)

COMO LLEGAR A SER CRISTIANO
by John Stott

CUANDO LA GUERRA NO ES JUSTA
by John Howard Yoder (in preparation)

ECONOMICA KOINONIA WITHIN THE BODY OF CHRIST
by Lindy Scott

EL SER HUMANO: VARON Y MUJER. SEGUNDA CONSULTA DE REFLEXION BIBLICA.
edited by Carmen Pérez de Camargo

MUJER: LA PARTICIPACION DE LA MUJER EN LA IGLESIA Y LA SOCIEDAD. PRIMERA CONSULTA DE REFLEXION BIBLICA
edited by Ruhama Ortiz de Mercado and Lindy Scott

POEMAS
by Rebeca Montemayor de Ulloa (in preparation)

***SERIES:* DIOS HABLA HOY (GOD SPEAKS TODAY) MONOGRAPHS OF THE LATIN AMERICAN THEOLOGICAL FRATERNITY - MEXICO**

HISTORIA SOCIAL Y POLITICA DE LA IGLESIA EVANGELICA EN MEXICO EN PERSPECTIVA BIBLICA
by Mariano Avila Arteaga

LAS MUJERES, LA IGLESIA, Y I TIMOTEO 2:9-15
by Lindy Scott

LOS EVANGELICOS MEXICANOS EN EL SIGLO VEINTE
by Lindy Scott

PRAXIS PASTORAL CON Y DESDE LOS MARGINADOS
by Sergio Ulloa Castellanos (in preparation)

REFLEXIONES SOBRE EL MINISTERIO DE TRANSFORMACION EN UNA ZONA MARGINADA EN LA CIUDAD DE MEXICO
by Frank Alton (in preparation)

UN ENFOQUE BIBLICO-TEOLOGICO DEL SER HUMANO: VARON Y MUJER
by Carmen Pérez de Camargo

Other books by Lindy Scott

Economic Koinonia within the Body of Christ

Las Mujeres, La Iglesia y 1a Timoteo 2:9-15

Los Evangélicos Mexicanos en el Siglo Veinte

Mujer: La Participación de la Mujer en la Iglesia y en la Sociedad (co-editor).

Impreso en :
RBC Comunicación
Leonardo de Vinci 19
Col. Mixcoac, C.P. 03910
☎563 47 39
México, D. F.